D1380909

St Antony's Series
General Editor: **Richard Clogg** (1999–), Fellow of St Antony's College, Oxford

Recent titles include:

Michael Addison
VIOLENT POLITICS
Strategies of Internal Conflict

Geoffrey Wiseman
CONCEPTS OF NON-PROVOCATIVE DEFENCE
Ideas and Practices in International Security

Pilar Ortuño Anaya
EUROPEAN SOCIALISTS AND SPAIN
The Transition to Democracy, 1959–77

Renato Baumann (*editor*)
BRAZIL IN THE 1990s
An Economy in Transition

Israel Getzler
NIKOLAI SUKHANOV
Chronicler of the Russian Revolution

Arturo J. Cruz, Jr
NICARAGUA'S CONSERVATIVE REPUBLIC, 1858–93

Pamela Lubell
THE COMMUNIST PARTY DURING THE CULTURAL REVOLUTION
The Case of the Sixty-One Renegades

Mikael af Malmborg
NEUTRALITY AND STATE-BUILDING IN SWEDEN

Klaus Gallo
GREAT BRITAIN AND ARGENTINA
From Invasion to Recognition, 1806–26

David Faure and Tao Tao Liu
TOWN AND COUNTRY IN CHINA
Identity and Perception

Peter Mangold
SUCCESS AND FAILURE IN BRITISH FOREIGN POLICY
Evaluating the Record, 1900–2000

Mohamad Tavakoli-Targhi
REFASHIONING IRAN
Orientalism, Occidentalism and Historiography

Louise Haagh
CITIZENSHIP, LABOUR MARKETS AND DEMOCRATIZATION
Chile and the Modern Sequence

Renato Colistete
LABOUR RELATIONS AND INDUSTRIAL PERFORMANCE IN BRAZIL
Greater São Paulo, 1945–60

Peter Lienhardt (*edited by Ahmed Al-Shahi*)
SHAIKHDOMS OF EASTERN ARABIA

John Crabtree and Laurence Whitehead (*editors*)
TOWARDS DEMOCRATIC VIABILITY
The Bolivian Experience

Steve Tsang (*editor*)
JUDICIAL INDEPENDENCE AND THE RULE OF LAW IN HONG KONG

Karen Jochelson
THE COLOUR OF DISEASE
Syphilis and Racism in South Africa, 1880–1950

Julio Crespo MacLennan
SPAIN AND THE PROCESS OF EUROPEAN INTEGRATION, 1957–85

Enrique Cárdenas, José Antonio Ocampo and Rosemary Thorp (*editors*)
AN ECONOMIC HISTORY OF TWENTIETH-CENTURY LATIN AMERICA
Volume 1: The Export Age
Volume 2: Latin America in the 1930s
Volume 3: Industrialization and the State in Latin America

Jennifer G. Mathers
THE RUSSIAN NUCLEAR SHIELD FROM STALIN TO YELTSIN

Marta Dyczok
THE GRAND ALLIANCE AND UKRAINIAN REFUGEES

Mark Brzezinski
THE STRUGGLE FOR CONSTITUTIONALISM IN POLAND

Suke Wolton
LORD HAILEY, THE COLONIAL OFFICE AND THE POLITICS OF RACE AND
EMPIRE IN THE SECOND WORLD WAR
The Loss of White Prestige

St Antony's Series
Series Standing Order ISBN 0–333–71109–2
(*outside North America only*)

You can receive future titles in this series as they are published by placing a standing order.
Please contact your bookseller or, in case of difficulty, write to us at the address below with
your name and address, the title of the series and the ISBN quoted above.

Customer Services Department, Macmillan Distribution Ltd, Houndmills, Basingstoke,
Hampshire RG21 6XS, England

Nikolai Sukhanov

Chronicler of the Russian Revolution

Israel Getzler
Professor Emeritus
Department of Russian Studies
Hebrew University of Jerusalem

in association with
St Antony's College, Oxford

First published 2002 by
PALGRAVE
Houndmills, Basingstoke, Hampshire RG21 6XS and
175 Fifth Avenue, New York, N. Y. 10010
Companies and representatives throughout the world

PALGRAVE is the new global academic imprint of
St. Martin's Press LLC Scholarly and Reference Division and
Palgrave Publishers Ltd (formerly Macmillan Press Ltd).

ISBN 0–333–97035–7

This book is printed on paper suitable for recycling and
made from fully managed and sustained forest sources.

A catalogue record for this book is available
from the British Library.

Library of Congress Cataloging-in-Publication Data
Getzler, Israel, 1920–
    Nikolai Sukhanov : chronicler of the Russian revolution /
    Israel Getzler.
        p. cm.
    Includes bibliographical references and index.
    ISBN 0–333–97035–7 (cloth)
    1. Sukhanov, N. N. (Nikolaæ Nikolaevich), 1882–1940.
    2. Revolutionaries—Soviet Union—Biography. 3. Journalists–
    –Soviet Union—Biography. 4. Editors—Soviet Union—Biography.
    5. Soviet Union—History—Revolution, 1917–1921.—Biography.
    6. Soviet Union—History—1925–1953. I. Title.

DK268.S93 G48 2001
947.084'1'092—dc21
                                                      2001046011

10   9   8   7   6   5   4   3   2   1
11   10 09 08 07 06 05 04 03 02

Printed and bound in Great Britain by
Antony Rowe Ltd, Chippenham, Wiltshire

For Dvorah
who lived with it

Sukhanov

Contents

List of Illustrations

Acknowledgements

The sketches of the leading figures of 1917 that appear in this book were made at the time by Iu. K. Artsybushev and were reissued in 1991 by Dr Dmitrii Pavlov in *Liki Semnadtsatogo*, published under his editorship in Moscow. I am deeply grateful to him for permission to use them.

Preface

My interest in Sukhanov was aroused some forty-five years ago
when I chanced upon A.J.P. Taylor's review in the (then) *New
Statesman and Nation* (21 May 1955) of a drastically abridged
English-language edition of Sukhanov's *Zapiski o revoliutsii* (Notes
on the Revolution). There, in an arresting passage, Taylor acclaimed
Sukhanov, the chronicler of the 1917 revolution:

> What should we not give for a record of Christ's life by a Roman
> philosopher who was himself waiting for a Messiah, who was
> deeply affected by Christ's personality and whose judgement was
> yet never submerged by belief? Nikolai Nikolaevich Sukhanov
> was a witness of this kind during the Russian revolution. His
> book is incomparably the best and most important account of
> those tremendous events from which spring most of the prob-
> lems of our world.

With an interest in European socialism and the Soviet experiment
that dates to my schooldays during the 1930s in Nazi Germany and
with my critical sense sharpened by my wartime experiences in
Eastern Siberia and Central Russia, I hastened to get hold of the book.
But, with Taylor's warning ringing in my ears that 'this translation
can be read for entertainment and interest', but that 'every scholar
must still go to the original text, I soon searched for and eventually
acquired a complete set of the then rather rare seven-volume original
edition. I had them expertly rebound and have ever since cherished
them as one of the treasures of my library. Above all, it was there that
I discovered Sukhanov's remarkable pen-portrait of Iulii Martov, the
Menshevik leader with whom I felt I could identify. Since many of
Martov's private papers and prolific writings were available in the
West, and his sister and party friends were generously willing to share
with me their recollections and opinions, I wrote a political biography
of my hero under the guidance of the late and very much missed
Professor Leonard Schapiro of the London School of Economics and
Political Science.

My experience in writing this book was very different. Little was known about Sukhanov in the West in the 1950s, and the Menshevik veterans whom I questioned in the 1960s were rather reticent and discouraging (as I later discovered, they had not even bothered to review his *Zapiski* in their *Sotsialisticheskii vestnik*, nor did they list in the bibliography of the Menshevik movement any of his writings from the end of May 1917 to October 1920, when he was a member of that party). In the Soviet Union, from the 1930s onwards and until the advent of *glasnost*, his *Zapiski* were held under lock and key in *spetskhranenie*, and historians were for many years wary of quoting them or citing them in footnotes.

In July 1992, while recovering from an operation, I was compelled to lie on my back for some five to six weeks, a period during which I whiled away my time by re-reading my treasured seven-volume *Zapiski* from cover to cover. Unknown to me at that point, this was the time when, thanks to *glasnost*, Dr Arkadii Kornikov was just publishing his richly annotated and meticulously indexed edition of the *Zapiski*. We were very soon in contact and I was deeply disappointed to learn from Dr Kornikov that virtually all Sukhanov's papers had disappeared. Determined nevertheless to write a study of Sukhanov, I put aside my long-term project on the soviets of 1917 and reconciled myself to working on a more limited political and intellectual portrait rather than a full-fledged biography of the man.

It is with pleasure that I acknowledge my deep debt to my colleague and friend Dr Arkadii Kornikov, chairman of the Department of History of the University of Ivanovo, for the generosity with which he helped me along in answering all my questions and proffering his valuable advice and vast store of information. If, throughout this book, I have used the original edition of the *Zapiski*, this is in no way a reflection on his excellent edition, but rather because of the limitations of my eyesight!

I am similarly deeply indebted to Professor Aleksei Litvin, chairman of the Department of History of Kazan University, who has unstintingly shared with me his unequalled knowledge of the archival materials relating to the Menshevik trial of March 1931, in which Sukhanov was one of the major defendants, and for supplying me with archival documents relating to the trial which he was then preparing for publication. I am also grateful to Professor Bella Galperina and the late, and warmly remembered, Professor Vitalii

Startsev, both of St Petersburg, for generously having made available to me the still unpublished third volume of the protocols of the Petrograd Soviet, which they edited. My sincere thanks are also due to Vladimir Naumov, Secretary of the Presidential Commission on the Rehabilitation of Victims of Political Repression, who was always ready to answer my questions and who made it possible for me to work on the file of the protocols of Sukhanov's preliminary investigations which is held in the Central Archive of the Federal Security Services of the Russian Federation. In the last ten years all these Russian colleagues have become cherished personal friends.

I warmly acknowledge the help given to me by the archivists of the Russian Centre for the Conservation and Study of Documents of Recent History (formerly the Marx-Engels Institute), the Archive of the Communist Academy, and the Central Archive of the Federal Security Service of the Russian Federation.

At the Hebrew University of Jerusalem, my colleague and friend Professor Dmitri Segal gave generous time to facilitating my communications with institutions in Russia and shared with me his rich knowledge of revolutionary Russia's radical *literati*.

Above all, Professor Jonathan Frankel of the Hebrew University and Professor Robert Service of St Antony's College, Oxford, highly respected colleagues and the warmest of friends, took off valuable time from their busy schedules to read and comb critically through my manuscript in draft form. I have benefited profoundly from their comments. But I owe my greatest debt to my wife Dvorah who has lived with this book throughout its making and to whom it is dedicated.

Glossary

batrak	hired agricultural labourer
bedniak	poor peasant
CEC–*TsIK*	Central Executive Committee of Soviets
Cheka/GPU/OGPU/NKVD	Soviet secret police, now renamed Federal Security Service of the Russian Federation
Comintern	Communist (Third) International, founded in 1919
Duma	elected Russian parliament
Glasnost	openness, publicity
Gosplan	State Planning Commission
Jacobinism	revolutionary-democratic movement and/or vanguard party aiming at seizure of power and establishment of minority dictatorship
Kadets	Constitutional Democrats
khodok	village messenger sent with errand or petition
Khlestakovshchina	a term of opprobrium derived from the very minor bureaucrat Khlestakov, the central figure in Gogol's comedy *The Inspector*: a vainglorious impostor, drunk with the sense of his own importance, he personifies boastfulness, cowardice, insolence, fickleness and pretentiousness. (Krylenko used the term in an endeavour to humiliate Sukhanov and make him look contemptible, odious, petty and ridiculous.)
kolkhoz	collective farm
kombedy	poor peasant committees
KPD	Communist Party of Germany

kulak	well-off peasant
Marx-Engels Institute	now renamed: Russian Centre for the Conservation and Study of Documents of Recent History
narodnik	populist, agrarian socialist
NEP	New Economic Policy (1921–27)
obshchina	peasant communal village
Octobrist	member of conservative-liberal party
Okhrana	tsarist secret police
Politburo	Political Bureau of Central Committee of Communist Party
PSS	Lenin, *Polnoe sobranie sochinenii* (fifth edition)
pud	weight – equivalent to 16.38kg
Rada	Ukrainian elected assembly
Revisionists	socialists starting from Marxist premises, but sceptical of certain important elements of Marxist doctrine
RSDRP	Russian Social Democratic Labour Party
Scheidemannism	a pejorative term used by socialist Internationalists during the First World War condemning the policy advocated by Philipp Scheidemann, leader of German social democracy, of *Burgfrieden* (civic truce) and of support for the war effort of the German imperial government in 'defence of the *Vaterland*'; also used by Bolsheviks and Communists to label socialist adversaries and critics.
skhod	communal village assembly
sovkhoz	Soviet state farm
Smolny (Institute)	from July 1917 seat of Petrograd Soviet and of Central Executive Committee of Soviets; during and after the October revolution the headquarters of the Military Revolutionary Committee, of Lenin, and of Sovnarkom
Sovnarkom	Council of People's Commissars

town duma	elected city council
trudovik	member of peasant party in Duma
zemstvo	rural, local self-government assembly
Zimmerwald	international, socialist, anti-war movement named after its first conference held in Zimmerwald, Switzerland, in 1915.

Introduction

This book is the product of a long-standing interest in Sukhanov, the chronicler *par excellence* of Russia's democratic revolution February to October 1917. Such a study of Sukhanov, who was vilified in the Soviet Union for more than half a century, would have been impossible before the advent of *glasnost,* which opened up materials relating to him in the Communist party archive of the Marx-Engels Institute, and in the archives of the Communist Academy and of OGPU. Since virtually all Sukhanov's private papers have disappeared, this book is an attempt at a political and intellectual portrait, rather than a fully-fledged biography, highlighting his role as an intellectually pivotal figure during the February revolution. At the centre of the book stands the seven-volume *Zapiski o revoliutsii* (Notes on the Revolution), a work now universally acclaimed as incomparable: a very honest, penetrating and incisive account of the events of 1917 as experienced by a deeply committed participant and believer whose judgement remained unclouded by doctrine or party-mindedness.

While Sukhanov personally knew all the leaders of the socialist parties and some of the other key figures, too, he never became fully the property of any one party or faction. He stands out as an independent-minded Russian revolutionary intellectual, an indomitable publicist, and a non-conformist agrarian economist. But he was equally a representative figure of the radical Russian intelligentsia, an intellectual community distinguished by a strong sense of civic duty and social responsibility, and by fearless opposition to the tsarist regime and the established order.

His first concern, as we shall see (in Chapters 1 and 5) was the modernization, on cooperative and mechanized foundations, of Russia's peasant agriculture which, he urged, should not be imposed from above but should rather be realized by the initiative of the peasants themselves. Moreover, he insisted that it was the traditional Russian village commune, the *obshchina*, that provided the ideal framework for Russia's agrarian revolution.

A prolific writer and a trenchant polemicist, he edited the prestigious, radical and self-consciously above-party *Sovremennik* before and during the First World War and Maxim Gorky's left-socialist *Letopis'* and its successor, the radical and oppositional *Novaia zhizn'* newspaper, during the period 1917–18 until its closure by the Soviet authorities on 16 July 1918. An agitator for Marxist–*Narodnik rapprochement* and unification before the war, he distinguished himself during the war in tsarist Russia as a daring, resourceful but lone voice of the Zimmerwald socialist peace movement (Chapter 1).

A founding member of the Executive Committee of the Petrograd Soviet in February 1917 and the ideologist of the 'dual power' of the revolution in its early days, Sukhanov joined Iulii Martov and his Menshevik-Internationalists in the second half of May 1917 and became a fierce critic of the Provisional Government and of the Menshevik-Socialist Revolutionary *bloc* that controlled the soviets until the October Revolution (Chapters 2 and 3). He proved an equally fierce and singularly courageous and hard-hitting critic of the Bolshevik October revolution and dictatorship in 1917–20 and was taken so seriously by Lenin that even as the Bolshevik leader lay on his deathbed he dictated his defence of the October revolution in a review of the *Zapiski,* published in *Pravda* and *Izvestiia*, which may well be regarded as his ideological testament.

After a five-year period of gradual accommodation with the somewhat more relaxed Soviet regime of the NEP years, Sukhanov took on the Bolshevik establishment on 4 December 1928 advocating a rational appeal to the peasants' economic interests as an alternative to Stalin's 'extreme measures' of brutal requisitioning. Two days later, his was the only voice raised in public criticism of proposals by Professor Vladimir Friche to impose an iron-clad preventive censorship on literature and publishing. To cap it all, came his unrelenting critique of the school of Agrarian Marxists in the Communist Academy who, since 1926, had been preparing the

Communist Party ideologically and psychologically for Stalin's final assault on Russia's peasantry in his double-pronged drive for collectivization and industrialization. 'To see for himself', in May–June 1930, Sukhanov undertook a private month-long study journey into the rural areas of the Volga, the Northern Caucasus, the Black Sea and the Crimea: his findings on the devastating results of collectivization have until very recently been confined to the pages of his OGPU file (Chapters 5 and 6).

Arrested on 20 July 1930, he was put on trial in March 1931 as a leading member of a fictitious Menshevik Union Bureau and sentenced to a 10-year term of imprisonment which was commuted in 1935 to exile in Tobolsk, Siberia (Chapter 6). Arrested again in September 1937, on a charge of spying for Germany and engaging in anti-Soviet agitation, he was shot on 29 June 1940. On 19 March 1992 he was rehabilitated in accordance with the law 'On the Rehabilitation of Victims of Political Repression' of 18 October 1991 on the grounds that the incriminating evidence had, for 'political motives', been 'fabricated'.

In an autobiographical essay dated 20 January 1927, Sukhanov – born in Moscow on 10 December 1882 – remembered his childhood and youth thus:

My father [Nikolai Samuilovich Gimmer] was a minor railway official. He suffered from alcoholism and died in 1903; I never saw him, nor did I ever know what is called a family. I spent some of my childhood with my mother, but the larger part with my grandmother. My mother [Ekaterina Pavlovna Simon] was a clever and able woman from a noble family, yet without intellectual culture, a midwife by profession. But I was never close to her. I was of weak physique and compared with my schoolmates I did badly in those activities that are characteristic of childhood and adolescence. I was of a contemplative disposition. My first memories: lack of money and endless, futile talks about divorce, partly in French so that I should not understand – but I did half understand and in the presence of strangers felt that I was the bearer of some shameful secrets.[1]

Thanks to the painstaking research of Dr Arkadii Kornikov, of the University of Ivanovo, who pieced together information on

Sukhanov's family, we know that the Gimmers, his father's family, were of German descent; that his great-grandfather was a Protestant pastor, while his grandfather, Samuil Philipovich Gimmer, was a physician who had practised in the Novgorod province and had acquired the title of Staff Physician and the rank of Titled Councillor with the rights of a nobleman. Sukhanov's father was listed as of Russian nationality and Russian Orthodox religion.

Sukhanov's mother, Ekaterina Pavlovna, also belonged to the service nobility. Her father was a retired army officer and her mother, Elizaveta Antonovna Simon, was a cultured, well-educated woman, an admirer of Lev Tolstoy with whom she frequently corresponded.[2]

Until 1896, when he was 14, Sukhanov attended high school in Moscow with his mother paying his way. He read a great deal and was passionately interested in the theatre and music. But in that year, as he recalled, a shadow was cast over his life by 'my mother's sensational court case, the substance of which served Tolstoy as material for his drama *The Living Corpse*.[3] Having left her drunken and dissolute husband in 1883 shortly after the birth of her son Nikolai and gone to live with her mother, she met Stepan Ivanovich Chistov whom she wanted to marry. But the Moscow Ecclesiastical Consistory refused her application for a divorce on the grounds that the evidence proving her husband's 'marital infidelity' was 'insufficient'. In despair, she persuaded her legal husband to feign suicide: a farewell letter was prepared and his clothes, complete with documents, were thrown down on the ice of the Moskva river while he made off for Petersburg with the money she had given him.

Unfortunately, the fake suicide was soon exposed by the police and the newly-wed couple were charged with bigamy. When the court case was heard in Moscow, it became a country-wide sensation, with all its details reported in the newspapers, including the seven-year sentence of exile to Yeniseisk province in Siberia handed down to the couple. But thanks to their case being taken up by A.F. Koni, a well-known lawyer in the criminal appeals department of the Senate, in 1898 Tsar Nikolai II, acting on the advice of his minister of justice, commuted the sentence to one year's imprisonment. While his mother was in the Butyrki prison and employed as a midwife, Sukhanov was left to fend for himself and began giving private lessons in the afternoons and evenings. He was apparently so successful at this, that the headmaster of his school asked him to tutor his own sons. Earning more than he needed to keep himself, he was able to spend the summer months of 1900 and 1901 travelling by boat along the Volga from Nizhnii Novgorod to Astrakhan, to the Urals, the Caucasus and the Crimea, and to Kiev, seeing for himself how Russia, and rural Russia in particular, lived. Distinguishing himself at his school , where he was the best student, he read deeply in history, classical antiquity, literature and religion. He was captivated by Tolstoy and his philosophy of self-improvement and rejection of culture, but that included

> a critical rejection of the political regime and of its economic structure which turned me into a left-wing radical and induced me to join illegal high school circles for general and political self-education. It was then that I made my first attempts at publishing in the school's journal which I edited and in the beginning of 1901 I read my first paper – on Chekhov's *Three Sisters* – to a well-attended meeting of Moscow's illegal high school circles. It was full of Tolstoyan ideas and was well-received. Thus, when I finished school and was awarded a silver medal [in June 1902], I had not only become a vegetarian but had also decided not to enrol in university. Not knowing what to do with myself, I left for Paris with the money I had saved, but had no particular aims.

In Paris, he enrolled for the academic year 1902–03 in the recently opened Russian College of Social Sciences which was headed by the historian Maxim Kovalevsky and staffed by émigré professors and lecturers, so that it already had a reputation in the conservative press as 'an academy of revolutionaries' while the liberal press saw in it 'an institution of a rationalist-liberal trend'. It was probably both, since it invited as guest lecturers such socialists as Victor Chernov, leader of the Party of Socialist Revolutionaries, Lenin, Georgii Plekhanov, 'Father of Russian Marxism', and Emile Vandervelde, leader of the Belgian socialist party, as well as the liberal Pavel Miliukov, leader of the party of Constitutional Democrats (Kadets). Sukhanov also attended many political talks by that galaxy of Russian revolutionaries, publicists and politicians who either lived in Paris or visited there, notably talks given by Lenin, Chernov, Trotsky and Martov.[4] As he recalled in his *Zapiski*

> Although I was not convinced by Martov, I vividly recollect the enormous impression made on me by his erudition, his powerful

intellect and his debating skill. I was surely no longer a fledgling then, but I felt that Martov's talks filled my head with new ideas; though I did not sympathize with him, I noted that he emerged the victor in his contest with the *Narodnik* 'generals'. Trotsky, who was then with Martov, in spite of all his showing-off, did not produce a tenth of Martov's effect and seemed no more than his echo.[5]

At the end of his year there, Sukhanov left Paris for Moscow determined to engage in revolutionary activity and on 25 July 1903 he enrolled in the Faculty of Philosophy and Philology at Moscow University which then boasted such luminaries as V.D. Kliuchevsky, A.A. Kizevetter, R.V. Vipper and V.M. Gere. But Sukhanov 'had entered the university with the sole purpose of avoiding police scrutiny as one who had no occupation'. He soon joined both the illegal central student organization and the underground Socialist-Revolutionary party organization and was busy in propaganda work and lecturing in the provinces. Having become a full-time propagandist, he quickly ceased to attend lectures and even failed to pay his university fees for the 1904 spring semester. Under daily police surveillance from 1 March to 25 April 1904, he was arrested on 25 May in a wave of arrests of members of the Moscow SR party. The printing type and a large quantity of illegal literature which the police found in his suitcase linked him directly with the illegal printing press that was tracked down and he was sentenced to a year and a half of imprisonment.[6]

The Taganka prison in Moscow became, so he wrote, 'the principal place and period of my education'. There, among other illegal publications, he made an intensive study of the social-democratic *Iskra,* notably 'the first-class articles of Plekhanov, Lenin, Martov and Trotsky, with pride of place going to Martov, that divinely inspired publicist'. More important still, it was in the Taganka prison that he wrote his first major article, 'On Our Agrarian Programme' which was his contribution to the agrarian debate of the SRs in preparation for their First Congress. In October 1905, he was – together with all other political prisoners – freed by a revolutionary crowd.[7]

1
Champion of the Russian Village Commune

Sukhanov had a deep and long-lasting political and social interest in agricultural economics. His public championship of the *obshchina*, the Russian repartitional village commune, dates back to 1905 and to his first published article, 'On Our Agrarian Programme', which appeared in *Revoliutsionnaia Rossiia*, the illegal ideological journal of the neo-*narodnik*, non-Marxist Party of Socialist Revolutionaries (SRs).[1] He wrote it while in the Moscow Taganka prison as his contribution to the debate on an agrarian programme in preparation for the first SR congress which was to convene at the end of December 1905 in Imatra (Finland). What distinguished Sukhanov's article was his staunch defence of the traditionally autonomous internal arrangements of the self-governing *obshchina* against those SR zealots who, come the revolution, would have forced the *obshchina* to prohibit the hiring of labour and the leasing of land. Sukhanov also took issue with their proposal that, in accordance with the 'self-labour principle', all periodically repartitioned communal land be allotted on an egalitarian basis in accordance with the number of working hands in a peasant household, rather than in accordance with the number of mouths to be fed as was the practice in most communes where land was redistributed regularly every few years among the peasant households. Such coercive legislation from above, Sukhanov urged emphatically, would 'create a perpetual antagonism between the population and the controlling agencies' which would be seen and resented as just another variety of tsarist 'police tutelage': if some peasant 'hired two or three *batraks* (farm labourers) and he himself would lie on the oven, the *obshchina*

7

might either tolerate or prohibit it, but why should that be regulated from the outside?' Sukhanov asked. Indeed peasants would in any case know how to get around such restrictive regulations.[2]

The *obshchina* alone is in a position effectively to regulate its members' internal economic relations. It alone is capable of assessing the interests and needs of every member since it has known all of them from birth, is familiar with their economic and family situations, their characters and weaknesses, and precisely how industrious, or otherwise, each is. It can always compel a household not to lease land, but rather to work it themselves and thus forego the hiring of a farm labourer. Alternatively, it can deprive a household of its allotment or take away from it the extra land it has leased.[3]

As for those SRs who had urged a prohibition of the leasing of land and the hiring of labour to prevent that polarization of the *obshchina* into a minority of capitalist farmers and a large class of agricultural labourers, as predicted by the Marxists, who welcomed the forward march of modern capitalism in the backward Russian countryside, Sukhanov argued that if the Marxists were right, then no legal enactments and prohibitions of the sort that some SRs advocated would halt the spread of capitalism in agriculture. Fortunately, that was not bound to happen, Sukhanov reassured his comrades:

We [SRs, as against the Marxists] stand on the firm ground of science ... It postulates a non-capitalist evolution of agriculture [as distinct from capitalist development in industry] whose socialization would proceed by way of co-operation [of peasant households] and thus by-pass a capitalist phase [in agriculture]. Few believe today in a capitalist future for agriculture ... true, all [comparative] studies of large and small farm holdings affirm the vitality and advantages of the former over the latter, but not of capitalist farms. They also prove wrong that Marxist scheme which posits a deep differentiation within the peasantry between a rural bourgeoisie, on the one hand, and an agrarian proletariat, on the other.[4]

Summing up the essentials of the SR agrarian programme, Sukhanov proclaimed his neo-*narodnik* credo. It envisaged, in the first place, as its political 'minimum programme', the establishment of a democratic, bourgeois-capitalist republic. This expectation from the overthrow of tsardom was one that the SRs shared, albeit with far less enthusiasm, with the Marxist social democrats. But what distinguished Sukhanov and the SRs from their Marxist rivals was the former's firm commitment to an immediate programme for the socialization of the land entailing 'the *liquidation* of private ownership in land, its transfer to public *ownership* and the equalization of its *use*'. As for the cultivation of the land (as distinct from its collective ownership), it would continue as before on a household or individual basis until peasants, attracted by the economic advantages of mechanization and co-operative farming, were prepared to band together.

Not surprisingly, Sukhanov refrained from spelling out the details of the somewhat vague SR plan for land socialization which was generally understood to mean that the land-fund would be vested more in organs of local self-government than in the state. This agrarian settlement, combined with the democratization of the political order and the necessary changes in the legal system, would lay the foundations for the SR maximum programme: 'the socialization of agricultural *production* and the social ownership of the means of production, i.e. the realization of our final aim [of socialism] in the village'.[5]

It is difficult to assess what influence Sukhanov's article had on the proceedings of the SR congress and on the programme it adopted.[6] Still, Mark Vishniak ('Pomortsev'), when referring to the SR literature on socialization, cited it alongside articles by Chernov, Aleksei Peshekhonov and G. Novotorzhsky.[7] The 22-year-old Sukhanov had good reason to feel pleased at being included in such distinguished company. Moreover, the question of whether to allocate land according to the number of producers, rather than consumers, in a household was widely debated, as were the questions of the leasing of land and the hiring of labour.[8] The arguments of such major figures as Osip Minor ('Solomin'), S.P. Shvetsov ('Pashin') and Nikolai Rakitnikov ('Bazarov') against 'regimentation' were certainly in tune with those of Sukhanov, including the warning against any reversion to an old regime-style of 'police tutelage over the life of the peasantry'. And when the vote was taken on the motion of the delegate from Nizhnii Novgorod to include in the SR programme a prohibition of the hiring of farm labourers, it was solidly defeated by 29 to 4 votes.[9]

While Sukhanov would continue intermittently to argue against SR zealots, against so-called Revisionists in Germany and Austria and against their Russian disciples who idealized the small independent peasant farm, the main thrust of his scholarly and polemical effort was directed against the traditional *'obshchinophobia'* of Russian (and later Soviet) Marxism. Formulated in the 1890s by Plekhanov, Peter Struve and Lenin, Russian Marxist agrarian thinking regarded the *obshchina* as a major obstacle to the modernization of Russia. That would come about as Russia developed a market economy and established a democratic, bourgeois, capitalist society as a necessary precondition to a socialist society. As distinct from the populists and the neo-populist SRs who extolled the egalitarian village commune as the ideal agrarian institution for the direct transition to socialism, by-passing capitalism, the Marxists decried and rejected the *obshchina* as a coercive collectively responsible framework. It had been created by the autocratic-bureaucratic tsarist police state to exact taxes and dues from the peasantry. With unconcealed glee, they pointed at a process of social differentiation within the village commune and its polarization into a minority of rural capitalist farmers and a large majority of agricultural labourers – a polarization that heralded its impending doom. They subjected the populist infatuation with the *obshchina* to a trenchant critique: it was 'naive and utopian' to rely on so primitive and reactionary an institution to serve as a basis for the realization of modern socialist ideas (Struve).

Lenin went even further in challenging the egalitarian proto-socialist character of the *obshchina* so dear to the populists: 'The *obshchina* was not an antagonist of capitalism, but, on the contrary, its very deep and solid foundation.' And in a memorable formulation that lasted into the agrarian debates of the 1920s when it became something like a Leninist dogma, he postulated:

> The old [communal] peasantry does not merely 'differentiate', it disintegrates completely, it ceases to exist, it is displaced by completely new types of village population: a rural bourgeoisie

(largely petty) and a rural proletariat, [i.e.] a class of agricultural commodity producers and a class of agricultural wage-earners.

And, for good measure, Lenin extolled 'the progressive historical role of capitalism in Russia's agriculture': it demolishes the local enclosure and restriction, the fragmentation of small agriculturists, it socializes agricultural production.[10]

Sukhanov, liberated from the Taganka prison together with others by a revolutionary crowd in October 1905, went on to take part in the December Moscow uprising. He spent the next few years on a study of the agrarian scene, producing two monographs published legally in 1908 and 1909 under the drab, but politically safe, titles *Ground Rent and the Principles of Land Taxation*[11] and *On the Problem of the Evolution of Agriculture: Social Relations in Russia's Peasant Economy.*[12] The first work carried a lengthy introduction by Chernov, the leader of the SRs, who warmly commended the young author to 'comrades who share [his] social-political credo and to all those interested in the great agrarian problem of our days'.[13] The second book constituted Sukhanov's major attempt (over 400 closely printed pages) to put the SR agrarian programme on a scholarly basis underpinned by data from *Zemstvo* statistics and the Army Registry of Horses. Sukhanov insisted that this work was 'the product of deduction' from his statistical study of 1,700,000 peasant households and he offered it more as a tentative 'hypothesis' rather than as a definitive work of scholarship. Taking issue with such Revisionists as Werner Sombart, Eduard David, Friedrich Hertz, Nikolai Oganovsky and Sergei Bulgakov, he argued the superiority of large mechanized farms over small peasant farms provided that they were based on the co-operative effort of independent farmers. Arguing against Russian Marxists such as Lenin and the Menshevik Peter Maslov, he urged the decapitalization of agriculture and the eventual elimination of capitalist farms contrasting them with the 'vitality and stability' of the Russian peasant farm.[14] This work, despite its fierce polemical style for which he subsequently apologized[15] profoundly to 'Peter Maslov and many other authors of various persuasions', including Lenin, earned him an honourable mention from the Academy of Sciences and the encouragement of his professors to pursue an academic career.[16] But in January 1911, accused of having engaged in 'revolutionary propaganda intended to incite student youth to ... a renewal of the revolutionary struggle in Russia ... ',[17] he was sent into a three-year exile under police surveillance to Archangelsk province, an unexpected turn of events which put an end to both his academic plans and his first marriage. For his wife, Sofia Shaternikova, sister of his close school friend Mikhail Shaternikov (to whose memory his book *The Evolution* was dedicated), left him and their two small sons, remarried and went to live in Poland.[18]

But Sukhanov's chief and controversial contribution is to be found in two articles published in 1910 and 1912 and in some subsequent articles in which he spelled out in detail what he regarded as the preconditions for the modernization and socialization of Russian peasant agriculture.[19] Time and again he insisted that the Russian peasant farm, though 'vital and stable' as compared with large capitalist farms which he believed were doomed, would remain backward and semi-pauperized unless the peasants themselves took advantage of the technical 'revolution of the means of labour' and organized together in co-operative production. The incentive would be the availability and collective use of farm machinery to replace the traditional methods of threshing with chains, mowing with a scythe, sowing by hand and winnowing with a shovel.

Without mechanization one cannot count on a social organization of agricultural production. Machines ....are intended for a large enterprise. It is absurd to acquire and employ a number of machines when one machine is adequate [to serve a number of households]. The households link, unite organically by the simple and inevitable transition to machine production in the interests of economy of labour. Decrees, contracts, [appeals to] virtues and customs, all forms of propaganda will be of no avail in [persuading peasants to relinquish their independence and merge their individual holdings into larger units] ... Moreover, this [modernized co-operative production] will create organs of self-government that will be equipped with material and scientific resources. The gradual linking and merging of the small-holdings will be inevitable in the interests of increased productivity of land and labour.[20]

Another – at least as important – necessary condition was, he urged, 'the conscious effort of the peasants themselves to band together in the interests of the economy of labour'. Such large units were the solution to Russia's agrarian problem and to the integration of agriculture into the socialist economy of the future. Unless both necessary conditions were met, the Russian countryside would stagnate and regress and turn into a multitude of isolated small peasant holdings, resembling nothing so much as potatoes in a sack which, as Marx put it 'make up a sack of potatoes and nothing more' – a nightmarish prospect for Sukhanov with his vision of large-scale, mechanized and co-operative agriculture which he extolled as 'the victory of human reason in economics'.[21]

The glaring omission in all this speculation on the forms of the merger of small farms was the *obshchina*, hitherto acclaimed by Sukhanov as 'a most precious legal and economic institution'. The chief reason for this omission was, it seems to me, Sukhanov's panicky reaction to the early success of Prime Minister Piotr Stolypin's agrarian legislation, particularly the laws of November 1907 and June 1910 which enabled, and even positively encouraged, 'the sturdy and strong peasants' as distinct from 'the needy and drunken', to opt out of their *obshchina* and, most important of all, to take with them their land allotment or its equivalent. As Sukhanov saw it, this opportunity would be seized by a number of groups: peasants with large land allotments, those who had left earlier without receiving compensation for their land allocation, those who were deeply in debt and yet others who had been resettled (*pereselentsy*). Noting that Stolypin's scheme of 'the fabrication of new landed property owners' had been quite successful, Sukhanov feared that it would 'sooner or later destroy the *obshchina* as a whole' and that fear was to remain with him whenever there was a question of permitting peasants to withdraw from the *obshchina* with their land or its equivalent. For although Sukhanov had not ceased to value the peasants' 'communal psychology, [egalitarian] customs and practices', as bound to facilitate their acceptance of a socialist agrarian programme, he did not think these virtues would be strong enough to withstand 'the real economic interests of those peasants who wanted to become peasant proprietors'.[22] Unlike many SR enthusiasts, Sukhanov was no naive utopian but had a healthy respect for market forces and economic interests.

As he put it a few months later, 'to use political power to establish norms that run counter to the trend of economic development is, of course, a utopia, but a utopia which is very injurious because it attempts to deflect the social movement from its true direction'.[23] Intimately linked with his socialist agrarian programme, which he hoped would prove acceptable to both Marxist social democrats and neo-*narodnik* SRs, was his campaign – waged mainly in the pages of the *Sovremennik*, a prestigious, socialist, self-consciously above-party political-literary journal to which he had contributed while still in administrative exile in Archangelsk – for the *rapprochement* and eventual unification of the Marxist and *narodnik* wings of Russian socialism. Having benefited early in 1913 from the amnesty in honour of the tercentenary of the Romanov dynasty, Sukhanov began working on the journal in St Petersburg, and in January 1914 became its editor together with Vladimir Stankevich.[24] At that time, the *Sovremennik* advertised itself as an 'inter-fractional organ which, as a matter of principle, will urge the necessity of the full organizational unity of all socialist trends'.[25] Sukhanov's chief message was that the traditional ideological differences between Marxists and *narodniks* had significantly softened and narrowed even over the most divisive agrarian question.

Turning to the Marxists, he urged them to stop seeing the SRs as nothing more than a petty-bourgeois party, but rather to recognize their serious commitment to revolution and to socialism. Similarly, they should accept 'the labouring peasantry' as a democratic and exploited class, sharing a common political and democratic interest with the proletariat, so much so that they 'therefore can be relied upon to support the entire so-called minimum programme of the proletariat' which aimed at the establishment of a democratic republic. While he believed that the ingrained *obshchinophobia* of Marxism had given way to a reluctant acceptance of the *obshchina* as a fact of life, and that it was 'no more a *casus belli*', he thought 'the still negative attitude of our social democracy to the *obshchina* remained a very sad fact'. This, he pleaded, invoking the example of the European comrades, must change:

> Anywhere in the West, this institution [i.e. the *obshchina*] would certainly arouse sympathy and support, and its violent destruction [by Stolypin's legislation] would provoke the severest condemnation. But with us, and in the name of the most fantastic aims, the most unfounded doctrinairism, a proletarian [i.e. social-

democratic] party adopts an ambivalent position regarding the *obshchina* and, in one of its sections [the Bolsheviks], is even prepared to cut itself off from the international [socialist] position and to take up instead that occupied by the *Junkers* and the reactionary bourgeoisie.[26]

A few years later, Sukhanov conceded that a number of legal economic changes in the organization of the *obshchina* were necessary: it must cease to be a closed estate organization but rather open up to include as equal members all those who lived in the territory of the village, even if they had not formerly been members. The strip system should be abolished, while the equalizing mechanism of repartition and of land use ought to be thoroughly standardized. There should be exemptions from compulsory crop rotation, and a system of compensation to individual peasants for their investments of labour and capital must be devised. Still, he insisted, all reforms must be subject to the one overriding condition: the preservation of the *obshchina*'s ownership of the land, which must be recognized as public and inalienable property – 'every patch of collective land' must be defended to the hilt, even against the peasants' own wishes.[27]

While Sukhanov pleaded with the Marxists, he also delivered some bitter home truths to his former party comrades, the neo-populist SRs. Arguing that the 'labouring peasantry', in its struggle against exploitation by usurers, forestallers and landowners, could choose between joining the socialist liberation movement or the co-operative movement, Sukhanov drew the operative conclusion that

the labouring peasantry is not by nature a socialist class, i.e. the peasant organization engaged in the defence of peasant class interests is not [necessarily] a movement which realizes the social ideal of collectivism. A socialist party cannot fuse with such a class nor can it link its fate with it. The labouring peasantry, by its nature, *may* be a friend of socialism, but it may also prove to be its enemy. [Therefore] a socialist party cannot be (and must not call itself) a peasant party. [By contrast], the only class that can by its very nature be regarded as collectivist is the proletariat ... it is indissolubly tied to the [socialist] movement as it can follow no other road to its liberation ... If it were necessary to attach a class label to the socialist party, then one would use the term proletarian party.[28]

On these grounds, Sukhanov enjoined the SRs, for the sake of *rapprochement* and the unity of the socialist movement, to give up seeing themselves as a 'peasant party' paying 'special attention to the peasantry', and to abandon the idea of 'the fusion of the proletariat with the toiling peasantry into one toiling people'. Were that renunciation to be made, he believed there would be an end to the fundamental difference in *Weltanschauung* between the Marxists and the *narodniks*, which had inspired justified (sic *I.G.*) suspicions in the Marxist side regarding the 'purity' of the scientific socialist principles of the *narodnik* side.

Sukhanov's initiative, outlined in some detail in his article 'On the Question of Our Disagreements', stimulated an intensive debate which lasted until the outbreak of the war and produced an unusually large number of polemical review articles and hostile comments in the 'fat journals' of the socialist intelligentsia.[29] Four reviews – by Stankevich, by the SR leader and theorist Rakitnikov, by Chernov and by Lenin – are of particular interest. They illustrate the extent to which Sukhanov had utterly failed in his persistent attempt to bridge the differences between *narodniks* and Marxists.

Stankevich, as perceptive as ever, spotted the inherent message in the article as being 'to unify or be devoured' (a slogan which he made the title of his own article). Alleging that Sukhanov had been less than even-handed in his treatment of the two sides, Stankevich went on to claim that Sukhanov, while still advocating the *narodnik* agrarian programme of land nationalization and the equalization of land usage, had 'resolutely broken with populism'. Would Sukhanov's 'Marxist arguments' in support of his agrarian programme cut any ice with the Marxists themselves, he wondered.[30] Some few years later, Sukhanov confirmed that Stankevich had not been that far off the mark, conceding that he himself had not regarded the two sides to the Marxist–*narodnik* dispute as equals but had instead expected that the *narodniks* would oust the non-socialist elements from their ranks and 'integrate' (or be devoured? *I.G.*) within the Marxist 'kindred milieu', being met half-way by the Marxists.[31]

Rakitnikov fastened on Sukhanov's point that the peasantry, unlike the proletariat, was not 'a socialist class by nature' and could even become an 'enemy of socialism'. That assessment was totally unacceptable to the *narodniks* because it turned the peasantry into 'second-class socialist citizens', Rakitnikov protested. He berated Sukhanov for being willing to compromise on *narodnik* theory in order to unify the parties and that, he urged, was out of the question.[32]

Chernov, Sukhanov's former mentor and patron, bitterly censured the article's 'rash attempt at the abolition of populism'. Defending populists old and new for their championing of the *obshchina* and their desire to by-pass capitalism, Chernov reminded Sukhanov that the populists were in the good company of Marx and Engels who had clearly dissociated themselves from the Russian liberals and their anti-*obshchina* views, berating them for behaving 'as if Russia had nothing better to do than dismantle [or privatize], as speedily as possible, the communal property of the peasants and plunge straight into capitalism'. But what may well have been most hurtful to Sukhanov, the champion of the *obshchina*, was Chernov's accusation that he had shown excessive zeal in prematurely burying the *obshchina* while it was still fighting for its survival; he must have smarted under Chernov's prediction that were there to be a reversal of the legal enactments which encouraged the privatization of collectively owned land, 'you will see how quickly many of the wounds inflicted on the *obshchina* will be healed'. Indeed, Sukhanov did see Chernov's prediction come true in the course of the 1917 revolution when, for whatever reason, the vast majority of 'separators' returned to their communal villages so that, on the eve of the October revolution some 98 per cent of Russia's peasants lived and worked in *obshchina*s (as compared with 80 per cent at the beginning of the century). In common with Rakitnikov, Chernov took special exception to the liberty with which Sukhanov rounded off 'sharp ideological corners' for the sake of '*rapprochement*'. The two fundamental problems on which Marxists and populists were deeply divided were 'the relationship between capitalist and non-capitalist development and the relationship between the proletariat and the rest of the army of workers', and that certainly included Russia's peasantry, Chernov lectured Sukhanov. Such disagreements, he urged, also led to sharp divergences on social philosophy and socialist practice. 'We [populists] insist on a socialist conception which is as unified as that of the orthodox Marxists. But it consists of different elements' such as those concerned with moral, psychological and juridical issues, while orthodox Marxists tended to ignore 'all factors except economics', Chernov concluded.[33]

As Stankevich had predicted, Sukhanov's initiative was at least equally unacceptable to the Marxists: Lenin launched a fierce attack on the campaign for unification 'conducted by the *Sovremennik* and its ringleader [Sukhanov]', stigmatizing it as 'the fighting method of the bourgeois intelligentsia against the workers'. Sukhanov, who preached 'the unity of *narodniks* and so-called Marxists and eliminates the distinction between Marxism and populism' was nothing but 'an empty wind-bag of which there are many in the *salons* of our liberal society.' For indeed: 'an abyss of theory and practice yawns between Marxism and populism!' And it was with glee that Lenin noted the complete absence of any positive response to

Fig. 1.1   Chernov

Sukhanov and 'the puny journal *Sovremennik'* from any Marxist circle.[34]

As so often in his life, Sukhanov had not only fallen between the stools but had seen his efforts end in complete fiasco.[35] As sharptongued Ekaterina Kuskova, a prominent member of the intelligentsia and a former colleague on the *Sovremennik,* noted when introducing him to guests at her *salon*: 'This is Nikolai Nikolaevich – formerly an economist and today a Mister Betwixt and Between *[byvshyi ekonomist, a nyne mezhstulenets].*'[36]

While Sukhanov, that independent-minded *Narodnik* now turning Marxist – he had apparently severed his organizational ties with the SRs in 1907–08 – may have thought of himself as a well-qualified campaigner for Marxist-populist *rapprochement*, his initiative was singularly ill-timed. On the Marxist side, by 1912 the perennial Bolshevik–Menshevik feud had become a full-blown split, so much so that the Mensheviks, the weaker and more conciliatory side in the conflict, appealed willy-nilly to the Bureau of the Socialist International to arbitrate and impose unity on the rival wings of Russian social democracy. Meanwhile, Lenin and his Bolsheviks, as party-minded and doctrinaire as ever, conducted a vicious slander campaign against the Mensheviks whom they called 'Liquidators', accusing them of burying the underground revolutionary Marxist party. They were certainly far beyond considering a *rapprochement* with the non-Marxist party. Lenin put it succinctly in a private letter denouncing the *Sovremennik,* [it is] 'the foul enterprise of a *bloc* of scoundrels, liquidators and *Narodniks* whom I shall abuse savagely' – and he certainly did.[37]

The very much worker-centred Mensheviks were far too intimidated by the Bolshevik campaign against them as 'liquidators of the party' to seek allies outside the orthodox Marxist camp, particularly eschewing any proximity to the SRs whom they regarded as a petty-bourgeois peasant party engaged in terrorism, a policy of which they thoroughly disapproved.

As for the neo-*narodnik* SRs, they were in deep crisis. They were still reeling under the blows dealt them by the unmasking of Evno Azef, the head of their terrorist Fighting Organization as a major police agent and by Stolypin's initially successful offensive against the *obshchina.* The Azef affair not only put an end to the SR policy of terrorist acts against high-ranking servants of the tsarist regime as a means to trigger a revolutionary mass uprising, it also discredited the gullible SR leaders who had patronized and pampered the Fighting Organization and its unsavoury head. Similarly, the mortal threat which Stolypin's agrarian legislation posed to the *obshchina*, and thus to the SRs' reliance on the communal traditions of the Russian peasantry, pulled the props from under the central plank of the SR doctrine. Small wonder that the SRs were on the defensive against their Marxist opponents who had severely censured their terrorism and had ridiculed their idealization of the *obshchina* and their infatuation with the Russian peasantry. To the SRs, Sukhanov's initiative was singularly embarrassing and in bad taste, so much so that Sukhanov complained that 'the *narodnik* press' had treated him as an outlaw.

While in Archangelsk exile, Sukhanov had fallen in love with and married Galina Flakserman, a young, enthusiastic Bolshevik with a rich revolutionary past. Together, and assisted by a group of exiles, they studied the statistical materials relating to the registration of homesteads for the year 1785 in Archangelsk province. Benefiting from the general amnesty in celebration of the tercentenary of the Romanov dynasty in 1913, they settled in Petersburg where both worked on the *Sovremennik*, with Sukhanov becoming its editor in January 1914. When the journal closed down late in 1915, Sukhanov joined the *Letopis'*, which had just been founded by Maxim Gorky, and soon became its *de facto* editor.[38]

The outbreak of war in August 1914 threw European and Russian socialists of all persuasions into ideological turmoil – confronting them with the painful dilemma of remaining faithful to their own anti-war and anti-imperialist commitments or rallying to the defence of their respective fatherlands. Whether they were Marxists or *narodniks*, they divided into two camps, the so-called defensists and the so-called internationalists. But for Sukhanov there was no such dilemma, he was an internationalist *par excellence* who threw himself body and soul into anti-war agitation, despite an early flirt with the idea that the defeat of Germany, which he expected, would ignite revolution there.[39] A spate of articles flooded from his pen to appear in, or be censored out of, the *Letopis'*, or published as brochures. Though officially exiled from Petrograd from May 1914, he managed to continue to live there – sometimes on someone else's passport, sleeping in different places and 'sometimes slipping in the shadows past the porter and the yard-man into his own apartment where his family was living'. He also managed to continue working under his own name (N.N. Gimmer) as an economist in the Ministry of Agriculture in the section that dealt with irrigation in Turkestan, as he reported with undisguised satisfaction in his *Zapiski*, noting that it was from that desk that he edited the *Letopis'* 'with the Damocles sword of police raids ever present'.[40]

The *Letopis'*, which listed among its editors and contributors a galaxy of Russia's left-wing intelligentsia was, right from the start, under the close surveillance of the police and the censors who suppressed many internationalist articles, poems and reports, including almost all the articles that Martov had sent in from abroad.[41] In a report to the press administration bureau, senior police officer Vladimir Trofimovich noted in November 1916 that the *Letopis'* had 'a radical oppositionist tendency with a social democratic colouring'. He pointed to what he claimed was its pro-German bias in trying to publish articles that praised Western, and notably German, culture as 'vastly superior to our Slav culture' and in insisting that 'the German military and economic might is incomparably greater than that of the Allies'. The anti-war agitation of English, French and Italian workers was reported sympathetically, he wrote, while the war was perceived as of 'no political or economic benefit to Russia'. Gorky, he went on, quoted the opinion of a workers' group that 'the defeat of Russia would improve the lot of the Jews and of the working class' and he claimed that 'inordinate space is given to the Jewish problem and Jewish interests are passionately supported'. Plekhanov's famous appeal to socialist deputies to vote in the Duma in support of war credits had been condemned and Plekhanov himself had been denounced as 'a traitor to the ideals and traditions of socialism', while 'all patriotic literature is fiercely denounced'.[42] If one allows for a conventional anti-Semitic bias on Trofimovich's part, his profile of the *Letopis'* was not that far off the mark. However, while the underlying assumption of Sukhanov's anti-war writings was the orthodox Marxist claim that the belligerents of both coalitions were tarred with the same imperialist brush, the main thrust of his writings was directed against the entire 'defensist' camp of liberal, radical, democratic and socialist supporters of the war. Thus, the liberals Pavel Miliukov, Fiodor Kokoshkin, Prince Evgenii Trubetskoi and Peter Struve, the radicals Nikolai Berdiaev, Sergei Bulgakov, Nikolai Yordansky, Aleksander Izgoev, Aleksander Finn-Enotaevsky and Mikhail Tugan-Baranovsky, and the socialists

Peter Maslov, David Zaslavsky and Georgii Plekhanov were all nailed down and mercilessly exposed by Sukhanov as seeking to provide the war with a new spiritual-ideological meaning and justification long after the earlier, spontaneous enthusiasm for the war had waned. He reserved particular venom for Berdiaev's and Trubetskoi's 'messianic-slavophile mission' which extolled Holy Russia as the natural defender and protector of weak and oppressed nationalities; and he ridiculed Miliukov for celebrating Russia as champion of the independence of all European countries threatened by German conquest and particularly for claiming that Russia's own 'independence' necessitated its control over the Straits of the Bosphorus. Using his expertise in economics and statistics, he poured scorn on his fellow economists Tugan-Baranovsky, Maslov, Finn-Enotaevsky and especially Yordansky who, abandoning their own 'scientific [integrity] in favour of war-time needs', had presented pre-war Germany as the exploiter of Russia by way of trade agreements, and had warned that should Germany win the war 'young capitalist Russia' would be thrown back and would turn again into a primitive old, semi-Asiatic, peasant *Rus*.[43] Sukhanov did not even spare his friend Stankevich, whose article 'Great Sacrifices are Needed' he castigated as sounding as if it came from the pen of one of 'the most single-minded spiritual supporters of the war among representatives of left-wing parties'.[44]

In Sukhanov's double-pronged battle against both the 'defensist' intelligentsia's ideologization of the war and the vigilant and merciless censor,[45] pride of place goes to his little book *The Left Groups and the War*, published, legally, in 1915 and 1916 thanks to his ruse of placing both at the beginning and at the end of this anti-war tract key statements quoted from the tsar's Imperial Manifesto and from the 26 July 1914 Address of the Duma's president. These explained why peace-loving Russia, to which 'designs of conquest are alien', was forced into war 'in defence of the just cause of the honour and security of Our Empire, protected by God'. In the body of his text, Sukhanov disposed one by one of all left arguments in support of the war, rounding off his polemical exposure by contrasting the defensive tsarist Manifesto with the Left's aggressive ideological justification of the war as a fulfilment of 'active national tasks and objectives':

> The principles stated in the tsarist Manifesto, embodying the idea of national defence, of the integrity and indivisibility of the

Fig. 1.2   Plekhanov

empire and of its territorial borders, the defence of the political and economic *status quo*, are of a very different order from the *active national objectives* which liberal commentators have tried to pin onto the war ... there can be no argument against the principles of the Manifesto, they have absolute validity for all those who uphold the idea of the *national state*.[46]

Sukhanov's victims were stunned and outraged and accused him of sailing under false colours, with some even trying to silence him by way of veiled denunciations. Yet, in no time at all, Sukhanov managed to issue four editions of the tract which his friend Alexander Kerensky jocularly described as 'a commentary on the Imperial Manifesto'.[47]

The legal publication of Sukhanov's anti-war brochures was apparently facilitated by the internationalist SR Sergei Mstislavsky, who put at Sukhanov's service his impeccable credentials and connections as officer and librarian of the Academy of the General Staff.[48]

It is difficult to assess the effectiveness of Sukhanov's anti-war campaign. Sceptical Stankevich, while conceding that Sukhanov's was the 'only audible critique of the war' in tsarist Russia, thought that it had provoked 'more abuse than serious objections and debate' and that its significance had been more of a 'historical nature'.[49] Still, Sukhanov's tract, which was also published in Germany, had a follow-up in Russia in a pamphlet *Why Do We Fight?* and his pamphlet against Plekhanov *On the Crisis of Socialism: Regarding the War Publications of G.V. Plekhanov* was published in two editions.

Sukhanov also took time off to lecture national independence movements such as those of the Poles and the Ukrainians who, allying themselves with one or the other war coalition, hoped thus to gain their independence:

> The freedom of national-cultural development, of a nation's growth, is not determined by the factual political independence of its state, nor by its might, nor by size and international weight, but by the *qualities* of its political organization.

The example he held up was multinational Switzerland where the German majority had shown no interest in joining the German *Reich*, while its French and Italian minorities had no inclination whatever towards 'secession'.

In tune with such radical internationalists as Rosa Luxemburg and the Bolsheviks Nikolai Bukharin and Georgii Piatakov, Sukhanov told the Poles that

> Poland, as an element of a free Russia, will, I have no doubt, enjoy far more favourable conditions for the national develop-

ment of the Polish people than a self-contained, oligarchic, aristocratic or plutocratic Poland. The task is therefore not to separate Poland, but rather to create free political conditions for its national development – it makes no difference whether [within the framework] of a politically independent state, or of a political entity which unites several nations ... If the choice is between a free *or* an independent Poland: we say a free Poland, even though it is not politically independent ... the preceding remarks are meant simply to indicate the points of departure of our reasoning and one would think – *sapienti sat.*: the struggle for independent national development is a struggle for democratism against a class state. The methods of that struggle are the usual methods of class struggle and none other.[50]

Lenin, in Zurich, seems to have been so impressed with Sukhanov's *The Left Groups and the War* that he repeatedly and impatiently insisted in March/April 1916 that his Bolshevik comrades make sure they get and study it. Indeed, he even considered, though rather reluctantly, a suggestion made by Grigorii Zinoviev that Sukhanov be invited to contribute to and possibly edit the Bolsheviks' *Sbornik Sotsialdemokrata*.[51] And as far away as Irkutsk, in August 1916, a group of political exiles reportedly used Sukhanov's tract for a 'heated discussion' of the war.[52]

Sukhanov himself in March 1918 was to look back with pride to his anti-war publishing activities in tsarist Russia when, all alone, he had faced 'the alarmist howls' of 'the entire bourgeois and boulevard press'.[53] If the near-impossible task he had set himself in tsarist Russia at war was to expose the defensism of the Left, then Sukhanov had good reason to feel proud of his achievement as the independent voice of the Zimmerwald socialist peace movement in Russia. Indeed, even as late as 7 March 1931, in his final speech at the Menshevik trial, he singled out as 'the best thing I did in my life' his 'internationalist Zimmerwaldist works' which, 'under tsarist censorship were almost the only legal anti-war publication'.[54]

2
Ideologist of the February Revolution

With the outbreak of revolution on 27 February 1917, the day of the mutiny of the Petrograd garrison which toppled tsardom, Sukhanov plunged immediately and for the first time in his career headlong into high politics. Indeed, as early as Friday 24 February, when whatever socialist leaders were then in Petrograd were still rubbing their eyes in surprise and disbelief, Sukhanov had already sensed and identified the beginning of the revolution and, fearing for its fate, was grappling with the problem of what should succeed tsarist autocracy. Thus it came about that Sukhanov, politically (and in his own words) a 'wild one', lacking any party organizational backing or special leadership experience or qualities, became for a time the leading ideologist of the Executive Committee of the Petrograd Soviet. He was the proponent of the transfer of power to the liberal bourgeoisie, and, in a way, the architect of moderately confrontational dual power when, on the morrow of the revolution, two rival centres of power emerged. These were the Provisional Government which grew out of the Temporary Committee of the Duma – formed in defiance of the tsar's prorogation of the Duma – and the Petrograd Soviet of Workers and Soldiers Deputies, consisting of elected delegates from factories, plants, insurgent army units and socialist parties and groups.

His considerations as to how to safeguard the revolution in its early days when its fate still hung in the balance derived from his understanding of the socio-political situation in Russia and not from a Menshevik-Marxist doctrine of bourgeois revolution as is often assumed.[1] His starting point was 'the complete fragmentation of Russia's democracy', by which he meant the absence of all and any stable and influential popular organizations such as socialist political parties, trade unions and democratic municipalities. All that 'the democracy' – that is, the organized lower classes as distinct from the *tsenzoviki* or privileged middle and upper classes – would be capable of improvising, he thought, would be 'combat organizations' but not 'real elements of state power'. But even were the democracy tempted to and capable of seizing state power, it would prove incapable of operating the state apparatus. Its bureaucracy, the rural *zemstva* and the municipalities would be willing to obey the orders of a Pavel Miliukov and a Prince Lvov and the Progressive *Bloc* of the Duma (an alliance of the liberal Progressives and Kadets with Left Octobrists and Nationalists, 300 out of the Duma's 420 deputies) – formed during the war years, but it would not take orders from socialists such as Nikolai Chkheidze, Matvei Skobelev or even Alexander Kerensky. Moreover, to establish their own state power and by-pass the Progressive *Bloc* of the Duma would turn 'the whole of privileged Russia', which in any case had reservations about the revolution, against the democracy and the revolution alike and drive it back into the arms of tsardom. This would mean 'the inevitable and immediate collapse of the revolution'.[2] Indeed Sukhanov found it easy to convince a majority of Mensheviks in the Executive Committee that a liberal bourgeois government was the best solution to the problem of power at present, wedded as they were to the doctrine of bourgeois revolution. That doctrine postulated that what backward peasant Russia needed immediately after the fall of tsardom was bourgeois-capitalist government and development until social, economic and political conditions for a socialist revolution were ripe so that socialists could in good conscience take power and build a socialist order. Sukhanov also had to make sure that Miliukov and his liberal associates in the Progressive *Bloc* were ready and willing to form a government. But his real task, as he saw it, was how to make sure that this bourgeois government would continue the process of democratization in earnest and not turn revolutionary Russia into something like the liberal bourgeois regimes of England and France. Indeed, Sukhanov expected something far more from the revolution. He, like many of his internationalist colleagues, expected the First World War to lead to an era in which capitalism would be liquidated and an international socialist revolution would take place. While he insisted that Russia lacked the strength and the necessary preconditions for a socialist transformation unless it formed part of and was assisted by a European socialist revolution, the vacuum created by the fall of tsardom could and already ought to be filled with 'a vast, unprecedented social content'.[3] Indeed, even before the outbreak of the revolution he had argued against the 'cult of the idea of a bourgeois revolution, the cult of political and social minimalism': it was, he believed, not merely harmful but *'short-sighted and utopian.*[4]

But his more immediate concern was the final victory over tsardom and for that the liberal bourgeoisie must be helped into power with a minimum programme that would be acceptable to both the liberal Duma Committee, the bourgeoisie and the socialist leaders of the democracy – the Executive Committee of the Petrograd Soviet. For Sukhanov was convinced that if the socialists wanted the 'propertied elements' to support the revolution and form a provisional revolutionary government, then 'all anti-war slogans would have to be temporarily struck from the agenda' and 'the Zimmerwald banner would have to be furled ... this was obvious to me as a Zimmerwald man myself'.[5]

Thus it came about that when negotiating the formation of the Provisional Government with the Duma Committee Sukhanov deliberately sidestepped the issue of war and peace. The minimum programme that he, together with the independent non-party social democrats Iurii Steklov and Nikolai Sokolov, drafted on behalf of the Executive Committee of the Petrograd Soviet laid down the following conditions for the Soviet's support: a commitment to full political freedom of speech, press and assembly, a complete amnesty for all charged with political, religious and terrorist crimes and military uprising, the lifting of all restrictions based on class, religion and nationality, the abolition of the police and its replacement by a people's militia, the retention of the Petrograd garrison troops in the capital, the ensuring of full civil rights to all serving soldiers and finally the launching of immediate preparations for the convening of a constituent assembly. Such minimal demands, Sukhanov felt sure, would be acceptable to Miliukov and his associates granted that 'in the given situation' they were willing to assume power with the backing of the Executive Committee of the Petrograd Soviet. All other concerns – such as an agrarian settlement, the proclamation of a democratic republic and a foreign policy which would 'strive to end the imperialist war' – were to be shelved until such time as the organized democracy had created 'a solid network of parties, trade unions, and democratized municipalities', since all attempts to deal with them now would require such compromises and co-operation with the government of Miliukov as to discredit the Executive Committee in the eyes of the popular masses. Indeed, Sukhanov did not think that a bourgeois government that was so out of tune with a revolutionized Russia would last longer than two to three months: he expected that it would be replaced by a government that represented the majority of the country, 'for instance, a petty-bourgeois Kerensky government'.[6]

When Sukhanov's scheme was placed before the Executive Committee there was a substantial minority of 'defensists' on the right who favoured the establishment of a coalition government in which socialists would be represented, and, at the left of the political spectrum, a small number of Bolsheviks who urged the formation of a 'provisional revolutionary government' of the democracy (without the bourgeoisie). Thus, when the vote was taken to empower the Duma Committee to form a government in which the Soviet would not participate, it was passed by only 13 to 7 (or 8) votes. But when the plenum of the Soviet with more than four hundred deputies present was asked to vote on the Executive Committee's resolutions on the transfer of power and on the programme of the Provisional Government, it voted overwhelmingly in favour, with only a mere 15 voting against.[7] 'The victory of the line of the Executive Committee [which he had done so much to promote] was decisive and complete,' Sukhanov noted with deep satisfaction.[8]

Similarly, as Sukhanov had foreseen, Miliukov and his colleagues of the Duma Committee did accept his liberal-democratic programme with but a few minor modifications and they published it on 3 March as the programme of the Provisional Government. The three conditions Miliukov insisted on were that the Executive Committee for its part simultaneously publish a proclamation welcoming the formation of the Provisional Government, approving its programme of reforms and promising its support 'on condition that it acted in the direction of these obligations', and that order be restored and relations between soldiers and officers be normalized, and that the decision on the future form of government be deferred until the convening of the Constituent Assembly.[9]

Both Sukhanov and Miliukov, the chief negotiators, were clearly pleased with the successfully concluded agreement and with the two proclamations which, according to Miliukov's express wishes, were 'printed and pasted [in the streets] on one common sheet one under the other' and also published side by side on the same front page in *Izvestiia revoliutsionnoi nedeli* of 3 March.[10]

> Everything is going well, said Miliukov. I, too, thought that things could not have gone better .... One could now think of having a rest and getting some food. We finally took leave, though we were to meet again in the not so distant future in the Marinskii Palace [the seat of the Provisional Government], although no more in the capacity of 'negotiators' but rather as representatives of two sides that were fighting each other tooth and nail. *Our 'agreement' was the arrangement of the conditions for the duel.*[11]

Not for nothing did Stankevich, one of the *trudovik* members of the Executive Committee and a remarkably perceptive and level-headed observer of the revolutionary scene, see in Sukhanov 'the ideologist of the revolution in its first phase'.[12] This was an assessment shared by Trotsky, who acknowledged Sukhanov as 'the moving spirit of the Executive Committee ... a theorist who stood head and shoulders above all its members at that time'. Indeed, Trotsky sneeringly continued, Sukhanov had done his best to 'throw both power and the war, as quickly as possible, over to the bourgeoisie'.[13]

Indeed, in a famous and often-quoted chapter of his *History of the Russian Revolution*, Trotsky pins the prime responsibility for what he calls the 'paradox of the February Revolution' – the Petrograd Soviet's transfer of power to the liberal bourgeoisie – squarely on Sukhanov. It was Sukhanov, Trotsky jeered, who 'devoted all his strength to having power handed over to the committee of the State Duma in the [doctrinaire belief] that the power destined to replace tsarism could only be a bourgeois power'.[14]

What Trotsky failed to mention was that in Sukhanov's '*a priori* scheme' only one half of the real power was surrendered to the national liberal bourgeoisie which was to be kept under vigilant Soviet control even as that power was expected gradually to diminish. Indeed, the point of departure for the 'organizational-technical scheme' which Sukhanov propounded in the Executive Committee on 4 March was his understanding of the course of the Russian Revolution: that the overthrow of tsarist autocracy which was taking place 'in the era of the collapse of capitalism' marked only its beginning; the Provisional Government was only the early, short phase of its consolidation, the revolution was bound to continue 'uninterruptedly' until 'the state passed into the hands of the democracy'; the Soviet, as the 'representative organ of the entire democracy must forthwith, subject to the limits imposed by 'necessary caution and common sense', fill the revolutionary period with 'the maximum social content'. It was in that spirit and with that expectation of Russia's revolution that Sukhanov's organizational-technical scheme sought to formalize relations between the Soviet and the Provisional Government and provide the institutional framework for the Soviet's vigilant 'pressure' and 'control' over the government and its activities.[15]

In the first place, he proposed, speaking in the Executive Committee on 4 March, that a Commission of Legislative Projects be set up with a considerable number of sub-commissions attached to it and staffed by 'socialist experts'; the commission's task was to prepare proposals for 'decrees and measures' in areas of social policy, economics and law. The Soviet, through its Executive Committee, or by way of the 'organized soviet masses', would by negotiation or pressure 'dictate' to the government a series of 'democratic reforms' which had been prepared by the Commission. That 'pressure' and 'control' from 'outside' was to be paralleled and complemented by a systematic penetration of the 'inside' of the state administration. This was to be achieved by 'ministerial councils' that would flank every ministry; in every such council the Soviet's representatives were to be in the majority, or at the very least on parity with other representatives, and they were to seek information on the activities of the particular ministry and master its business and advise the minister on measures that they considered he should adopt. Thus, according to Sukhanov's plan, the Soviet's representatives would gradually take over some of that business with the final aim of 'conquering the state apparatus'. The chairmen of the Soviet sections in the ministerial councils were to combine and form a *collegium*, a kind of shadow-cabinet, that was to work in the closest contact with the Executive Committee and coordinate the activities and the information gained by the various ministerial councils. Thus it would be able to face the Council of Ministers and exert 'pressure and control' over general policy.[16]

The question of whether this institutionalized bridling of the Provisional Government and the Soviet's penetration of 'all the pores of state administration' would be at all acceptable to the government was one that Sukhanov apparently did not consider, nor did he report the heated arguments that took place over his project in the Executive Committee. He seems to have taken it for granted that Miliukov and his colleagues in the government would do anything to hang on to power. Thus, in early April, when Victor Chernov complained that they had handled the government roughly, Sukhanov tried to calm him down by saying that 'they will not leave unless they are removed by force'.[17] What is clear is that his scheme did not envisage idyllic 'co-operation and contact' between the two partners to dual power, but rather rivalry and conflict: 'the most legal, rightful and historically inevitable class struggle between the revolutionary democracy and the government of the privileged'. In that struggle, the Russian democracy, having created 'a solid network of class organizations, political parties, trade unions, democratized municipalities and soviets, would be invincible when confronting the united front of capital and imperialism'.[18]

Sukhanov's ambitious scheme was largely stillborn; but it tells us a great deal about his understanding of dual power and of his scenario for the Russian revolution taking place within the context of the era of the 'collapse of world capitalism'.[19] The only major institution that came out of these plans was the Liaison or Contact Commission with the government which was elected on 7 March with a watered-down mandate. It had originally and significantly been planned as an 'Observation Committee'[20] True, a large Commission of Legislative Projects was elected which included some of the best brains and experts of the Executive Committee, but although it was expected to set up a number of sub-commissions very little came of that.[21]

The extent to which Sukhanov was wedded to his confrontational conception of dual power can be traced in his efforts to commit the Petrograd Soviet to embark sooner than he had originally expected on an active peace policy and put pressure on the Provisional Government to revise the foreign policy inherited from tsardom. Encouraged by Nikolai Chkheidze, chairman of the Petrograd

Soviet, on the evening of 3 March, to think about issuing an address to the European proletariat 'in the name of the Soviet and the revolution',[22] Sukhanov was goaded into action by Miliukov's telegram to the Allies sent on 4 March. That telegram gave an account of the revolution and of the restoration of order as if it had all been the work of the Duma Committee: the role of the Petrograd Soviet was all but ignored save for a passing and ambiguous mention. Moreover, it conveyed to the Allies the 'firm decision of the people and the national representative body' (that is, the Provisional Government) to make all efforts and sacrifices 'to achieve a decisive victory over the enemy'.[23] Nudged by an insistent Sokolov, Sukhanov promptly drafted a brief statement meant to correct Miliukov's account and at the same time to urge the Soviet to 'react energetically to the statement of the Provisional Government'. But for whatever reasons, Steklov, the editor of *Izvestiia*, broke his promise to publish it.[24] On the next evening, 5 March, Sukhanov rang Gorky to urge him to compose An Address to the Peoples of the World, convincing him of the 'historical significance' of such a document. Receiving the text the next day, he realized that Gorky had missed the point, being primarily concerned with culture and its international prospects rather than with peace or politics. Having tried unsuccessfully to rewrite it, he then quickly drafted another text, as a spare and 'just in case'. This contained, he thought, 'what should have been said even though it was badly said'.[25] At the session of the Executive Committee on 8 March, both drafts were heatedly debated. Sukhanov's draft was accepted and then handed over to him and Steklov for further revision. On 11 March, the revised text was again debated and approved in the Committee with Sukhanov warding off all attempts from right and left to make some significant changes, including that of Iu. Kudravtsev who wanted the last line of the Address – 'proletarians of all countries unite' – deleted on the grounds that this was a party slogan.[26] (For complete text in English translation *see* Appendix One).

At last, on 14 March, a special festive session convened in the vast overcrowded hall of the Naval Cadet Corps to issue the Address to the Peoples of the Whole World. It was opened by Chkheidze who congratulated the 'comrades and workers' on having accomplished in three days of revolution the great feat of 'liberating Russia, making her free and leading her into the family of civilized nations'.

Now, they could 'send word to the whole world and to the [Socialist] International that Russia has ceased to be the *gendarme* of Europe'. With Sukhanov, who was scheduled to introduce the Address, delayed by the breakdown of the car bringing him, it was Steklov who deputized for him with a verbose, meandering impromptu speech and a faulty reading of the Address that deeply distressed Sukhanov when he finally arrived. In the lengthy debate that followed, 'Papa Chkheidze', whom Sukhanov really liked, also annoyed him profoundly, when, endeavouring to answer the attacks of some Germanophobic speakers, he read into the Address a refusal to negotiate peace with the government of Emperor Wilhelm: 'We will negotiate only with the German people themselves once they have emulated our example and removed Wilhelm: and his clique; until then, we will continue to fight: that, comrades, is what this document says!'

But Sukhanov shared the general elation when the resolution proclaiming 'Poland's right to full independence' was debated and

Fig. 2.1   Chkheidze

speaker after speaker, Russian, Georgian, Ukrainian, Pole, Jew and Lithuanian, affirmed their internationalist credo and commitment to peace. It was left to the Georgian Menshevik Akaki Chkhenkeli to rise to the occasion and make a speech befitting what was after all the finest hour of Sukhanov and (arguably) of the Russian Revolution.[27]

Years later the 'defensist' Stankevich proudly defended the Address against critics and cynics, including Lenin. 'It would be an extraordinary mistake', Stankevich wrote:

> to assess this historical document as a literary work inspired by the intelligentsia's divorce from Russian life. True, Sukhanov composed it under the influence of Zimmerwald and Kienthal, but the Address united a vast spectrum of people with very different motives. Above all, its internationalism was not something alien brought in from outside; rather, it reflected the genuine mood of large circles of the intelligentsia, of entire organizations and political movements. The vocabulary of its internationalism found a resounding echo within the popular masses. There was undoubtedly no war in the psyche of the people.[28]

Two years later, a sobered Sukhanov reduced the passionate prose of the Address to two basic propositions:

> Conscious of its revolutionary strength the Russian democracy declares that it will by all means counteract the imperialist policies of its ruling classes and it calls upon the nations of Europe to join in common, resolute action for peace. We will staunchly defend our freedom against any reactionary onslaughts, internal or foreign; the Russian Revolution will not retreat before the bayonets of the conquerors and will not allow itself to be crushed by military force.

In short, Sukhanov insisted, the Address affirmed an anti-imperialist commitment to peace and to the military defence of revolutionary Russia as long as that peace was not yet achieved. The Address was also meant as a firm reply to the imperialist foreign policy statements of Miliukov and the Provisional Government.[29]

Sukhanov, together with his internationalist associate Iurii Larin, and backed on 17 March by a meeting of Zimmerwaldists ranging from the Menshevik-Internationalists to the Bolsheviks, followed up the Address with a resolution calling for a 'nation-wide campaign' to 'wring from the government a renunciation of annexations' and thus bring it into line with the peace policy of the Petrograd Soviet. This, as Sukhanov explained to the Executive Committee on 22 March, was intended as a practical measure to 'change the entire international situation. Bellicose liberalism is [unacceptable]. The meaning of our revolution is being perverted.'[30]

The idea of mobilizing the masses to put pressure on the Provisional Government to revise its foreign policy seems to have found wide support in the Executive Committee: even such 'defensists' and moderate Menshevik leaders as Boris Bogdanov, Kuzma Gvozdev, Mark Liber, Matvei Skobelev, Chkheidze, and Genrikh Erlikh signed the resolution.[31]

Indeed, the Menshevik Organizational Committee, in a resolution of 19 March, had already urged 'the mobilization of public opinion and the organization of the working class and of the democracy of the entire country to pressure the government and compel it officially and unconditionally to renounce all plans of conquest .... and to persuade the Allies to issue the same declaration and take such steps as would lead to peace negotiations'.[32]

A meeting of delegates of more than one hundred front-line units who crowded into the office of Duma President Mikhail Rodzianko on 24 March and listened to a debate on relations between the Provisional Government and the Soviet illustrates what Sukhanov expected from his nation-wide campaign. Having heard Sukhanov trounce the spokesmen of the Republican Union of Officers who argued for the continuation of the war 'until victory', 87 out of 104 delegates adopted the following resolution drafted by Sukhanov:

> This meeting is of the opinion that free Russia cannot desire the enslavement of other peoples and urges the Provisional Government to proclaim to all nations that it does not strive for any conquests whatever and that it will conduct war solely for its defence [and only] as long as Germany and Austria do not proclaim that they too do not strive for conquests and agree to discuss peace terms without the annexation of territories and without the payment of reparations.

In short, to strive towards a negotiated peace rather than war 'until final victory'.

The meeting also sent a delegation of three officers and three soldiers who delivered the resolution to Prince Lvov and War Minister Alexander Guchkov who told them that the government was 'dealing with the problem raised in the resolution'.[33]

Sukhanov's plan for a nation-wide campaign and indeed his ideological leadership, which rested on that left-wing coalition which had dominated the Executive Committee since its foundation, was challenged by the Georgian Menshevik Iraklii Tsereteli, celebrated hero and martyr of the Second Duma, and his group of so-called Siberian Zimmerwaldists – consisting of the former Bolsheviks Vladimir Voitinsky and Nikolai Rozhkov, the SR leader Abram Gots, and the Mensheviks Fiodor Dan, Semion Vainshtain and Konstantin Ermolaev, who arrived in Petrograd on 19 March from Irkutsk. Within a few days, they had wrested control of the Petrograd Soviet from the Internationalist *bloc* vesting it instead in a newly formed Menshevik-SR *bloc* of so-called 'revolutionary defensists' that controlled Russia's soviets until October 1917.

Thus, as early as 20 March, Tsereteli, in a programmatic speech in the Workers' Section of the Petrograd Soviet, formulated a conception of the Russian Revolution and of dual power which ran counter to Sukhanov's. The workers of Petrograd, he said, were to be congratulated on having joined with 'all the living forces of the country, the revolutionary army, the peasantry and the entire progressive bourgeoisie' to overthrow the autocracy. He complimented them on their self-restraint in handing over power to the bourgeoisie because of their sober understanding that 'what is happening in Russia is a bourgeois revolution'. That bourgeois revolution could lead to the complete victory of democracy, but not yet to the final aim of a social revolution, even though it constituted a phase of that revolution. The Soviet controlled the activities of the bourgeoisie in power and was pushing it on along the road of revolution, thus ensuring that power was used in the interests of the people. While it was true, Tsereteli continued, that the proletariat was 'the reliable, unshakeable bulwark of liberty', other classes, too, were interested in that freedom and they, all together, 'must support the power of the revolutionary government', 'the entire plenitude of executive power must therefore belong to the Provisional Government so long as that power strengthens the revolution'.[34]

Fig. 2.2   Tsereteli

Apparently, Chkheidze there and then told Tsereteli that he might have gone too far and had perhaps 'somewhat dampened the ardour of the audience with his insistence on the bourgeois character of the revolution and on the revolutionism of the Provisional Government'. Yet this was no new departure for Tsereteli: as early as 4 March, when he was still in far-away Irkutsk, he had already sent a cable to Prince Lvov, the head of the Provisional Government, expressing his political philosophy of 'a nation-wide accord' in Russia's bourgeois revolution.[35] As chairman of the Irkutsk Committee of Public Organizations, to which he had been elected as a matter of course upon the outbreak of the revolution, he 'greeted the formation of the Provisional Government', assured it of the Committee's recognition and support for 'the struggle against the remnants of the old power' and expressed 'the firm belief that the consistent realization of the hopes of the democracy will rally all the living forces of the country in the fervent struggle for a new Russia'.[36] Remarkable in that cable was the absence of even so much as a mention of the Petrograd Soviet. The 'weak and pale' language, the 'restraint and moderation' of this telegram remained a puzzle to Vladimir Voitinsky, Tsereteli's close friend and associate, as he noted in his memoirs, written in 1923, where he spent two pages explaining it.[37] Even in a separate telegram to Chkheidze, Tsereteli reminded the Petrograd Soviet that 'the consistent realization of the hopes of the democracy will rally all the living forces of the country in the intensifying struggle for a new Russia'.[38]

When Sukhanov, on 21 March, finally tabled his resolution in the Executive Committee, he explained that it derived from the obligation of the Address of 14 March to 'fight the imperialism of their own country'; this was particularly necessary now since Miliukov had just told the entire world that Russia continued to be fully committed to the 'old war aims' and to agreements with the Allies, while the bourgeoisie was intensively campaigning for 'a war to the finish', all the time invoking the official statements of the Provisional Government. Even Chkheidze, he added unwisely, had, in his comment on the Address on 14 March, weakened its anti-imperialist meaning. There was, indeed, 'the greatest danger' that the revolution might be diverted into an 'endless war', presaging military defeat and complete economic collapse. Contrary to what his critics maintained, the democracy's peace efforts, he urged, would not weaken the front nor impair the defence of the country, but would rather strengthen the war effort by making it clear that this was a purely defensive war. Concluding his speech, he expressed his confidence that their peace efforts would find support among the German proletariat and thus undermine the *Burgfrieden* (civic truce) in the enemy coalition so that, with the entire European proletariat co-operating, a democratic peace could be negotiated and achieved. Turning to the defensists, he said that the Soviet's peace effort was not merely the road of the International but also of 'true patriotism' – for it guaranteed the 'real defence of the country'.[39]

Sukhanov was shocked when Tsereteli pounced on him without a warning and attacked the resolution and his speech in its support as a 'nonsensical, pernicious venture'. Sukhanov, he complained, had not even so much as mentioned the need to support the army, its discipline and military efficiency, the work of the defence industries nor the question of repulsing the enemy. There was no question, Tsereteli lectured Sukhanov, hinting at his critique of Chkheidze, that 'the democracy which, from the start of the revolution, had been master of the country, was objectively interested in putting an end to the war and was deeply opposed to imperialism'. That was far more significant than 'all the declarations of Miliukov'.

> If we only put the problem sensibly, the Provisional Government will be compelled to accept our programme. But if the Provisional Government rejects it and pushes the issue to the breaking point, the vast majority of the country will support us. It is of decisive importance that our peace policy also be accompanied by measures which will safeguard our country against utter defeat.

The Soviet must therefore abandon a policy of 'irresponsible opposition' and regard defence as one of the revolution's principal tasks, as a precondition to a democratic peace and the safeguarding of the revolution's achievements. In conclusion, Tsereteli moved a resolution which countered Sukhanov's resolution and was little more than a call for the mobilization of both the rear and the front for defence.[40]

There ensued such a fierce debate, with so many demanding the floor, that the session was adjourned to the next day when, just before the debate was about to begin, Tsereteli, in a conciliatory move, approached Sukhanov with a compromise resolution which combined both their resolutions, evenly balancing calls for both peace and defence. That resolution was passed by a vast majority. While this was acceptable to Sukhanov and the Left, they still felt that it lacked any practical commitment and therefore proposed an amendment which included a statement in support of the peace campaign. Tsereteli countered that amendment by proposing that the Executive Committee's Contact Commission should approach the government with a demand that it issue an official declaration that 'the new Russia renounces all conquests and reparations'. The Soviet, he tried to reassure them, could, if necessary, start a peace campaign at any moment it chose. When put to the vote, Tsereteli's proposal gained the support of a significant majority.[41]

That majority which rallied to Tsereteli and replaced Sukhanov's campaign for a drastic change in the government's foreign policy with polite diplomacy and negotiation with the Provisional Government was a humiliating defeat for Sukhanov in whose view it marked, a 'turning point in the entire policy of the Soviet and, what's more, in the further course of the revolution'.[42] It certainly put an end to Sukhanov's ideological leadership and the 'hegemony' of the Left in the Executive Committee. Henceforth, it was the charismatic, prestigious and authoritative Tsereteli and the SR-Menshevik *bloc* that supported him which controlled and shaped the policies of the Petrograd Soviet and of the soviets.

As a direct follow-up of Tsereteli's compromise resolution of 22 March, the Contact Commission of the Executive Committee secured a meeting with a delegation of the Provisional Government in the evening of 24 March. At issue was the Soviet's urgent demand that the government issue an official statement renouncing all territorial claims and conquests. This was a particularly urgent matter now because of Miliukov's repeated affirmations of Russia's loyalty to all agreements with the Allies and to their common war aims. What the Executive Committee found particularly objectionable was Miliukov's policy statement of 22 March made at a press conference where he envisaged 'the merger with Russia of all Ukrainian lands' as well as 'the acquisition of Constantinople and the Straits ... which has always been regarded as the immemorial national task of Russia'.[43]

It was only after two days of inconclusive haggling between the delegations over the wording of the government declaration that at last a draft was presented to the meeting by Prince Lvov. Tsereteli, who as a matter of course had assumed the chairmanship of the

Contact Commission, declared the document unsatisfactory: it did not spell out clearly that 'Russia renounces all claims to foreign territories', he said, insisting politely but firmly that it be amended to that effect.[44]

That did not satisfy Sukhanov: apparently feeling that he was not bound by Tsereteli's diplomatic style, he was eager to expose the pomposity and emptiness of the document's hackneyed phrases about free Russia not desiring 'domination over others', 'the appropriation of their national possessions' nor 'the enslavement and humiliation of anyone'. Thus he reminded the meeting, notably members of the Provisional Government present there, of the pious words of the Tsar's Imperial Manifesto which had accompanied Russia's declaration of war. Quoting by heart, though not quite accurately, he said:

> The Lord sees that it is not for the sake of vain mundane glory, nor for violent oppression that we have taken up arms, but rather solely for the sake of defending the national possession of the State of All the Russias.

This sharp juxtaposition provoked the indignation of Mikhail Tereshchenko, the minister of finance, who shouted : 'What! Does someone in this hall permit himself to insult the ministers of the revolution and compare them with Nicholas ll. This is absolutely intolerable!' And with that, he stormed out of the room.[45]

The next day (27 March), when the document was being studied in the Executive Committee, 'arousing deep dissatisfaction', Tsereteli, who was anxious 'not to make the [question of the war] a matter of conflict' with the government 'at present', urged that all the document lacked was 'clarity and a few concrete touches'. Once these were inserted, one would be able to regard the 'demands of the democracy as having been fulfilled and a major victory having thus been obtained'. He told the meeting he would telephone Prince Lvov or Vladimir Nabokov (head of the chancellery of the Provisional Government). He soon reported back with satisfaction: 'I have spoken to Prince Lvov – they have revised [the document] in the spirit of our suggestions.'[46] Indeed, on 28 March the government published a Declaration of the Provisional Government addressed 'To the Citizens [of Russia]' which included the addition of just six words 'no violent seizure of foreign territories'.[47]

Next day, speaking at the Conference of Soviets on the question of the war, Tsereteli hailed the Declaration as 'an enormous victory of the entire democracy', for not only did it mark 'a turning point in Russia's foreign policy, but it is also a torch tossed into Europe so that those ideals that presently only glimmer there will flare up brilliantly as they have flared up here to illuminate our entire life'.[48]

Naturally enough, Sukhanov did not quite share Tsereteli's enthusiasm for the government declaration of 28 March. His assessment, like that of most internationalists in the Executive Committee, was that while 'objectively, it was the first positive act to be taken by any of the belligerent countries since the start of the war, yet its real significance was that it created a new situation for further struggle'. That was the point made by Larin: 'We must complete what has been started', by Victor Grinevich: 'It is only the first step; it must not remain an isolated renunciation, but become a general act!', and by Piotr Iurenev: 'This first step must not remain the last.'[49]

Sukhanov suffered his first major personal defeat on 24 March when the Executive Committee's policy statements were voted on in preparation for the All-Russian Conference of Soviets due to open in Petrograd on 29 March. In a vote to decide who was to report on the revolution in Petrograd, Skobelev beat him by 13 votes to 9. Steklov, competing with Sukhanov to report on 'the Soviet's attitude to the Provisional Government', beat him by 14 to 11. But more important still was his defeat by Tsereteli (17 votes to 7) for the privilege of reporting on the Executive Committee's 'attitude to the war'. In short, Sukhanov had been ousted from a position of direct influence on high politics. It was small comfort that he was unanimously elected – amid general amusement – to be the Soviet's spokesman on the 'agrarian question' which, at the time, was of no particular interest to him, or to the Executive Committee, so much so that he delegated the *de facto* chairmanship of the agrarian committee of the Conference to Professor I.V. Chernyshev.[50]

Still, when he and Chernyshev presented the Executive Committee's report on the agrarian question to the Congress's agrarian section, which consisted largely of soldiers-SRs who, as Sukhanov had feared were 'chauvinists on the war question ... but demagogical radicals on the land question', it was rejected out of hand and a 'conditional' 'preliminary and very general' resolution was adopted which was referred 'to the localities for discussion'.

True, at the centre of the resolution stood 'the alienation, without compensation, of all privately owned lands above a certain norm'. That norm was to be fixed in every region by 'local democratic committees'. These lands were to be 'handed over to the toiling people', yet no clue was given as to the institutions – state and/or municipalities – in which these lands were to be vested. What was clear was that 'the final resolution of the land question would be the prerogative of the Constituent Assembly'. Until it convened, all land transactions were to be frozen, while in this interim period, land committees, in which peasant organizations predominated, would fix land rents, regulate wages, lease land that was lying idle or have it worked by hired labour and prevent arbitrary seizures of land.[51]

When, on 9 April, Sukhanov tabled and explained the agrarian resolution to the plenum of the Petrograd Soviet, it provoked 'a heated debate' and it was decided 'to defer the adoption of the resolution on the land question until such time as the matter has been discussed in detail during a future meeting of the Soviet'. Apparently, Sukhanov's misgivings about dealing with the land question at that time were more than well-founded. Perhaps he may have derived some consolation from the Conference's demanding 'the suspension of the [Stolypin] law of 14 June 1910 on withdrawal from the *obshchina*', a law that he had very much resented.[52]

As for his all-absorbing interest in high politics, that was now reduced to rearguard action as member of the Conference's Commission on the War under Tsereteli's chairmanship. The commission was due to prepare the Conference's resolution on the war, a document that was also to serve as its response to the government Declaration of 28 March. In that commission, Sukhanov and his associate Larin 'fought to the bitter end' for every word of the resolution; not only did 'we have the unpleasant experience of remaining in the minority', as he complained to the Executive Committee, but they were even told by Tsereteli: 'Why are you wasting time? Can't you see that your efforts are leading nowhere and that all your amendments are being rejected!'[53]

That was not quite true: a comparison of both Tsereteli's original draft and his Conference speeches with the final 'Resolution on the Question of the War', which was adopted on 30 March, suggests that Sukhanov and his associates did succeed in injecting some Zimmerwaldism into the resolution. Indeed, Sukhanov got his way when securing an amendment passed by 19 to 14 votes which specifically included a commitment 'to strive towards the speediest ending of the war' and saw in 'an official renunciation of all programmes of conquest by all governments a powerful means of terminating the war'. Sukhanov was certainly delighted with the final resolution on the 'Attitude to the Provisional Government' passed on 1 April. Though it eschewed all talk of class struggle, it was very much in tune with his confrontational understanding of dual power rather than with Tsereteli's pet concept of 'the mobilization of all the living forces of the country' by which he meant an 'all-national accord' uniting the proletariat and the army 'with a large part of the bourgeoisie'.[54]

Altogether, Sukhanov, with some reservations, remembered the Conference as 'the best Soviet congress ever: it consolidated the democracy on the proletarian platform of Zimmerwald'. That joy was soon complemented by Sukhanov's delight at the outcome and resolutions of the Congress of the Western Front Armies in Minsk (7–10 April). These marked the climax of 'the sovietization of the army' – its acceptance of the leadership of the soviets and the adoption of the resolutions of the Conference of Soviets.[55]

As for Tsereteli: he was so thrilled with the success of the Minsk congress – to which he certainly contributed in no small measure – that on his return to Petrograd he felt the need to share his delight with .... Sukhanov![56]

The 'sovietization of the army' was largely completed by 18 April, so that the army, the real power in the land, was – to Sukhanov's deep satisfaction and delight – now under the control of the soviets. The political and ideological permeation of the army by the soviets was realized by way of a network of elective cells in companies, regiments, divisions and army corps which had, since 30 March, grudgingly been given official recognition by Defence Minister Alexander Guchkov and Chief-of-Staff General Mikhail Alekseev.[57]

But although Sukhanov and Tsereteli saw eye to eye on these spectacular achievements, relations between them in the weeks preceding the so-called April Crisis were still characterized by their divergent, if not incompatible, understandings of dual power and their attitude to the Provisional Government. While Sukhanov told the Executive Committee on 2 April that he was convinced that 'we are moving inexorably towards an open rupture [with the government], not today but tomorrow ... ',[58] Tsereteli was later to recall that 'nothing presaged the April conflict in the days that preceded it. On the contrary, it looked as if the entire course of events was contributing to the strengthening of ties between the Provisional Government and the Soviet democracy.'[59] Their differing attitudes came into the open in the dispute over the procedures and the role of the Contact Commission. Sukhanov reported to the Executive Committee on 5 April that the last session of the Commission 'made a most distressing impression on me ... the function of our delegation was reduced to the mere registering of what had already been done by the government. The Commission was presented with *faits accomplis* to which they were expected to assent.' He proposed that in future all negotiations with the government be made public. This is what was registered in the protocols of the Executive Committee; but in his *Zapiski* he also quoted the following account of the goings-on in the Contact Commission's sessions:[60]

> Our delegation has it out with the Council of Ministers in private, intimate tones, especially recently. We put questions to the government and make requests (on a par with any other organizational group). The ministers hear us out, state some facts, add their views and for the most part turn down our requests. We do not react at all and do not even report on our negotiations to the Executive Committee. Generally, the Soviet does not react to Government actions which go against its wishes.

Sukhanov urged the Executive Committee to pay special attention to the work of the Contact Commission and oblige it to make regular and detailed reports and give its proceedings an official character by, for example, keeping proper minutes of its sessions and a precise record of all its resolutions and the government's replies to them. In the *Zapiski* he makes the further claim that he also proposed electing a panel of 'one notary and two clerks' to be present at the sessions. The Contact Commission was not there to conduct 'intimate conversations with highly placed personages', but was simply an intermediary between two class enemies, two sides that were locked in 'natural and legitimate litigation'.[61]

Naturally enough, Tsereteli did not agree with Sukhanov's report, as he told the Executive Committee on 5 April: 'We did receive complete satisfaction on a number of issues. True, on some questions we did not, but we have received no definite instructions to regard these as "conflict issues", and certainly this is no reason for changing the entire system of our relations with the government as Sukhanov urges.' For his part he proposed : let us 'not tie the hands of the Contact Commission, but reserve the right to demand that in certain cases the Contact Commission should take minutes of its negotiations with the government'.[62] Chkheidze does not seem to have shared Tsereteli's trust in the Provisional Government; so much so that he urged: 'they should not have direct dealings with the government: such dealings should be in writing and they should insist on written replies by the government'.[63] Sukhanov's proposals were rejected by a small margin. The compromise reached was that sessions should be recorded and the minutes be signed by all members of the Soviet delegation.[64]

Sukhanov's dissatisfaction with the procedures followed by the Contact Commission turned into an angry outburst during one of its sessions when, in reply to his query, he was told by Miliukov that Fritz Platten, Lenin's man in Switzerland, had been refused entry into Russia on the grounds that 'he had rendered a friendly service to an enemy country by organizing Lenin's journey through Germany'. Sukhanov took up the cudgels for both Lenin and Platten.

> The explanation of the Minister for Foreign Affairs totally dumbfounds me: for who is Lenin? Lenin is a Russian citizen who, in spite of the complete political freedom that exists in Russia was still unable to return to the country other than with the help of Platten. If Lenin is a criminal, why was he not arrested at the border? Why is he even now at liberty? But if Lenin enjoys the full rights of a citizen any assistance given to him to return to his country can only be considered as a service to him and also as a service to our Ministry of Foreign Affairs which has proved unable to fulfil its functions with regard to ....

Sukhanov was brusquely interrupted: the ministers raised a hubbub with the left Kadet Nikolai Nekrasov, minister of transport, shouting even louder than all the others: 'That's enough! Listen here Nikolai Nikolaevich, stop it! We just don't see eye to eye here. That's quite enough!' But what seems to have shocked Sukhanov far more was the reaction of his comrades. 'Lowering their eyes, they kept a deadly silence. *Not a soul* supported me. Apparently, from the point of view of the Soviet members, I was guilty of the greatest tactlessness and impropriety – not for the first, nor the last, time.'[65]

Sukhanov's running feud with Tsereteli now centred on the question of 'the next step' or follow-up to the government's Declaration of 28 March, and, connected with it, whether the soviets ought to support the government's Liberty Loan. While Tsereteli had hailed the Declaration as a 'turning point in Russia's foreign policy', Sukhanov and the left-wing opposition in the Executive Committee had urged that it was not worth much unless some 'further steps were taken', in other words an official government Note to the Allies informing them of the Declaration, which so far had been addressed only to the Russian people.[66]

The question of Soviet support for the Liberty Loan was debated for the first time in the Executive Committee on 7 April. Sukhanov was of the opinion that active endorsement and support of the loan would be tantamount to 'our unconditional backing of the war'. Therefore, the loan should be neither supported nor opposed.

Tsereteli attacked Sukhanov's position as 'indeterminate'. 'We are a force and we have no right to refuse. We regard the country's defence as the cause of the entire democracy. The defeat of our front is the defeat of the revolution.' When the vote was taken, 21 voted in support of the loan, 14 against and 8 'not to hinder'.[67]

The Left, however, was not prepared to put up with such a narrow defeat. Next day, 14 members – Sukhanov among them – signed a declaration demanding that the decision to support the Liberty Loan be reconsidered: the decision, they claimed, marked a drastic change in the policy and public statements of the Petrograd Soviet; it had not been co-ordinated with the socialist parties and had been taken by a small quorum. Thus, they 'insist' that the decision be brought before the plenum of the Soviet following preliminary discussions in the Executive Committee and among the socialist parties.[68] When this declaration was placed before the Executive Committee, it was suggested that it 'not be debated',[69] a decision perhaps taken in the wake of Victor Chernov's report that in 'the West', the government Declaration of 28 March had 'passed unnoticed'. Chernov therefore proposed that the government be requested to inform the Allies of the Declaration by means of 'a diplomatic Note'. Speaking in the Contact Commission, Chernov argued that the Declaration had been meant only 'for internal consumption', and thus the Allies were 'under no obligation' either to take note of it or respond to it.[70]

With Miliukov only very reluctantly agreeing to send such a Note, Prince Lvov urged Tsereteli and the Executive Committee to speed up support for the Liberty Loan. A general meeting of the Petrograd Soviet was convened on 16 April to debate the loan. But the meeting was told by Chkheidze that the Executive Committee had decided to defer the debate for three days until the promised Note would, according to schedule, have been drafted and despatched to the Allies. Tsereteli supported Chkheidze's statement, telling the assembly that 'the Soviet must not decide the question blindly'. The Note would mark a 'third victory' for the Soviet, one to stand alongside the first – the Address to the Peoples of the Whole World of 14 March – and the second – the Government Declaration of 28 March. Thus 'by giving money for the war, the proletariat will know that it does not make the grant for the purposes of conquest or the enslavement of other peoples'.[71]

With the debate on the Liberty Loan postponed by three days, Sukhanov was free to prepare for 18 April, the day when revolutionary Russia was to celebrate the First of May with festivities for which Sukhanov was the main planner and organizer;[72] it was also to be publication day for *Novaia zhizn'*, the new daily owned by Gorky that Sukhanov was to edit together with a small group of *Letopis'* colleagues such as Vladimir Bazarov, A.N. Tikhonov, V.A. Stroev and Boris Avilov. Not for nothing did Sukhanov refer to *Novaia zhizn'* as 'the organ of the *Letopis'*'. *Novaia zhizn'*'s contributors represented a broad and impressive section of radical and socialist intelligentsia: publicists, writers, political commentators, economists and sociologists. Inscribed on its masthead was the proclamation that it was a 'social-political and literary social-democratic newspaper'. Its first editorial, 'Our Tasks',[73] outlined a very detailed programme which lodged it firmly on the left wing of 'the democracy', somewhat to the left of Martov's Menshevik-Internationalists, but, as we shall see, at a clearly defined distance from Lenin and the Bolsheviks. It was deeply committed to the anti-imperialist ideal of a 'revived proletarian International' and to the Zimmerwald watchword of a 'peace without annexations and indemnities' which it understood to mean that the inhabitants of occupied territories and of disputed border areas should 'decide their own future in free referenda', and that the reconstruction of war-ravaged areas should, by international agreement, be the obligation of all belligerents. The war should be ended by way of negotiations and 'organized forms' and not by the destruction and weakening of 'the fighting strength of our revolutionary army'.

Novaia zhizn' was committed to the 'immediate aim' of completing the 'democratic revolution' and the achievements of that revolution's social and political objectives. It saw in the soviets 'the chief engines of the revolution' and supported them as 'the natural centres which rally and organize the popular masses'. It warned against 'the fatal mistake' of the soviets now assuming sole revolutionary power and thus endangering the revolution, the reason being that both the peasantry and the working class were seen as scarcely ready to shoulder political power, while the premature establishment of their dictatorship would provoke violent resistance among all strata of the bourgeoisie at a time when Russia was at war and in the throes of a terrible economic crisis. Therefore, *Novaia zhizn'* believed that the soviets ought for the time being to support relations with the bourgeois government but at the same time maintain 'unremitting control' of its activities. In order to achieve all this the masses must be organized, the watchword of the day being 'organization, organization, organization', for without powerful trade unions, the 8-hour working day and all the achievements of the revolution could not be safeguarded, nor would the democracy be able to cope successfully with the economic crisis without the support of vigorous organs of self-government. Likewise only a well-organized peasantry would be capable of pushing a democratic agrarian reform programme through the Constituent Assembly and realizing the transfer of all lands into national possession. But above all, the political parties must be revived and rejuvenated so that they could infuse their spirit into all organizations. While *Novaia zhizn'* was committed to 'the old banner of the RSDRP', it regarded the 'old factional divisions as out-dated' and believed that there must be room within the RSDRP for 'all shades of revolutionary internationalist socialism'. With the task ahead being the consolidation of the democratic revolution's achievements and the paving of the road to socialism, it was imperative to foster carefully a new consciousness, a new attitude to man and a new socialist culture and thus 'prove ourselves worthy of our victory over the old regime'.

To sum up, with its emphasis on the need to complete the democratic revolution, with its warning against the 'fatal mistake' of the soviets assuming 'sole revolutionary power'; with its readiness to co-operate with – but firmly control – the bourgeois government; with its insistence on an agrarian reform which would be enacted through the Constituent Assembly; with its call for a revived and pluralist RSDRP including 'all shades of revolutionary internationalist socialism', with its commitment to the 'revival of the proletarian International', to peace-making through 'organized forms and negotiations' (to the exclusion of sabotage and other forms of direct action), and to the maintenance, as long as the war lasted, of 'the fighting strength of our revolutionary army' and finally with its emphasis on a humanist socialist culture, it had thus clearly marked itself off from the revolutionary maximalism of Lenin's *April Theses*, from his narrow and uncompromising party-mindedness (*partiinost*), from his call for the destruction of the Second International, from his general agenda of class and civil war and from his rabble-rousing demagoguery. Thus, much à la Sukhanov, *Novaia zhizn'* advertised itself as a radical, independent and fiercely internationalist, anti-war organ, close to – but slightly to the left of – what became the Menshevik-Internationalist faction. Small wonder that soon after Martov's arrival on 9 May, Sukhanov accepted his invitation to join the Menshevik party.

While Sukhanov was still basking in the glory of the First of May celebrations, 'that truly bright people's festival', and celebrating the birth of *Novaia zhizn'*,[74] Miliukov's Note to the Allies of 19 April came as a stunning reminder that the foreign policy of the Provisional Government was still resolutely committed to the continuation of the war 'until decisive victory' rather than its ending by negotiation. As the wording of the Note put it, the government was insistent on the 'fulfilment of the obligations that we have undertaken towards our Allies', the 'victorious conclusion of the present war' and the setting up of 'those guarantees and sanctions required to prevent future bloody conflicts'.[75] In short, the peace policy of the Petrograd Soviet had been openly challenged and the government's Declaration to the Citizens of Russia of 28 March had been rendered worthless.

Fig. 2.3 Miliukov

Sukhanov was the last speaker at the combined session of the government, the Executive Committee of the Petrograd Soviet and members of the Duma Committee which was convened on the night of 20–21 April for the purpose of 'clarification' (in Sukhanov's view what was required was 'an ultimatum').[76] Quoting, with 'maximum tactlessness' (to use his own words), from the ministerial reports which had all testified to 'the complete ruin of the economy' he hammered his message that it was not merely absurd but 'criminal and unpatriotic' to even dream of waging a war 'until total victory' over Germany was achieved and until all the imperialist aims of the Allies were realized. To proceed with such a war would 'undermine the economic foundations of the country even further and enslave Russia to the Allies'. 'The Russian democracy can no longer take responsibility' for such a policy, and therefore the Executive Committee's 'promise to support the Provisional Government can no longer be honoured'. What Russia desperately needed in order to repair its ruined economy was 'a policy of peace'.[77]

While Sukhanov's main concern was Russia's overriding need for peace, he also realized that Tsereteli and the majority of the Executive Committee were most anxious to minimize the political crisis and to accommodate the government by accepting a mere note of clarification.[78] Thus, next day, in his article 'The Democracy and the Provisional Government', Sukhanov began to speculate on possible political solutions to what he called 'the internal crisis' of the government. Conceding that the Provisional Government had so far lived up to the demands and programme of the democracy insofar as its internal policies were concerned, he insisted that in its foreign policy it had 'continued and even sharpened the foreign policy of the autocracy'. Obviously, the democracy could neither trust nor tolerate a government which was now deliberately throwing the country into the throes of a never-ending war. That, Sukhanov urged, did not necessarily mean that power must be transferred to the democracy. What was really needed were 'correctives' to the composition of the government. Miliukov, 'who is not merely the standard bearer but the very progenitor of the war programme of the autocracy', had proved incapable of implementing 'a democratic peace programme'. But such a programme should be acceptable to all strata of society including a majority of the government: while it was true that the bourgeoisie could not tolerate any 'undermining of the foundations of the bourgeois order', yet under the pressure of grim necessity it should be capable of concluding a peace 'without [the acquisition of] Galicia, Constantinople, Armenia and Eastern Prussia', all so dear to Miliukov. However, should the 'governing group' regard itself as powerless to do that, then one should consider the formation of a coalition government comprised of those left elements in the government who were committed to the ending of the war together with other extra-government left groups. But if the government preferred instead to resign, then the democracy must willy-nilly assume power.[79]

Predictably, the day after the government's clarification note had been approved by the Soviet, Tsereteli again put the endorsement of the Liberty Loan on the agenda, urging that since 'the incident has ended in the victory of our democracy' and the clarification had been accepted, it was 'now necessary to resolve the question of the loan'.[80] Sukhanov, knowing full well that a majority of the Executive Committee favoured the loan, reminded them and a fuming Tsereteli that support for the loan had been made conditional upon 'a change in the government's foreign policy' and that no such change had occurred. To the contrary, they were now in even a worse position than on 28 March when the government had promised to take 'further steps'. They were now in the middle of an internal government crisis and only when that was resolved, he told the Executive Committee, should they give the money. Otherwise – 'hold back'.[81] When the vote was taken in the Executive Committee, Sukhanov and the opponents of the loan were defeated by 33 to 16 and when a resolution in support of the loan was put to the Soviet plenum, it was passed by no less than 2,000 against a mere 112 votes.[82]

Writing in next day's *Novaia zhizn'*, Sukhanov decried as a political mistake the Soviet's support for what he called the 'War Loan', but in his *Zapiski* he saw the vote even more bleakly as marking the 'end of a month of castrated, formal Zimmerwaldism'. From then on, as he saw it, 'a new banner of social patriotism flew over the Soviet democracy, and with it, over the Russian revolution: *the period of Soviet Scheidemannism had begun'*.[83]

Later, pondering in his *Zapiski* the defeat of the 'Zimmerwald line', he speculated whether it had been predetermined by 'the preconditions of the revolution', specifically its 'original sin – the petty-bourgeois structure of Russia, the broadly all-national character of the revolution', with the peasant-soldier taking centre stage from the very outset. Was it because of that, he wondered, that the efforts of the Zimmerwaldists in the Soviet were running counter to the 'laws of history'and were therefore utopian and doomed. Conceding that the formation of the 'new Soviet majority' – which consisted largely of peasant soldiers, intelligentsia and petty-bourgeois-philistine elements – was both 'natural and inevitable', he insisted that this by no means meant that the struggle for peace as such was beyond the strength of the peace movement. Since peace was a 'democratic cause', it could have been promoted by a united front of the petty-bourgeois and proletarian masses against the imperialist bourgeoisie. Therefore the struggle for the Zimmerwald line 'was not bound to fail – it was only terribly difficult and apparently had proved to be beyond the strength of those who had actually waged the fight. So let us not rail against the laws of history, but rather be fair to those who, in an unequal fight, suffered defeat in what was the only correct course of the revolution.'[84]

While the Menshevik leaders were still trying to help the government to rescue Miliukov, Sukhanov, both in *Novaia zhizn'* and in the Executive Committee, argued for the establishment of a coalition government, dumbfounding both his left-wing associates and even Tsereteli, who wondered whether this represented some Machiavellian ruse. In the end, he decided that the unexpected move was due to that 'combination of doctrinaire leftism with a large dose of impressionism' that characterized Sukhanov.[85] Not too bad an explanation, if one complements it by recalling Sukhanov's shrewd understanding that only the formation of a coalition government would oust Miliukov and Guchkov, a view he had advocated as early as 21 April.

On 27 and 28 April, both in *Novaia zhizn'* and the Executive Committee, and perhaps in response to the resolution of the Menshevik Organizational Committee of 24 April which had rejected coalition as both 'inexpedient and harmful',[86] Sukhanov examined the traditional socialist objections to coalitionism and urged that they were no longer valid. One reason for these objections, he thought, was the bad experience of French socialism in 1899 when a French socialist leader, Alexandre Millerand, had joined the bourgeois government of Waldeck-Rousseau and had soon forgotten his socialism. In the light of that experience, socialists had set their faces against 'Millerandism', embodying their opposition to it in resolutions of the Socialist International in 1900 and 1904. More recently, there had been the anti-war principles of Zimmerwald which were incompatible with shouldering the responsibility for conducting the 'imperialist war'. But both were irrelevant in Russia's present political situation which made a drastic change in foreign policy both imperative and feasible: the April Crisis had demonstrated the colossal strength of the organized democracy as contrasted with the apparent weakness of the Provisional Government, for it was the Soviet alone which had prevented civil war and restored order even in the midst of mass demonstrations for and against the government. What was on the political agenda, Sukhanov urged, was a 'coalition ministry to end the war'. Such a ministry, even if the democratic ministers were to comprise only a minority, must be free of all those who did not share a commitment to European peace; its composition would have to reflect both the shift in the balance of power towards the democracy and the direction of external and internal policies in tune with the revolution. Such a ministry should be committed to international peace and to a number of internal reforms. But should the government be unwilling to adopt this policy, then 'we ourselves must create such a state power around a clearly defined programme and implement it ourselves.'[87]

Having thus commended the entry of socialists into a coalition government, Sukhanov was all but the odd man out in the left-wing opposition in the Executive Committee in endorsing and voting for coalition. It was, apparently, his fervent commitment to peace, his insight that an all-bourgeois government was out of place in revolutionary Russia and therefore doomed, and, of course, his independence of mind, that enabled him to brush aside all Marxist and radical socialist taboos on coalitionism.

In the editorials of *Novaia zhizn'* on 2 and 3 May, Sukhanov and his associates set out the following conditions for entry into a coalition government: in the first place, there must be an active foreign policy aimed at the speedy achievement à la Zimmerwald of a general peace 'without annexations and indemnities based on the self-determination of nationalities'; secondly, decisive measures must be taken to democratize the army, while concurrently strengthening the military front to defend 'liberty'; thirdly, there must be a number of social, economic and financial reforms; fourthly, the convening of the Constituent Assembly must be speeded up; and lastly and most importantly, the socialist ministers must be responsible to the Congress of Soviets and, until that body was convened, to the Petrograd Soviet. *Novaia zhizn'* singled out points one and three as of 'decisive importance'. In a number of editorials; it drew attention to the Soviet plenum's overwhelming (2000 to 100 votes) endorsement of coalition on 5 May. *Novaia zhizn'* welcomed the new coalition government (of six socialist ministers and nine so-called bourgeois ministers, most of them liberal-conservative *intelligenty*) as one pledged to peace, to the organization of production and to a rational use of the land, and concluded on an optimistic note: 'The democracy now has its democratic government; it will depend on the democracy to make that government powerful enough to strengthen and broaden the achievements of the revolution.'[88] In the same issue *Novaia zhizn'* reminded its readers that the Executive Committee had been promised that 'many responsible posts are to be filled by representatives of the socialist parties serving as deputy ministers and directors of departments and would thus exert practical influence on the country's administrative affairs'.[89] It seemed as if some of Sukhanov's early hopes might be realized.

On 5 May, the programme of the coalition government was published. Its preamble committed it to work 'energetically' for the realization of 'the ideas of liberty, equality and fraternity' and its first point aimed at 'a peace without annexations and indemnities and at the right of nations to decide their own affairs' and at the achieving of an agreement with the Allies 'on the basis of the Declaration of 28 March'. Its second point promised the democratization of the army and, more problematic for Sukhanov and his *Novaia zhizn'* colleagues, 'the development of its military strength, both defensive and offensive, as the Provisional Government's most important task'.[90]

It took only five days for doubts to surface in Sukhanov's mind and he began to publish a series of articles in which he scrutinized the new government's foreign policy, starting with the first two points in its programme. In theory, there was no contradiction between the two, he wrote, in fact they had been the policy of the Petrograd Soviet from the very beginning: that is, 'as long as the war had not ended politically, it must be serviced technically'. But it was up to the democracy to make sure that the two points did not come into conflict in practice. That was no easy matter as the first point was the result of a compromise accepted only reluctantly by the bourgeoisie who hoped that an offensive would at last be launched, while the second point constituted '*the very heart of the bourgeoisie's programme'*. The democracy must therefore make sure that no new offensive was launched for the old war aims which must be replaced by official proposals of peace according to the Zimmerwald formula. Defence Minister Kerensky's efforts to restore and raise the army's fighting capacity for both defensive and offensive operations must be paralleled and complemented by Foreign Minister Tereshchenko's efforts to induce the Allies to revise the war's aims.[91]

In the following articles, Sukhanov warned day in and day out against the exclusive preoccupation with the idea of 'practical pre-paredness for an offensive', while not even lip service was being paid to the promised peace offensive and the revision of the war's aims.

A sense of particular urgency and frustration runs through these articles, apparently the result of his early premonition and final real-ization that a military offensive was under way and was bound to put an end to the great expectations he had of the Russian revolu-tion as peace-maker. He attacked both his old friend Kerensky and, with particular venom, Tereshchenko for abjectly submitting to the Allied foreign policy rather than declaring officially that revolution-ary Russia was not bound by the old tsarist treaties. Since the Allies had shown no interest in revising the war's aims, Sukhanov, in tune with his friend Martov and his close colleague Bazarov, was in fact considering a break with the Allies, and, should the Germans attack, the waging of a 'separate war' to defend revolutionary Russia. On the eve of the offensive, Sukhanov made sure that his implacable opposition to it and his campaign for peace could not be misinter-preted as 'disorganization of the war': he called on soldiers to obey even those orders which sent them into the attack; for as long as the war lasted, they must strengthen the army's organization and fighting capacity and its firm discipline – 'this is the line of *Novaia zhizn'*.[92]

When the offensive was finally launched on 18 June, Sukhanov wrote that for once he agreed with Tsereteli, who had declared: 'the revolution has staked everything on one card, the offensive'. But he also wanted to remind him that he had done nothing to bring Russia's war aims in line with democratic principles before 'putting the fate of the Russian revolution on that one card'. Sukhanov rarely missed an opportunity to needle Tsereteli.[93]

During the political crisis caused by the walk-out of the Kadet ministers from the government on 2 July and the subsequent violent Bolshevik-led demonstrations against the government and the leaders of the Soviet under the slogan of 'All Power to the Soviets', Sukhanov spoke in support of Martov's urgent motion to form a 'government of the democracy' to replace the coalition government. There was no point, Sukhanov argued, in trying, as Tsereteli intended, to rebuild the coalition government ; it had been 'a fiction rather than a state power' and its activities had been nothing but 'sabotage and disruption'. He appealed to the Soviet plenum 'to reject decisively' Tsereteli's proposal to defer the decision for two weeks until representatives of Russia's soviets could be convened to deal with the crisis.[94]

Prior to the July Days (for Sukhanov's version of the Bolshevik role in the July Days, *see* Appendix 2, and, for his account of the 4 July siege of the Executive Committee by the workers of the Putilov plant, *see* Chapter 3 below), his chief preoccupation in *Novaia zhizn'* had been with foreign affairs and peace, but from 11 July until the Bolshevik October revolution he concentrated mainly on the problem of power. True, in the Executive Committee he consistently supported Groman's radical plans 'for the organization and regulation of the national economy'; but he, the radical, had restrained himself in order not to embarrass Groman and prevent him from gaining the support of the moderates in the Executive Committee. Only once does it seem that he took time off to comment on agrarian matters when he reacted sharply to Agriculture Minister Chernov's draft law prohibiting land sales: it was riddled with loopholes, he wrote, it did not prohibit land sales to foreigners nor did it prevent fictitious deals which split large estates into small peasant holdings in an effort to protect landowners against future confiscations.[95]

The July Days were followed by a lengthy political crisis when the Soviet's leaders were renegotiating the formation of a coalition government, but this time from the position of weakness that the violent demonstrations had inflicted upon them. In his article 'Crisis', Sukhanov showed himself more than ever worried by a general move to the right which he feared might strengthen the *haute bourgeoisie*, diminish the role of the social movement and channel the revolution into those bourgeois-democratic forms which characterized Western Europe. In the present situation, he feared that the efforts of the Soviet leadership to reach agreement with the bourgeoisie might take Russia in that direction and also produce an impotent government, even were it to assume 'exceptional powers'.[96] A few days later, on 19 July, in an article significantly headed 'In Search of a State Power', Sukhanov drew attention to the fact that the Soviet leaders' guidelines in their negotiations with their bourgeois partners were 'diametrically opposed to' and incompatible with the conditions stipulated by the Kadets: it was precisely because the democracy's programme was so odious to the Kadets that they had walked out on 2 July. Worse still, even such bourgeois non-Kadet candidates for a coalition government such as Ivan Efremov, Prince Georgii Lvov, or even P.N. Pereverzev – a marginal SR – were completely out of tune with the democratic programme. Indeed the Kerensky–Tsereteli utopian attempt to broaden the *political* base of state power could only be realized at the cost of 'narrowing the *social* base of the entire revolution'. Equally utopian was the demand of the bourgeois negotiators that the soviets be stripped of their political role and turned into 'pure and simple class organizations'. Sukhanov was convinced that as long as the revolution was not dead, the soviets 'remained the source and authority of state power'.[97] At the same time, in a characteristic passage, Sukhanov spelled it all out:

> History hardly knows another example in which a ruling group whose power does not rest on bayonets or on personal influence, but rather on real class relationships, finds itself in such a tragic and absurd situation in which it has not the slightest idea of what to do with that power and hence it is in search of 'dead souls' with which it can create the appearance of coalition. But that power was given by the soviets, and it was not given in order that it be handed over to the enemies of the revolution.

The only possible state power in Russia now was a 'dictatorship of the democracy' which would draw its authority from the soviets and unflinchingly realize the democratic programme.[98]

With a heavy heart, Sukhanov recorded in the *Zapiski* how the Menshevik leaders Tsereteli and Dan had marched off to the Malachite Hall of the Winter Palace during the night of 22–23 July to offer the Soviet leaders' acceptance of the Kadet conditions which put an end to the Soviet's control over the socialist ministers in the projected second coalition government:[99]

Yes, this was that very same almighty Soviet which could once dismiss the revolutionary government in five minutes and which even now had the backing of the real strength of the country .... thus it had both in word and deed removed itself from high politics.

When the second coalition government was finally formed on 25 July, Sukhanov, in an unsigned editorial, noted that Tsereteli, the central figure who had given some stability and consistency to the democratic component in the previous coalition government, was absent from its ranks. True, he wrote, alluding to Krylov's fable, as in the past 'the revolutionary cart was drawn by the swan, the crab and the pike', but now the swan's wings had been severely clipped and its spine injured, while the crab and the pike who had lately been feasting on carrion were bright, cheerful and vigorous as never before.[100] On 22 August, Sukhanov used the Menshevik Unification Conference to accuse the leaders of the Petrograd Soviet of having abandoned the two principal points of the Address to the Peoples of the Whole World of 14 March: 'the struggle for peace and the struggle against imperialist governments'; to illustrate his point, he singled out the Soviet's support of the Liberty Loan as marking 'the break with Zimmerwald'. Countering Tsereteli's defensive argument that everything possible had been done to achieve peace, and nothing further could be done until the international proletariat joined the struggle, Sukhanov reminded him that the record did not show that 'we were ready to break with the Allies for the sake of peace and present them with an ultimatum to enter peace negotiations'. And a break with the Allies would not have meant a separate peace; it might even have led to a separate war, although one that 'we undoubtedly could have waged, provided that we had dissociated ourselves beforehand from the present [imperialist] war'.[101]

Not surprisingly, during and in the wake of the Kornilov mutiny – the abortive attempt to seize power made by General Lavr Kornilov, commander-in-chief of Russia's armed forces – in late August and early September, Sukhanov and with him *Novaia zhizn'* resumed his call for 'a dictatorship of the democracy': the Central Executive Committee of the Soviets would declare itself 'the sole source of state power', while 'the principle of the dictatorship of the democracy would be realized through the democratic organizations'. Not only was any form of coalition government now 'unthinkable', when the entire bourgeoisie, represented by the Kadet party and its mouthpiece, the *Rech'*, had been guilty of underwriting Kornilov's plot, but the democracy must now also clamour for the Kornilovites to be put on trial: 'not in the name of abstract justice, or out of malice and revenge, but for the sake of the democracy's self-preservation and the victory of its cherished goals. Its cry must be: "Long Live the Fearless Severity of Revolutionary Justice against its Enemies."' Piotr Palchinsky, the governor-general of Petrograd, most likely prompted by Kerensky, closed down *Novaia zhizn'* 'for preaching lynch justice' and until 9 September the paper appeared as *Svobodnaia zhizn'*.[102]

In the wake of the Democratic Conference of mid-September – convened by the Central Executive Committee of Soviets to deal with the political crisis and specifically with the question of coalitionism – when the composition of the new government was being negotiated, Sukhanov, in an unsigned editorial – 'In the Clutches of Power'[103] – weighed a number of solutions to the problem of power: a simple continuation of coalition government; a homogeneous government of the moderate democracy (that is, Mensheviks and SRs); his own favourite, a wall-to-wall coalition of the entire democracy, including the Bolsheviks; or, and this seems to have been his real worry, a Bolshevik dictatorship which he thought would be the worst way out of the situation. While he does not seem to have been aware of Lenin's two letters of 15 September to the Bolshevik leaders in which he unsuccessfully summoned them to ready themselves for the seizure of power, yet from his reading of the Bolshevik *Rabochyi put'* he may well have guessed that such plans had surfaced in the party from time to time and had then been disowned or explained away. Sukhanov certainly expected the Bolsheviks to have a majority at the planned Second Congress of Soviets and was well aware that their resurrected slogan of All Power to the Soviets was nothing more than a cover for a Bolshevik 'dictatorship of the proletariat'. While he had no doubt that the Bolsheviks were capable of seizing power, he was equally sure that they would not be able to maintain themselves in power. The outcome of the Bolshevik adventure, he feared, would be 'the utter rout and crushing of the revolution'. For, once in power, the proletariat would be isolated from all the 'real, living forces of the democracy' and would prove unable to master the mechanics of the state apparatus and put it in motion in an extremely complex situation. Politically, they would be unable to withstand 'the onslaught of hostile forces' which would not merely sweep away the Bolshevik 'dictatorship of the proletariat, but the revolution as well'. In his opinion, the only state power that made sense in the present situation was a 'truly honest' coalition within the democracy, for it alone would be capable of realizing a common minimal programme and enjoy the support of 'all the living forces of the democracy'.

Lenin took issue with the warnings of Sukhanov's editorial in a lengthy treatise significantly called 'Will the Bolsheviks Maintain Themselves in State Power?'[104] It was not so much part of his ongoing polemic with the 'quarter Bolsheviks' of *Novaia zhizn'* (he did not know that Sukhanov was the author of the editorial), but rather his major attempt to convince and cajole his reluctant Bolsheviks to dare to take the plunge into the October revolution. Dealing point by point with what he identified as *Novaia zhizn'*'s six arguments against the Bolshevik seizure of power, he insisted firstly that the proletariat was not isolated; to the contrary, because of the experience of coalitionism it enjoyed the sympathy of the majority of the population, nor secondly, was it isolated from the 'living forces of the democracy' as many erstwhile Menshevik and SR supporters 'now favour a pure Bolshevik government'. Thirdly, while it was true that the proletariat could not master the technique of the [existing] state apparatus, it could 'smash all that is oppressive, hidebound and irremediably bourgeois in the old state apparatus and replace it with its own new apparatus, the soviets of workers, soldiers and peasants deputies'. Fourthly, that apparatus would be 'put into motion' by 'the mighty enthusiasm of genuine, popular creativity', and it would be administered by the 240,000 members of the Bolshevik party. Fifthly, while it was true that 'the situation is exceptionally complex', 'any revolution is a very fierce, mad and desperate class struggle and civil war. No great revolution in history has managed without civil war.' Finally, rebutting Sukhanov's argument that the proletariat would be incapable of withstanding the assault of the hostile forces which would sweep away both the dictatorship of the proletariat and the entire revolution, Lenin was adamant that since 'all the necessary conditions for revolution were there', there was no force on earth that could stand in the way of the Bolsheviks provided they did not allow themselves to be intimidated and would succeed in taking and holding on to power until the victory of the world socialist revolution.

Sukhanov repeated his warnings in a signed editorial on 1 October appealing (tongue in cheek?) to the Bolsheviks not 'to allow themselves to be provoked' into offensive steps which would unleash civil war. He reminded them of the fiasco of the July Days when they had gone into the attack all on their own and contrasted that defeat with the spectacular success of the Kornilov Days when the united democracy had defended the revolution. The 'obvious lesson' that Sukhanov wanted the Bolsheviks to learn was that 'the democracy is invincible in civil war when it takes up a defensive position relying on the support of the most influential organs of the population', but it suffers defeat when it charges headlong into 'an offensive initiative and loses the support of the mass of the wavering and uncommitted'.[105]

Lenin took up that challenge in an 'Afterword' where he wrote: 'You gentlemen of *Novaia zhizn'* who yourselves report daily on the growing ruin of the country, do you really think that it will agree to wait until the Constituent Assembly and the Congress of Soviets meet?' and he accused them of responding 'to the formidable problems of civil war with confused phrases and constitutional illusions'.[106]

When the third and last coalition government was formed on 25 September thanks to the indefatigable efforts of Tsereteli, Sukhanov pointed the finger of scorn in an article entitled 'The Victory of Tsereteli',[107] a victory which for him marked yet another resounding defeat for the revolution:

> We have no doubt that Tsereteli, the creator of that coalition government, will as before serve as its loyal knight and act as its commissar within the democratic organizations. But we doubt that this coalition, this wretched offspring of cowardice and opportunism will long survive.

This attack on Tsereteli's coalitionism was paralleled by his attack on Tereshchenko and the government's foreign policy which he denounced as 'subservient to the unlimited war aims of the Allies' when what was really on the democracy's agenda was the ending of the war.[108] He continued his attack on Tereshchenko on 5 October in an angry reaction to the renewed postponement of the planned conference with the Allies in which a revision of the war aims was to be on the agenda. Sukhanov sneered: There [at the conference in Paris] the Allies would 'graciously revise the war aims of Russia', that is, dispose of Constantinople and the Dardanelles, of Armenia and Galicia. And they would even 'dispose of their guarantees of Russia's territorial integrity', but not of their own war aims: Syria, Mesopotamia, Trieste, Alsace-Lorraine. In response to that 'new challenge', it was the 'patriotic duty' of the democracy to campaign for 'immediate, general, democratic peace proposals to the nations of Europe'.[109] He made the same point in an article on 20 October in which he took the side of Defence Minister General Alexander Verkhovsky who had come out for a drastic change in foreign policy and for a democratized army which must not fight 'for some Mesopotamia for the English merchants'. Sukhanov, expressing the hope that 'this still-born coalition would fall apart, urged that the democracy then immediately set up its own government which alone could save the country. This was his last article before the Bolshevik October revolution which brutally dashed all his hopes that the coalition government, which he had done his best to discredit, might be replaced by 'a democratic state power'.[110]

3
Chronicler of Russia's Democratic Revolution

Thanks to his seven-volume *Zapiski o revoliutsii* (Notes on the Revolution), Sukhanov has been universally acclaimed (since *glasnost*, even in the former Soviet Union) as the chronicler *par excellence* of Russia's democratic revolution from February to October 1917 and his *Zapiski* have been recognized as an indispensable historical source.[1]

Sukhanov began to write his *Zapiski* in July 1918 just when 'by the will of the "Communist" authorities I was made unemployed, removed from my literary work by the closing down of *Novaia zhizn'* [on 16 July 1918] and from political activity by my expulsion [on 14 June 1918] from the central Soviet institution (TsIK) where I had been active from the first moment of the revolution'.[2] He completed the first volume, which covers the early days of the revolution, in November 1918 and the last volume, which takes the story to the October revolution and the 'dictatorship of the Russian Communist Party', on 30 August 1921.

The first volume, he claims, was based almost exclusively on what he himself remembered of the first days of the revolution when, as a founding member of the Executive Committee of the Petrograd Soviet and of its Contact Commission with the Provisional Government, he was 'in the very crucible of the great events and in the laboratory of the revolution'.[3] In order to refresh and check on his memory for the following six volumes, he also consulted the newspapers of 1917, notably his own *Novaia zhizn'*, and some of the major participants such as Trotsky, Anatolii Lunacharsky, Fiodor Dan, Vladimir Voitinsky and Vladimir Antonov-Ovseenko.[4] Yet what characterizes the entire work is the accuracy and honesty of Sukhanov's accounts of events, scenes and even speeches, an integrity vouchsafed by such contemporary adversaries as Miliukov, Sergei Melgunov, Tsereteli and Trotsky. While Melgunov admits that 'inevitably one has to rely on Sukhanov's account for one's own narrative' of the early days of the revolution,[5] Tsereteli, referring to a major episode of the July Days, testifies to Sukhanov's 'almost stenographic accuracy ... since he was in the habit of jotting down in his notebook all those characteristic episodes at which he was present'.[6] Miliukov concedes that he used Sukhanov's *Zapiski*, 'though they were written from the opposite standpoint ... to confirm the objectivity of my own account' and he condescended to commend Sukhanov's 'seven volumes as a useful complement to the three volumes of my own account'.[7] Even Trotsky, while sneering at Sukhanov's 'frayed *Zapiski*', made extensive use of them for his own *History of the Russian Revolution*, so much so that Stalin would accuse him of having written his history of the October revolution 'according to Sukhanov'.[8] Better still, Trotsky paid Sukhanov the ultimate compliment of simply copying some of his own speeches verbatim from the *Zapiski* including that of 25 October 1917 which consigned Martov and the Mensheviks to 'the rubbish bin of history'.[9]

But there is more to the *Zapiski* than their reliability and indispensability as a historical source. Their author, though close to Martov, but slightly to his left, and himself belonging to the small radical non-Bolshevik Left, was exceptionally familiar with the wide range of political issues, ideologies and personalities at the centre of the revolution and was blessed with a sharp and critical eye and pen. With his penchant and talent for sharp analysis, he was rarely satisfied with merely telling a story or describing an event, which he does superbly well, instead he used them to drive home a point. True, Sukhanov assures the reader time and again that his *Zapiski* were 'personal reminiscences and no more', mere 'disorderly jottings of an eye-witness' and should not be taken 'as history or even as the most superficial and unpretentious historical outline'.[10] But he may be protesting too much when claiming that 'they are not the fruit of reflection, even less so of study – they are the fruit of *memory!*' of one who had the good fortune to live through the 'unforgettable days, the grand events of the epoch, the greatest in the history of mankind' and he felt he must write 'his own story'.

For I saw, I remember, many, many things that were inaccessible to and remain unknown to contemporaries. And who can guarantee that this will not remain unknown to history. Moreover, who can guarantee that other participants and witnesses will correctly illuminate the matter and that another witness account will not prove of value to historians.[11]

Nothwithstanding Sukhanov's disclaimers, whether in self-defence against contemporaries whose feathers he knew he had ruffled, or just in quest of freedom to say bluntly what he had to say, the *Zapiski* constitute an eye-witness account of how 'the wondrous epic' of the February revolution was turned into 'an amazing tragedy unprecedented in history'.[12]

While the rise and fall of Russia's democratic revolution of February to October 1917 is the unifying theme of the *Zapiski*, its main thesis is Sukhanov's *J'accuse*: his indictment of the Menshevik and SR leaders, above all Tsereteli and Dan, as bearing major responsibility for the tragic Bolshevik outcome of the revolution. With their control over the soviets and through them over the revolutionary army, they were the real power in the land and 'could have led the revolution wherever they wanted'. But they deliberately and incorrigibly pursued a policy of co-operation with the potentially counter-revolutionary 'bourgeoisie' and of political coalitionism with the Constitutional Democrats [Kadets], their incompatible ally.[13] They thus prepared the ground for the Bolshevik conquest of the masses, their takeover of the soviets and their perversion of the revolution.

It is that unifying theme and thesis that binds together what looks deceptively like a long string of reports of events and scenes, portraits and silhouettes, comments and analyses into a unique and idiosyncratic but felicitous blend of chronicle, historical memoir and contemporary history.[14]

Pride of place in the *Zapiski*, apart from the political portraits of the *dramatis personae*, must be accorded to some of the major scenes of the revolution at which Sukhanov himself was present and which he recorded with an immediacy which captures their drama and import. Cumulatively they combine to illustrate Sukhanov's major theme and to support his principal thesis: for the *Zapiski* are nothing less than a work *à thèse* which he repeats time and again, that the soviets, led by the *bloc* of Mensheviks and SRs, had all the power in the land and that their leaders, notably Tsereteli and Dan, frittered it away. In his chapter 'The People Demonstrates Its

Strength and Power', Sukhanov takes the reader on a euphoric tour of Petrograd celebrating the First of May 1917. True, it had been a beautiful spring day and he and his colleagues, racing against time, had just managed triumphantly to bring out the first issue of *Novaia zhizn'* in no fewer than 100,000 copies, but there was more to it than that: this chapter is very much the work of Sukhanov the believer, writing in the latter part of 1919 and nostalgically eulogizing the revolution that he had lost:

> This was not a tour [when he travelled along the streets like a 'victor on his estate'] but a 'divine poem' and unforgettable symphony made up of sun rays, the silhouettes of the fabulous town, the festive crowds, the somewhat off-key sound of the Internationale and some indescribable emotions from within – all that is gone now and is not likely to return .... Yes, this was an unexampled manifestation of the people's boundless strength and achievement and this was a spring that filled the gigantic breast of Petersburg with waves of fresh enthusiasm, of unclouded hopes, with the wholeness of a rock-hard faith not drawn from some made up fairy tale but from the tangible world ... What we saw in the Nevsky [Prospect] exceeded by far anything that could have been organized. This was truly a bright, all-national festive day and all its brilliant organization, with decorations never seen before, fades before the lively animated active tangible participation of all these hundreds of thousands of people on this First of May.[15]

More soberly, Sukhanov illustrates the extent of the Soviet's power in his account of the emergency session of the Petrograd Soviet on the evening of 20 April, convened to decide what action should be taken in answer to Miliukov's 'treacherous' Note to the Allies of 18 April[16] which reaffirmed Russia's loyalty to their treaties and war aims and its own determination to 'bring the World War to a decisive victory'. Sukhanov savoured to the full the tension and the drama of the scene in the centre of which stood the initially hapless but ultimately resourceful Stankevich. A leading *trudovik*, and by no means a radical, Stankevich had failed to gauge the angry and militant mood of the assembly which had been whipped up by a radical orator who had called for the overthrow of the

Provisional Government. In an attempt to calm tempers, Stankevich began: 'Some make a simple decision and say we must topple the Provisional Government and arrest it.' And no sooner had he uttered this half-sentence than a good half of the audience burst out in stormy applause. An obviously 'disconcerted' Stankevich quickly regained his composure and warning against 'needless bloodshed, chaos and disorganization' which were 'unsuitable, unnecessary' for resolving the political crisis he turned again to his audience:

> Why, comrades, should we come out [against the government] and against whom are we going to use force and fire our guns? Aren't you and the masses that support you all the power there is, and what you decide is what will be. Look there (at this point Stankevich stretched out his arm and pointed at the clock on the wall, drawing after him the eyes of all in the hall): It is now five minutes to seven and you decree that the Provisional Government shall be no more, that it must resign. We shall ring through that message by phone and within five minutes the government will surrender its powers, and by seven o'clock it will have ceased to exist. What use is there then in violence, insurrection and civil war?

Sukhanov recorded a 'sensation' in the hall and a burst of 'stormy applause'. But it was not just the result of rhetoric, Sukhanov urged: Stankevich had accurately sized up the situation as one in which the Soviet, in the form of its Executive Committee, held the entire real power and could lead the revolution in whatever direction it desired. And it was with delight that Sukhanov registered that it was the Executive Committee which, during the April Crisis, ordered General Lavr Kornilov, with guns and troops, back into the barracks, decreed and effected the restoration of order and thus prevented the violent demonstrations and counter-demonstrations from escalating into civil war; 'only the Soviet could do that' and tell the soldiers that 'only the Executive Committee has the right to give you orders'.[17]

He enlarged on this theme until it became the *leitmotiv* of both his articles in *Novaia zhizn'* – and in the last four volumes of his *Zapiski*: although the Soviet leaders controlled the vast network of soviets and a multiplicity of organizations such as co-operatives, Red Guards, trade unions and, above all, the Army, they would not use that power to advance the revolution, plan and control its economy, give satisfaction and benefits to the masses which supported them and, most important for Sukhanov, pursue a peace policy. Instead, he charged, they were hell-bent on collaboration with the 'propertied elements' and on coalitionism with the Kadet party which, frightened by the revolution,was turning counter-revolutionary.[18]

Small wonder that looking at the high-water mark of the February revolution from the sad vantage point of 16 October 1919, Sukhanov remembered how 'high into the heaven [the revolution] reached and how boundless, diverse and bright, colourful and beautiful were its horizons; such, exactly, was the face of the Russian land in those days'.[19]

But already in the following chapter, with its heading 'The Soviet Lays the People's Power at the Feet of the Bourgeoisie', Sukhanov tells the story of how the leaders of the Soviet began to dissipate that power by making one concession after another to the Provisional Government in the wake of the April Crisis from which they had emerged the victors. They declared 'the incident as settled', pledged support for the 'Liberty Loan' just after the Provisional Government had torpedoed the Soviet's peace policy, and termed the government 'deserving of support', when, in the opinion of Sukhanov, what it deserved was 'execution'. Worse still, the Soviet's Address to the Army of 30 April, ominously and for the first time referred to 'the possible need of an offensive to resist or prevent an enemy offensive' and told soldiers that, having vowed to defend Russia's freedom, they 'cannot just sit it out in the trenches', and must not 'rule out offensive operations'. Sukhanov, deeply committed as he was to an active peace policy, saw in all this nothing less than the Soviet's 'capitulation' and the beginning of its slide into social-patriotism and *'Scheidemannism'*.[20]

If, until May 1917, Sukhanov had attacked the Soviet majority leaders for making concessions to the Provisional Government, from mid-May on, after they had joined that government as junior partners, he castigated them for their unbending devotion to coalitionism. It was that, he asserted, which drove workers and soldiers into the arms of the Bolsheviks: 'He who watched the policy of coalitionism also saw the success of Lenin. These were two sides of the same coin.' In Sukhanov's opinion the contest between Lenin and his Bolsheviks on the one hand and the leaders of the Soviet majority on the other, fought out within the soviets, formed the substance of the period June to October 1917.[21]

Sukhanov's account of how 'Lenin overcomes and overpowers the February revolution'[22] begins with Lenin's arrival in Petrograd from Swiss exile on 3 April. Together with Chkheidze and Matvei Skobelev, members of the praesidium of the Executive Committee, who had been delegated to represent the Petrograd Soviet, Sukhanov travelled to the Finland Station to witness Lenin's arrival. It proved to be a major event.[23]

Having passed the military units and crowds massed along the platform on his way to the Tsar's Room, Sukhanov registered the welcome home which the Petrograd Bolsheviks had done their best to make 'not merely a demonstration of loyalty [to their leader] but also a show of strength'. Sukhanov, who knew his Bolsheviks, was not in the least surprised:

> They generally shine in organization, always intent to make the most of appearances, to display their goods from their best side and to throw sand into people's eyes ... They had prepared a triumphant welcome ...

Sukhanov recorded both the scene and the speeches:

> Lenin walked, or rather hurried, into the Tsar's Room, in a round hat, his face chilled [from the cold] and a luxurious bouquet of flowers in his arms. He stopped still in the centre of the room in front of Chkheidze ... and here a [glum-looking] Chkheidze delivered his welcoming speech, keeping to the spirit, the letter and even the tone of a sermon: 'Comrade Lenin, in the name of the Petersburg Soviet of Workers and Soldiers Deputies and of the revolution as a whole, we welcome you in Russia. We consider that the principal task of the revolutionary democracy now is the defence of our revolution against all encroachments from both within and without; this goal urgently requires the closing of the ranks by the entire democracy and not disunity. We hope that you, together with us, will pursue these goals ...'.

Fig. 3.1   Lenin

While Sukhanov himself was 'stunned', Lenin stood there as if
nothing that 'concerned him to the slightest degree had happened.
He looked around, gazed up at the ceiling, adjusted the bouquet

which was rather ill-suited to his figure' and spoke without even looking at, but rather turning away from, the delegates of the Executive Committee:

> Dear comrades, soldiers, sailors and workers! I am happy to greet in you the victorious Russian Revolution and to greet you as the advance guard of the world-wide proletarian army ... The predatory imperialist war marks the beginning of civil war throughout Europe. The time is not far distant when, at the call of our comrade Karl Liebknecht, the people will turn their weapons against the capitalist exploiters. The day of the world-wide socialist revolution has already dawned .... Germany is seething ... the whole of European imperialism may crash any day now. The Russian Revolution which you have wrought has heralded the start of a new epoch. Long live the worldwide socialist revolution.

While Sukhanov agreed with Lenin in principle that they were living in an age of world revolution, he still felt that 'there had burst on us something ... novel, harsh and stunning'. It would not do 'just to hail the world-wide revolution' and not to say a word about the historic realities of Russia's revolution. What made this scene not merely memorable but also of historic importance was the confrontation between Lenin and Chkheidze which foreshadowed the split and the conflict which Lenin was subsequently to impose on the 'revolutionary democracy', towards his 'victory over the February revolution'.[24]

But first of all Lenin had to reconquer his party, and Sukhanov ponders at length how, soon after his arrival, Lenin succeeded in prising the Bolshevik leadership away from the 'old social-democratic Bolshevism' whose spokesman in Petrograd was Lev Kamenev, and instead made them accept the *April Theses* and his new Bolshevism. Not surprisingly, in the centre of Sukhanov's analysis, stands Lenin 'the Thunderer', the founder and leader of the Bolshevik party:[25]

> First of all, there can be no doubt that Lenin is an extraordinary phenomenon, a man of exceptional spiritual force: his calibre is of first-class world magnitude. He represents an unusually felicitous combination of theorist and popular leader of a movement.

If yet more terms and epithets were needed, I would not hesitate to call Lenin a man of genius, keeping in mind the meaning of the concept of genius. A genius, as is known, is an 'abnormal' person, whose head is 'not in order' – more concretely, he is a person who operates within an extremely limited sphere of intellectual activity, where that activity is carried out with unusual force and effect. Such a man is extremely narrow-minded, a chauvinist to the marrow of his bones, devoid of any understanding or grasp or capacity of the simplest and generally common things. Such was the genius of Tolstoy who, in the felicitous (even though not quite accurate) expression of [Dmitri] Merezhkovsky, was simply not clever enough for his own genius. Undoubtedly, Lenin is such a man as this, to whose mind many elementary truths are inaccessible, even in the area of socio-political movements, and from this derives the endless series of his most elementary mistakes both in his period as agitator and demagogue as well as during his dictatorship; yet, on the other hand, in a certain area of ideas, of a few 'fixed' ideas, Lenin displays such amazing force, such super-human thrust, that his colossal influence among socialists and revolutionaries has already been secured by the mere qualities of his nature.

Sukhanov's story of the alienation and bolshevization of the workers and garrison of Petrograd which he attributes to the 'compromising' policies of the leaders of the Soviet majority reaches a climax in his accounts of the peaceful demonstration of 18 June and of the violent disorders of the Bolshevik-led protest demonstrations of the July Days. He noted that the demonstration of 18 June, called in support of the First Congress of Russia's soviets then convening in Petrograd, had a clearly Bolshevik 'political profile': column after column, with hardly an exception, marched under banners and placards with Bolshevik slogans such as 'All Power to the Soviets!' 'Down with the Ten Capitalist Ministers!' (the 'bourgeois' majority of the coalition government) and 'Peace to the Hovels, War on the Palaces!' – 'a sharp slap in the face of the Soviet majority', he observed with glee.[26]

While Sukhanov's lengthy account of the July Days is replete with remarkable scenes such as the kidnapping on 4 July of Victor Chernov, the SR leader and minister of agriculture, by irate anarchist sailors and his spectacular rescue by Trotsky,[27] Sukhanov excels in capturing the anger and despair of the workers of the Putilov armaments plant as they massed before the Tauride Palace on 4 July while the Soviet was in session.[28] Some had been looking in vain for Tsereteli and all seemed intent on a show-down, if not worse, with the Soviet leadership. Sukhanov saw some forty worker-delegates, many armed with rifles, storming in:

> One of the workers, a classic sansculotte, in a cap and short belt-less blue blouse, leaped onto the speaker's podium, trembling all over with rage and, brandishing his rifle, shouted ... : 'Comrades, how long are we workers going to put up with treachery?! You [turning to the Soviet delegates] have assembled here to confer and make deals with the bourgeoisie and the landlords ... you are busy betraying the working class. Well, you'd better know that the working class won't put up with it! All thirty thousand Putilov workers are here down to the very last man. We are going to get what we want! No [deals] for the bourgeoisie! All power to the Soviets! ... Your Kerenskys and Tseretelis are not going to fool us!' Chairman Chkheidze, [Sukhanov noted] under whose nose the rifle had been brandished, remained completely calm and self-controlled. In answer to the ranting of the sansculotte .... Chkheidze leaned forward from the platform, stretched out his hand and slipped into the man's trembling hand yesterday's Appeal .... . 'Here comrade, I beg you, please take this and read it! It tells what you and your Putilov comrades should do. Please read it and don't disturb our work!' The Appeal said that all those who had gone into the streets should return home, otherwise they would be traitors to the revolution. The ruling group and Chkheidze [Sukhanov noted] had nothing better to offer to the representatives of the popular masses in this highly charged moment ... The perplexed sansculotte, not knowing what else to do, took the Appeal and was then without much difficulty pushed off the rostrum. Soon his comrades too were persuaded to leave the hall; order was restored and the incident was over ... but to this day I can see that sansculotte on the platform of the White Hall, shaking his rifle in the faces of the hostile 'leaders of the democracy' in his attempt to express the will, the yearnings and the anger of the proletarian lower strata who sensed treach-

ery but were powerless to fight it. This was one of the finest scenes of the revolution and, together with Chkheidze's gesture, one of the most dramatic.

Sukhanov watched with fascinated apprehension how the Bolsheviks exploited the unpopular policies of the Soviet leadership and the misery and frustrations of the masses with that demagoguery which was the 'natural' line of the Bolshevik committee men and agitators. It was thus that they expressed 'their dedication to the party and the revolution'.[29] As an example of early Bolshevik demagoguery, Sukhanov recorded the address of Alexandra Kollontai at the First of May Concert Meeting in the Mariinsky Palace where she had insisted on speaking far earlier than scheduled as she claimed that she could 'electrify the atmosphere'.[30]

> 'Comrades [she said, waving her clenched fists and jumping up and down as she was wont to do], they tell you day in and day out: Soldiers to the trenches! Workers to your lathes! ... But aren't the trenches defended and aren't there as many lathes at work as the owners wish?! ... But you, comrades, don't forget something else: it is indeed workers to the lathes – to work, and soldiers to the trenches – to die. But what about the bourgeoisie, the landowners? Landowners – home – to a comfortable rest on their estates?! And the bourgeoisie – to the loot stuffed in their coffers?! ... '.

The crowd in the brilliantly illuminated imperial theatre went into raptures. It was not just that Kollontai had captured their mood, she had injected them with a certain 'political programme', Sukhanov noted.

If that was Bolshevik demagoguery 'in embryo', it reached 'unprincipled', 'uninhibited' and 'shameless' heights in the propaganda speeches not only of rank-and-file agitators, but even of the leaders during the last few weeks before the October Revolution,[31] Sukhanov records. Their gospel was class hatred: 'Now the rich have everything and the poor have nothing.' But soon the tables would be turned and 'everything will belong to the poor and this is the promise of your own workers' party; it alone fights the rich and their government for land, peace and bread'. This was 'the line' of the numerous mass meetings held on the eve of the October

Fig. 3.2 Kollontai

Revolution. The one that Sukhanov attended and recorded took place on 22 October in the People's House where Trotsky was the main speaker.[32]

> Trotsky at once began to heat up the atmosphere .... As one who was present there I testify that this is exactly what was said:

'Soviet power will put an end to the suffering in the trenches; it will give land and heal the country's wounds .... It will send a soldier, a sailor and a woman worker into every village to requisition bread from the rich and send it *gratis* to the towns and to the front ... Soviet power will give everything that there is in the country to the poor and to the men in the trenches. You, bourgeois, you have two fur coats – give one of them to the soldier who freezes in the trenches. You have got warm boots ... stay at home, a worker needs your boots.' All around me the mood verged on ecstasy. It seemed as if the crowd would of its own accord break into some religious hymn. Trotsky formulated some general short resolution along the lines of 'We shall defend the worker-peasant cause to the last drop of our blood.' 'Who is in favour?' The thousands-strong crowd raised their hands to a man. I saw the raised hands and burning eyes of men, women, youths, soldiers, peasants and typically petty-bourgeois figures. Were they in a trance? Did they see through a raised curtain a tiny corner of some 'promised land' for which they longed? Or were they rather in the grip of the political hour, under the influence of socialist rhetoric? .... Do not ask! Accept it at face value .... Trotsky went on speaking, the vast crowd still held their hands aloft. 'Let this vote of yours be your vow', Trotsky shouted. 'Vow that you will support the Soviet with all your might and main and at the cost of any sacrifice, for this is the Soviet that has taken upon itself the great burden of bringing about the victory of the revolution and providing you with land, bread and peace!' And still the crowd stood with arms raised aloft. It agreed ... it vowed .... Once again, accept that this was how it was: it was with an unusually heavy heart that I gazed on this truly magnificent spectacle.

And Sukhanov sums it up and drives home his point that the October Revolution was not just a military conspiracy, a belief with which the Mensheviks (except Martov) and the SRs 'consoled themselves for months', but that it also had mass support:

Throughout Petersburg the scene was repeated time and again. Everywhere there were the same reviews and vows. Thousands, tens of thousands and hundreds of thousands of people. Properly

Fig. 3.3 Trotsky

speaking, this was already an uprising. The thing had already started.[33]

Indeed, surveying the support which Lenin could muster in many of the provincial soviets, the Petrograd Soviet and garrison, the Moscow Soviet and the front-line troops in the north, and even in some municipalities, Sukhanov concluded that 'the overturn under these conditions certainly did not resemble a military conspiracy or a Blanquist experiment'.[34]

Sukhanov the political portraitist is every bit as perceptive and imaginative as Sukhanov the reporter of some of the revolution's major scenes. He has immortalized himself by creating a gallery of major and minor revolutionary figures, the gems of which are his superb, empathetic, yet for all that, critical, profile of Martov,[35] whom he loved deeply, and a less empathetic and far more critical profile of Kerensky, a friend of long standing whom he fought bitterly in 1917.[36] Nor was this surprising, for he brought to his portraiture an unusual combination of talent and the advantage of the independent-minded intellectual who, in the course of his prolific journalistic work, had become familiar with and gained access to a wide range of intellectual circles and political camps. He certainly indulged himself in the privilege of the memoirist to indict and judge his fellows, especially those who, he believed, had ruined Russia's democratic revolution. They were, he said, at liberty 'to defend themselves, to contradict me and to expose me'. Tempering all this was his empathy with and singular pride in the Russian radical and revolutionary intelligentsia whom he knew so well. Indeed the more one knows from other sources about Tsereteli, Dan, Kerensky, Miliukov, Lenin, Trotsky, Lunacharsky or Chernov, to mention just a few, the more convincing Sukhanov's character sketches appear.

Sukhanov the portraitist seems to have made a valiant effort to separate the immediate 1917 impression he had of his characters from what he later perceived them to be when he sat down to write his *Zapiski*. A striking example is his boldly unflattering vignette of Stalin as he appeared to him during the early months of the revolution compared with the Stalin of July 1919 in whom he recognized

one of the most central figures of the Bolshevik party and perhaps one of the few individuals who held (and until this

Fig. 3.4 Kerensky

Fig. 3.5   Martov

minute still holds) in his hands the fate of the revolution and of the state. Why that is so I do not presume to say: influences in the irresponsible upper spheres that are remote from the people and from publicity are so intricate! At any rate one is truly puzzled with regard to Stalin's role. The Bolshevik party, in spite of the low level of its 'officers' corps' and of its ignorant and accidental mass, had a whole line of outstanding figures and worthy leaders among its 'generals'. However, Stalin, during the time of his modest activity in the Executive Committee of the Petrograd Soviet early in 1917, gave the impression – and not only to me – of a grey blur which would now and then loom up dimly and vanish without leaving a trace. There is properly speaking nothing more to be said.[37]

In the same vein, when Sukhanov wrote the third volume of his *Zapiski* late in 1919, he stuck to the original portrait of Dan that he had initially drafted under the impact of Dan's political role in 1917 as a central figure in the Menshevik–SR *bloc* that controlled the soviets. Indeed, Sukhanov was quite perplexed when Dan later claimed [in 1919?] – after the two had become allies – that he too had, albeit behind the scenes, 'always been in opposition' – but Sukhanov made no concessions.[38]

Referring to his account of the bitter dispute between Lunacharsky and Tsereteli on the last day of the Democratic Conference on 20 September as to whether or not the term 'assists' (*sodeistvuet*), intended to define relations between the future Pre-Parliament and the Provisional Government, had been inserted surreptitiously into the text of the conference's final resolution, Sukhanov asks:[39]

> Was this a conscious intrigue? Am I accusing someone of conscious deceit, of deliberate unworthy 'machinations' for the sake of honour and power? Oh, No! ... I am deeply convinced that this was not the case. We have not lived through the last one hundred and fifty years [since the French Revolution] in vain. Our revolution, from beginning to end, was headed by selfless, deeply idealistic people.

And Sukhanov thought instead that it was all a matter of hasty and sloppy last-minute drafting at three o'clock in the morning.

In a similar vein, when surveying the 'exceptionally brilliant' composition of the Pre-Parliament as it opened on 8 October, he noticed that the Constitutional Democrats had sent all their best talents: 'propertied Russia gave all its riches'.[40]

But the 'democratic' section clearly outdid its adversaries with its intellectual and cultural political baggage accumulated throughout decades of struggle, exile, imprisonment and emigration. It was a great school from which our socialist leaders graduated and our movement was so rich in major leaders that our intellectual influence loomed and still looms large in European socialism.

With his special weakness for the art of rhetoric in a year of great oratory, Sukhanov's *Zapiski* contain a good many speeches which might otherwise not have been recorded. Explaining why he reproduced almost in its entirety the speech Trotsky delivered at the Democratic Conference in mid-September as well as a short summary of Tsereteli's speech in reply, Sukhanov said that he wanted readers to savour 'the art of rhetoric and the political thought of our time and thus realize ... that the heroes of our revolution have left the celebrated leaders of the epoch of 1789 far behind'.[41]

While Sukhanov's gallery of major and minor revolutionary personalities deserves separate study, the portraits of the two Menshevik leaders Tsereteli and Dan must be singled out for an understanding of the central thesis of the *Zapiski*: these, as Sukhanov explicitly states, 'are built entirely from beginning to end on the basis of the mistakes of Dan and his associates'.[42]

While Sukhanov seems to have been baffled by Dan and his role in 1917, his portrait of Tsereteli, that 'truly fateful figure of the revolution', is simple and cogent:[43]

I have no intention whatever of detracting from Tsereteli's 'idealism' or 'nobility': but to me he seems like a horse that, having the bit between its teeth moves blindly on, totally oblivious of hills or ravines. In the grip of one idea, or rather one little glimmer of a utopian idea [*ideika*], this remarkable leader of the human herd was a very minor political thinker ... that *ideika* held that there are responsible and irresponsible 'propertied elements' (*tsenzoviki*),

living and dead forces. Thus guided he was blind to all else other than the creation of a solid *bloc*, of a united front of the democracy [in alliance] with those responsible living forces ....
Yet what characterizes Tsereteli is not just his blind galloping on, but rather that even in that he has shown some enviable and unusual courage and single-mindedness. In pursuit of his aims, he engages in very questionable intrigues and does so quite deliberately and unhesitatingly and when it is necessary even admits quite openly to doing so, saying: 'Take it as it is, follow me if you so wish, or go against me ... '. These characteristics have by no means diminished his authority and popularity and many have even seen in them 'a trace of nobility'. As for myself, I shall not quarrel with that.

Sukhanov ponders for more than seven pages over Dan's role in 1917 and his partnership with Tsereteli. He is puzzled by what seems to him to be a basic contradiction between Dan as a major left-wing socialist intellectual and theorist, a veteran professional revolutionary, a leading party politician and organizer, and Dan the man who bore such heavy responsibility for the 'fateful and criminal mistakes of the year 1917'. What, Sukhanov wonders, were their respective roles in that political partnership, and what was its historical impact. Without Tsereteli, Dan would probably not have adopted coalitionism; nor become a 'theoretical and practical mainstay of the opportunist Soviet majority which ruined the February revolution'. And he continues: without Dan, Tsereteli could not have managed, and certainly not if Dan, remaining faithful to his Zimmerwald position, had gone against Tsereteli and headed the left-wing opposition in the Soviet. In other words, had it been Tsereteli rather than Martov whom Dan had turned against, 'the balance of forces in the Soviet would have been changed significantly'. But Dan had thrown all his weight and talents into supporting coalitionism – 'the line of the Soviet majority'– and had pursued that line consistently to the bitter end even when others, for example the staunch coalitionist Boris Bogdanov, secretary of the Workers' Section of the Petrograd Soviet, had already abandoned it. Worse still, Dan had been a partner worthy of Tsereteli's steel in ignoring the wishes of the popular masses and in using tough, repressive methods against the left-wing opposition in the soviets.[44]

Sukhanov, it becomes clear, was certainly also using the portraits to square accounts with his major 1917 adversaries in the Petrograd Soviet who had pushed him aside, rendered him ineffective and, for good measure, sneered at him. Indeed, at the end of his dramatic account of the voting in the Petrograd Soviet on 30 August and 9 September – a vote which ousted the Menshevik-SR praesidium, and marked its take-over by Trotsky and the Bolsheviks – he describes with unconcealed glee the defeat and exit of those who with foolhardy conceit had put continued support for their policy of coalitionism to a vote of confidence. This was, he believed, 'the beginning of a new era in the history of the revolution':[45]

> The overthrown rulers filed down in silence from the platform under the triumphant gaze of a thousand-strong mass. Only Tsereteli, giving way to his Caucasian temperament, could not refrain from a parting shot and stern warning : 'We leave this platform with the conviction that we have held high and with distinction the banner of revolution! Our only hope is that you will hold it as high for even half the time we held it!' he shouted.

And Sukhanov rounds it all off with a scathing political obituary of the man who was his major adversary in 1917:

> Bound hand and foot by his worthless *ideika*, Tsereteli was a bad politician. I shall not comment on his subsequent actions which were no less inglorious than what had come before. I only wish with all my heart that they really prove to be his last. Even almost four years of Bolshevik state power have yet failed to erase from my mind the bitterness of my memories of that man who once stood at the head of the revolution. May those four years weigh leaden on his political grave.[46]

While Sukhanov concedes that he knew little of what was going on among the 'upper echelons of our bourgeois intelligentsia', that being 'some small part of the revolution which I did not see and cannot therefore reflect in my notes', he made up for it by studying their newspapers. To cite just one example of his firm grasp of the line of the 'bourgeois' newspapers during the post-July Days period:[47]

These papers apparently thought the Bolsheviks were already down and out and had therefore written off the humbled, fallen and despised enemy. Now the Kadet *Rech'* and its boulevard echoes began to strike out at Chernov, Tsereteli, the Mensheviks and the SRs and at the soviets altogether. This was inevitable, quite consistent and far-sighted, for in the interests of a bourgeois dictatorship which then seemed possible and near at hand, it was precisely the Soviets who had to be wiped off the face of the earth. For from the point of view of the plutocracy, it was they who embodied the original sin of the revolution, who were the source of 'dual power', the root of the evil.

Sukhanov took seriously the ideological commitments of his opponents, certainly those of the leaders and upper echelons of the socialist parties, but also those of the Kadets. Miliukov seems to have fascinated him and convinced him of the sincerity of his own and his party's single-minded and stubborn commitment to the 'national liberal' idea of a Great Russia to which he would sacrifice the 'real Russia' and the great revolution 'himself falling victim to his own blinkered chauvinism'.[48] The *Zapiski* record two characteristic scenes: speaking in the Pre-Parliament on 8 October, Miliukov had proclaimed Constantinople and the Bosphorus Straits as 'our national cause!' He went on to compliment the Allies on their commitment 'to a new world community with justice as its foundation and liberty as its corner-stone'. A sceptical Sukhanov called out: 'You yourself do not believe in what you are saying!' Miliukov turned towards the Left, put his hand to his heart and replied: 'This is my deep conviction. I have always believed in this and I still do believe in it!'[49]

In another scene, Sukhanov records the show-down in the Pre-Parliament between the Right and the Left. Peter Struve had just unburdened himself of a very impressive and bitter broadside against the Left – 'the *profession de foi* of a highly cultured and talented reactionary' – when someone from the benches of the Left interjected: 'Kornilov!' Quick as a flash Struve answered: 'Kornilov? That is an honest name and we are ready to lay down our lives for him!' From the Right came loud applause.

I got up to survey the camp of the [Kornilovite] mutineers. As if in reply, Miliukov rose, clapped demonstratively and shouted in our direction: 'Yes! Kornilov is indeed an honest man!' Following Miliukov, the Right rose to their feet as one man; opposite, the Left too was on its feet and for a moment the two forces confronted each other like cocks ready to throw themselves into a fight.[50]

Sukhanov adds that this incident helped him to a better understanding of the 'inner meaning of the Kornilov affair and the role of its heroes'. Indeed, he took the abortive Kornilov *putsch* seriously and claims to have taken its measure right from its outset as a move that aimed at the establishment of a 'bourgeois dictatorship' that would replace the 'sham dictatorship' of Kerensky and thus 'put an end to the revolution'. He certainly rejoiced in the solidarity of the entire 'revolutionary democracy', including the Bolsheviks, in the face of a threatened counter-revolution.[51] But he also appreciated the comic side of the mutiny when the 'Wild Division', Kornilov's most loyal military force, surrendered to the praesidium of the Soviet, offering a full confession of their guilt. Sukhanov savoured to the full the exotic spectacle to which Martov had alerted him:[52]

The hall was crammed with quilted jackets, Caucasian fur caps, felt cloaks, braid decorations, waxed black moustaches, eyes wide with astonishment and the smell of horses. They were the elected, the cream, headed by 'native' officers, in all perhaps some five hundred men. The crowd kept absolutely silent while delegates from individual units, clutching bits of paper, made speeches in broken Russian. On the whole they all said one and the same thing. In naive, high-flown language they sang the praise of the revolution and vowed their devotion to it even unto the grave, even to the last drop of their blood. Not a man in their units, not one of their people, had gone – or would go – against the revolution and the revolutionary authority. It had all been a misunderstanding that could be simply cleared up by establishing the truth. The 'Wild Ones' delivered solemn vows.

Not one of the speakers failed to underline with special pride that the All-Russian revolution was headed by their [Caucasian] countrymen who were now receiving them on behalf of the 'great' Soviet .... Every one of them devoted part of his speech and sometimes a good half of it to Chairman Chkheidze and especially to Tsereteli. Some even addressed him using 'thou' and 'great leader'. Tsereteli answered his countrymen with a very sympathetic speech delivered with an extraordinary warmth of tone ... and he welcomed the 'Wild Ones' as natives of those same Caucasian mountains from which he himself came.

Sukhanov's attention, however, is not confined to the personalities and oratory of the political elite; he is also deeply interested in the popular masses of soldiers, workers and peasants, watching them at mass meetings, studying their faces at demonstrations and listening to the speeches of their delegates. He marvels[53]

> Where did these orators appear from? I am not talking about the politically conscious or semi-conscious or about the local political leaders who, within a matter of only two weeks were already used to the speaker's platform and the listening crowd; the people I mean are the grey ones, those with black earth on their boots, who are incomparably more interesting.

Many of those 'grey men' appear in his pages, beginning with a group of workers whom to his delight he overheard as early as 25 February formulating 'brilliantly' the programme of the revolution as being: 'bread, peace with the Germans and equality for the yids'.[54] Two days later, when the Soviet had only just assembled and appointed its praesidium, proceedings were interrupted time and again by soldiers' delegates who demanded that the floor be given to them to make their reports.[55]

> Standing on stools, rifles in their hands, agitated and stammering, they strained to make the coherent report they had been charged to deliver, intent on telling their story in this unfamiliar, to them unreal, atmosphere .... possibly quite unaware of the significance of the events on which they were reporting. One after the other, and using simple clumsy language, the soldiers' delegates told the stories of what had happened in their units. Holding their breath, the assembled delegates listened as children do to a wondrous fairy tale that they already know by heart .... 'Our instructions are to tell you that we do not want to serve against the people, but rather want one and all to join our fellow workers in defending the cause of the people. For that we are

ready to lay down our lives. Our general meeting has instructed us to greet you: Long Live the Revolution!' And with that, the faltering voice of the speaker was drowned out by the thunderous applause of the assembly.

The exception was a young soldier who 'had obviously graduated from a party propaganda school'. He burst through the cordon of guards and ran into the centre of the hall, brandished his rifle above his head and shouted: 'Comrades and brothers, I bring you fraternal greetings from the lower ranks of the Semenov Guards Regiment. We are all, to the last man, resolved to join the people against the accursed autocracy, and we vow to serve the people's cause to the last drop of our blood.'[56]

His performance was all but matched by a village-messenger (*khodok*) who appeared before the Workers' Section of the Soviet as early as 7 March.[57] A shrewd little peasant from the Ust-Izhorsk rural district, he knew exactly how to get himself the floor and 'greet the fraternal workers and congratulate them on their victory and organization'. He was the first who proclaimed in the name of the peasantry the slogan of 'All Land to the People!' and naturally enough, he too got a warm reception. He was soon followed by a front-line soldier who demonstrated his unit's loyalty and dedication to the Soviet by delivering to it, thrown together in a dirty sack, all the men's medals, Georgian Crosses and all:[58] 'In this sack are all the decorations that we have won with our blood; we have decided to send you the most precious things we have. Not one of us has kept anything back.' There was a moment's total silence as the audience seemed to hold their breath, but then there burst forth a storm of thunderous applause. Then again there was the soldier who, to the delight of the entire audience in the Soviet, described how his unit had celebrated the revolution by calling on their German enemies in the trenches opposite to join in and finish off their Wilhelm.[59]

It is hardly surprising that it was Sukhanov, still very much a Populist at heart, who, late in the evening of 1 March, spotted the following scene which he subsequently recorded with such warmth and empathy:

There was Nikolai Sokolov sitting and writing at a table surrounded on all sides by soldiers, some seated, some standing and leaning on the table, all prompting him and dictating what he should write. Through my mind there flashed that description of Tolstoy at his school at Yasnaya Polyana where he together with the children there used to make up stories. It appeared that this was a commission that had been elected by the Soviet to draft a 'Soldiers' Order' – there was no formal agenda, no discussion, they all spoke and were completely immersed in the work of formulating their collectve opinion without any voting. I stood there and listened with tremendous interest ... having finished the work, they put a heading on the sheet: 'Order Number One'. This is the history of the document which earned such resounding fame .... the Order was in the fullest sense a product of 'popular creativity' and in no way the malevolent concoction of a particular individual or even of a leading group [as was insinuated by a hostile 'bourgeois press'] ... nor can Sokolov be considered to have been its author ... he was only the technical executor of the plans of the masses ... this was perhaps the sole independent act of political creativity of the General Assembly of the Soviet throughout the revolution.[60]

In a more ominous scene, Sukhanov describes how he watched a unit of soldiers in the triumphal procession which accompanied Lenin from the Finland Station to the Kshesinskaia Palace on 3 April. Together with them, he listened to Lenin who, from a second-floor balcony, harangued the crowd that had massed in front of the palace:[61]

'Capitalist robbers!' Lenin shouted [hoarse already] .... 'They kill off the people of Europe for the sake of the profits of a bunch of capitalists;' ... 'Defence of the fatherland is nothing but the defence of one group of capitalists against the other.' The 'celebrating' soldiers reacted angrily. One shouted: 'That one up there ought to be hoisted on a bayonet for this! Listen to what he's saying! If he came down we would show him! Yes, we'd show him alright ... For this the German has [paid him]...'.

Addressing many a soldier delegation genuinely worried about the Soviet's peace policy, Sukhanov patiently, if not always successfully, explained to them just what the 14 March Address to the Peoples of

Fig. 3.6   Sokolov

the Whole World meant. One front-line soldier, having heard his explanation, agreed that the government ought to renounce 'the conquest of foreign lands', but proffered the advice that one should 'appeal by telegraph to the Soviet of Workers and Soldiers in Berlin', offering them peace. When Sukhanov explained to him that there was as yet no such institution in Berlin, and that this would come only after a revolution there, the soldier found it difficult to believe that of all countries 'Germany, which he understood was an advanced country which had overtaken Russia, should have no Soviet of Workers and Soldiers Deputies.'[62]

Only a few months later, Sukhanov overheard a peasant delegation plead with Kerensky to pass a law prohibiting land sales and thus ensure that the nation's land be preserved intact.[63] They were obviously not convinced when Kerensky told them that they 'need not worry, the government will take measures. The government and I will do our duty.' But, 'such a law was promised long ago', they told Kerensky. What they wanted now was a law and not a promise. Whereupon Kerensky 'very angry and almost stamping his foot, shouted "I have said that this will be done, and it will ... You need not look at me so suspiciously!"'

Sukhanov was also present when a young officer heading a delegation of front-line troops told Prince Lvov of 'their devotion to the revolution and readiness to die for it'. Then, in a text obviously learned by heart but not quite mastered, he added:

> We have been charged to convey greetings to the Provisional Government and to the Soviet of Workers and Soldiers Deputies. We have been charged to tell the Provisional Government that we hold it in highest esteem and have full confidence in it and will support it in-so-far-as (*postol'ku poskol'ku*) it fulfils ....

Lvov, who was known to be both a kind man and a gentleman to boot, could not take this painful reminder of the Soviet's much resented formula of conditional support, cut the man off in mid-sentence, turned on his heel and stalked off.[64] To cap it all, Sukhanov overheard a drunkard in the street late in the evening chanting in 'the deep bass of an arch-deacon' the prayer for peace: 'Let us pray to the Lord for peace all over the world, without annexations and contributions.'[65] The jargon of the revolution had well and truly sunk in.

When the October revolution came, Sukhanov recorded three scenes which make the reader share his premonitions and despair when watching its early events from the vantage point of the Bolshevik-dominated Congress of Soviets. When at last the Congress opened at eleven o'clock on the evening of 25 October, Sukhanov scanned 'the gloomy and indifferent faces of the crowd of the [soldiers] grey in their great-coats and of black-soil [peasants] that filled the assembly hall':[66]

What struck the eye was an enormous difference: the Petersburg Soviet, notably its Workers' Section, consisting of average Petersburg proletarians, compared with the crowd of the Second Congress, looked like the Roman Senate which the ancient Carthagenians took for an assembly of gods. With a mass like *that*, with the vanguard of the Petersburg proletariat, it seemed indeed possible to be tempted into an attempt to illuminate old Europe with the light of a socialist revolution [in Russia]. But the incomparable [Petersburg] type is an exception in Russia: even the Moscow worker is as different from the Petersburg proletarian as the hen from the peacock. But here at the Congress, the hall was filled with a crowd of a very different order. Out of the trenches and the darkest backwoods, completely crude and ignorant people had crept out, devoted to the revolution out of spite and despair, their 'socialism' was hunger and an intolerable thirst for rest. Not bad material for experiments – but such experiments would be risky.

What followed then was Martov's immediate and desperate attempt to defuse the crisis caused by the Bolshevik *coup d'état*. He appealed for a 'peaceful resolution of the crisis by the formation of an all-democratic government'. He urged that a delegation be elected to negotiate with all socialist parties.[67] Trotsky, who stood next to Martov, made short shrift of that proposal with a speech that Sukhanov recorded word for word as if to underline the Bolshevik leaders' steely determination to 'go it alone'.[68]

'A rising of the popular masses,' Trotsky barked out, 'needs no justification: what has happened is an uprising not a conspiracy. We have hardened the revolutionary energy of the workers and soldiers of Petersburg; we openly steeled the will of the masses and they marched under our banner and we have won. And now we are told: Renounce your victory! Make concessions! Make an agreement! With whom, I ask! With whom should we have an agreement? With those wretched groups [of Mensheviks, SRs and the Bund] that have walked out [of the Congress], or with those [like Martov] who make this proposal? But we have had a full view of them. No one in Russia is with them any more. Are the millions of workers and peasants who are represented here at this

Congress expected to make an agreement as equal partners with those who are ready to barter them away to the tender mercies of the bourgeoisie? No! A compromise is no good here. And to those who have walked out, and to those who come with such proposals we must say: You are pitiful individuals, you are bankrupts; your role is played out; go where you belong from now on – into the rubbish bin of history' .... 'Then we shall leave,' Martov shouted from the platform, amid stormy applause for Trotsky.

In the last major scene recorded in his *Zapiski*, Sukhanov, who had walked out with Martov but had come back as a mere spectator, makes the reader feel his predicament when watching the Bolsheviks celebrate Lenin's decree on peace, of which he certainly approved, and their victory, which he both disapproved of and feared.[69]

I had no difficulty in finding a vacant place in the back rows where, it appears, the public was seated. Alas! For the first time since the revolution I was attending such an assembly as one of the public and no longer as a fully-fledged member [of the Soviet Congress]. I found this extremely saddening and painful. I felt torn and separated from everything that I had lived by for the past eight months, months which were the equal of as many decades. The decree on peace was put to the vote and passed unanimously ... and there was an unmistakable heightening of the mood.

After Lenin had concluded his speech, Sukhanov reports:

Prolonged ovations were followed by the singing of the Internationale, then Lenin was again cheered: 'Hurrah!' they shouted, throwing their caps up in the air. They sang the Funeral March in memory of the victims of the war, and again burst into clapping, shouting and throwing up their caps once again. The entire praesidium, with Lenin at its head, stood up and sang, their faces alight, exalted, their eyes afire, and they too clapped and shouted 'Hurrah!' and flung up their caps. Yet the mass of delegates was even more interesting: its mood was even more exalted: the overturn had gone more smoothly than most of them had expected – it already seemed complete.

But I did not believe in the victory, the success, the 'rightfulness', the historical mission of Bolshevik state power. Sitting at the back, I watched the triumphant celebration with deep concern. How I longed to join in and merge body and soul with that mass and its leaders! But I could not ....

Not even Lenin's Decree on Peace, essentially the Soviet government's offer of a negotiated peace addressed to 'the belligerent governments and their peoples', of which Sukhanov very much approved, could reconcile him to the Bolshevik *coup d'état*; nor could his fears of a Bolshevik Jacobin dictatorship be assuaged by Lenin's Decree on Land, which he would gladly have underwritten. Knowing his Bolsheviks, Sukhanov's immediate and overriding concern was his attempt to prevent them from 'going it alone'. Thus, in an interval in the debate on the Decree on Land, he contrived to prod the Left SR leaders Boris Kamkov and/or Vladimir Karelin to convene an impromptu meeting of their faction which he was given leave to address as an 'honoured guest'. In an impassioned speech, he hammered the 'necessity of a united democratic front and the formation of a state power out of a *bloc* of socialist parties'. He even went so far as to condemn sharply the parties that had walked out of the Congress, including his own faction. But to no avail. Whatever the reason, neither the audience of some 150 Left SRs, nor I.M. Malkin (Sokolovsky), the member of the Central Committee who replied, responded to his appeal in any way.[70]

Having taken his story from 'the moment of the fall of the old regime to the dictatorship of the All-Russian Communist Party', Sukhanov wanted to continue even though he regarded his seven volumes as complete on their own.[71] With practically all his papers having disappeared, there is no way of knowing whether he ever tried to extend his memoirs into the early Soviet period. Still, apart from his articles of exposure and indictment published in *Novaia zhizn'*, and his vitriolic interjections and statements in the Central Executive Committee until June/July 1918 when he was finally silenced, there are here and there in the *Zapiski*, notably in volumes 6 and 7 written in 1920/21, but also in volumes 3 and 4, written in 1919/1920,[72] acute observations and reflections on the 'Bolsheviks in power'. They are in tune with a talk he gave in April 1921 in the House of the Press to an audience which consisted largely of Communists.[73] On that occasion, they abused him for his 'boring social-democratic [i.e. Menshevik] speech' on 'the impossibility of socialism in Russia' and the need for 'a dictatorship of the majority'. Further, in his letter of resignation from the Menshevik party, written on 10 December 1920, he reassured his former comrades that this by no means implied that he had made his peace with the regime or was 'in solidarity with the policy of Bolshevik state power'.

True, these are scattered references, but taken together they constitute a well-considered assessment and condemnation of the Bolshevik regime in the light of Sukhanov's experience of 'four years of Soviet state power', a period that he defined – and detested – as 'War Communism'.

Sukhanov takes the Bolsheviks to task in his *Zapiski* not so much for making the October revolution, but for 'going it alone' and establishing a minority dictatorship.[74] He accepts that 'a new revolution was admissible, the uprising was legal and the liquidation of the existing [Kerensky] government was necessary', but 'only *on condition*' that this was done under the auspices of 'a united front of the democracy', committed to 'the liquidation of the political and economic domination of the bourgeoisie and the landowners'. But that certainly did not mean 'the destruction of the old state and a rejection of its heritage' nor a root and branch 'liquidation of the economic and social foundations of the old society'. While the Bolshevik seizure of power in itself 'had a very good chance of being victorious', the Bolsheviks had no idea of 'what to do with their victory and with the state they had conquered': 'I assert that they had no conception of nor plans for coping with the consequences of being in power' except that they would 'let the peasants grab the land', were prepared 'immediately to propose peace', had 'most confused conceptions of workers' control' and had the 'most fantastic thoughts on how to pump bread [out of the village] with the help of "a sailor and a woman worker"'.[75]

And Sukhanov continues:[76] of course there were also Lenin's ideas, 'borrowed entirely' from the practice of the Paris Commune and Marx's *The Civil War in France* and 'from the Anarchist Kropotkin' regarding the seizure of banks, the destruction of the credit system, the manning of the government apparatus by workers, the election of officials and the equalization of salaries. Sukhanov concludes again:

But the Bolsheviks did not know what to do with their victory and the state that they had conquered. They acted *against* Marx, *against* scientific socialism, *against* common sense and *against* the working class when, by way of an uprising under the slogan All Power to the Soviets, they endeavoured to give the Central Committee of their party total state power in Russia.

Thus, controlling 'the entire wealth of the state and determining the fate of millions', they implemented their 'absurd experiments' from their 'primitive chancelleries' protected by 'palisades of bayonets' without rendering any account whatsoever to the people, unleashing a reign of terror and mass arrests 'shedding blood like water in torture chambers' and turning the Smolny into a 'supreme police headquarters and prison', and, in accordance with 'the cannibalist principles ... of that Asiatic internationalist, Lenin', closing down newspapers on an unprecedented scale with arguments 'more primitive and less literate' than those of their tsarist predecessors.

Worse still, Sukhanov maintains,[77] they were now leading the masses, 'the proletariat, the soldiers, the peasants,' against the entire old world and presuming to use their party of the proletarian vanguard, surrounded by 'millions of accidental, unreliable fellow travellers' to create 'a new, never-before-seen proletarian state and a new never-before-seen economic order' – and all this in 'our ruined, half-barbarous petty-bourgeois, economically fragmented country ... and against the will of all organized petty-bourgeois elements and the entire bourgeois front'. And the consequence of doing all that in the desperate 'conditions of war and starvation', Sukhanov maintained, must perforce be 'the destruction of the productive forces of the country'.

Lenin was a most eager reader of the *Zapiski*:[78] nagging his secretaries and wife Nadezhda Krupskaya, he made sure that he received each volume immediately on publication. Having read volumes 1–4, and perhaps volume 5 (he received it on 13 January 1923), he decided to square accounts with Sukhanov, the Mensheviks and Kautsky, and all those 'Marxist pedants', who, like Sukhanov, had presumed to question the Marxist credentials of the October revolution.

In volumes 3 and 4 of the *Zapiski* Sukhanov had ridiculed Lenin who, 'as if by magic', 'by Leninist will and command' had plunged the 'backward, fragmented, ruined country of the *muzhik* into socialism'. And all this 'independently of the West and before the coming of a world-wide socialist revolution'. He had denounced that 'magical jump' into socialism as contrary to 'the basic principles of Marxism, of scientific socialism and of the fundamentals of the present-day social-democratic programme and tactics'. For good measure, he poked fun at that 'utopian construction of the state' which Lenin had 'fiercely defended in his *State and Revolution*' and which, soon after, in the light of the bitter experience of practice, Lenin himself had thrown out as 'infantile delusions and useless trash', while in lieu of an 'economic programme' Lenin had simply relied on 'the direct creativity [of the masses] from below' and on the 'plundering of the robbers' loot'.[79]

While Lenin in power treated his Menshevik adversaries, even Martov and the 'Sukhanovs', with contempt, he strangely enough took very seriously their critique of his October revolution and made sure he received Martov's and Axelrod's anti-Bolshevik articles published abroad. Having gone to considerable lengths to procure a full set of the Menshevik émigré *Sotsialisticheskii vestnik*, he ordered it kept in a '*secret* box'.[80] On 16 and 17 January 1923, Lenin dictated from his sickbed a polemical review of the *Zapiski* to the secretary M.A. Volodicheva.

Taking issue with Sukhanov and all those who à la Kautsky had condemned the Bolshevik revolution as 'a foolhardy attempt to plant socialism in an uncivilized country', Lenin justified his 'October' by proposing a novel method for creating 'the basic prerequisites for civilization'. Lenin argued for a historical sequence for Russia and 'the countries of the East' very much at variance with that of 'Western European countries':[81]

If a definite level of culture is required for the creation of socialism (though no one can say precisely what that definite level is since it is different in every West European country) why can't we first use revolutionary methods to conquer the [political] prerequisites for that definite level and then, using worker-peasant state power and the Soviet order, move on and catch up on other nations.

In short, in such countries as Russia, 'situated on the borders of the civilized countries of the West and the countries of the entire East', the revolutionary state would first of all create such 'political prerequisites' as for instance 'the expulsion of the landowners and the Russian capitalists' and then begin to create the missing material and cultural conditions for 'the foundations of a socialist society'. As if in answer to Sukhanov's repeated taunt that the Bolsheviks in 1917 had no programme or plan of what to do with their power, Lenin quoted Napoleon's dictum:

> *On s'engage et puis ... on voit* and translated freely into Russian that means that 'first one must enter into serious combat and then things will become clear'; so we, in 1917 entered into serious combat and there we saw such details as the Peace of Brest-Litovsk and the NEP etc. And now there is no doubt but that basically we have been victorious.

Lenin concluded: 'It does not occur to our Sukhanovs, not to speak of the social-democrats to their right', that some revolutions, notably in the East, may diverge from the West European model and that a textbook written according to Kautsky, useful in its time, could not have foreseen the 'diverse forms of development of world history'. And, running true to polemical form, Lenin pronounced as mere 'fools' those who still failed to be convinced.

Even had Sukhanov wanted to, without a newspaper and lacking a seat in the Central Executive Committee he had no way of replying to Lenin's argument, and in any case, by the time Lenin's review was published, he had already made his peace with the October revolution. Sadly, too, the prominence the review gave to Sukhanov and to his critique of Lenin and of the Bolshevik revolution ensured that the *Zapiski*, after provoking early interest, were soon to disappear into limbo while their author was fated (quite undeservedly) to be elevated in Soviet encyclopedias and books to the position of 'one of the leaders and theorists of Menshevism'. Worse still, as we shall see, Lenin's censorious review was used in 1926 by M. Kubanin of the Communist Academy as the motto for his vicious attack on Sukhanov which may well have been the opening shot in the campaign of delegitimation against him. In December 1927, at the Fifteenth Congress of the Communist Party, no less a dignitary than Lazar Kaganovich quoted Lenin's critique of the *Zapiski*, as did Alexander Shlikhter at the Conference of Agrarian Marxists late in December 1929.[82]

As for the Mensheviks, they very much resented the *Zapiski's* severe criticism of their performance in 1917 and did not even review it in their *Sotsialisticheskii vestnik*; nor were Sukhanov's writings of the 1917–20 period, when he was an active member of the Menshevik party, so much as mentioned in the bibliography of Menshevik writings. As so often, Sukhanov fell between the stools.

4
In Opposition to the Bolshevik 'Jacobin' Dictatorship

What Sukhanov had dreaded most and had incessantly warned against happened on 25 October: the Bolsheviks seized power, securing a semblance of soviet legitimacy through the Second Congress of Soviets in which, together with their Left SR allies, they had a significant majority. The relatively small Menshevik contingent at the Congress, of which Sukhanov was a member – less than one hundred deputies compared with three hundred Bolsheviks and two hundred SRs – now had to decide whether it would stay on or leave in protest against the Bolshevik *coup d'état*. In the end, both major Menshevik factions, the Revolutionary Defensists now led by Fiodor Dan (Tsereteli had left for the Caucasus), and Martov's Menshevik-Internationalists, walked out of the Congress during the night of 26 October; thus, as Sukhanov was later to complain bitterly, 'they gave the Bolsheviks a monopoly over the Soviet, the masses and the revolution'. He himself had agitated passionately against the walk-out among the Menshevik-Internationalists, but was defeated by a 12 to 10 vote and had to swallow his misgivings and join Martov in leaving the congress.[1]

Thus, deprived of a seat in the Central Executive Committee (CEC) elected by the congress, Sukhanov had to confine his oppositional role to the pages of *Novaia zhizn'* until the beginning of December, when he 'corrected his mistake' and joined the CEC as a representative of the Union of Paper Mill Workers. That act was in open defiance of the Menshevik party's Central Committee which had enjoined members, and specifically Sukhanov, 'not to accept mandates from non-party organizations'.[2]

But in the meantime, he came to grips with the Bolsheviks in power in an article of that name which appeared on 29 October 1917. Even then, he had first to square accounts with his old adversaries Tsereteli and Kerensky who had 'invested all their energy and their diplomatic talents in supporting the wretched counter-revolutionary coalition government', and had, thereby, he complained, been the true begetters of the overturn of 25 October. 'The Bolsheviks in power,' he wrote, 'is no mere comic opera: what we are faced with is a truly great tragedy, threatening the country with endless misery and the collapse of the revolutionary achievement.' Yet for all his fierce objections to both the methods and policies of the Bolsheviks, he could see no way to liquidate the Bolshevik adventure other than by compromise and agreement. Those who thought that the regime of Lenin and Trotsky could be overthrown by 'armed force' were deluding themselves, he wrote. True, he believed the regime was ultimately doomed, but that was not because of any external military threats, but rather because of its 'inherent defects'. The policy of the coalition government and the resultant despair of the people had driven the masses of workers and soldiers into the arms of 'these consummate demagogues and political infants'. But 'these masses cannot give the Bolsheviks a state apparatus and the ability to put this apparatus into motion'. Bolshevik power was thus condemned to do no more than tick over idly and would soon disintegrate unless it was broadened to include the entire democracy.[3]

The next day, he pinned his hopes on the so-called *Vikzhel* (acronym for the All-Russian Executive Committee of Railway Workers) negotiations of socialist parties with the Bolsheviks which he believed could end the civil war within the socialist camp. But it did not take him long to realize that the talks were doomed to founder on the Bolsheviks' adamant refusal immediately to eschew terror. And even then, he continued to toy with the idea that dissident leading Bolsheviks, led by Kamenev and Zinoviev, might still be capable of bringing about 'the formation of a broadly-based government of the democracy on the ruins of Lenin's cabinet'.[4]

On 7 November, a deeply depressed Sukhanov admitted that no agreement with the Bolsheviks was possible in view of their 'official declarations that only a government manned by the Bolshevik party is a real soviet government and that in Russia there can be nothing other than a soviet government'. Moreover, that government of People's Commissars had been endowed with absolutist rights by the CEC of Soviets which had, in turn, left for itself nothing but 'the mighty instrument of moral pressure'. There was, then, no soviet power in Russia but only 'the dictatorship of the honourable citizens, Lenin and Trotsky, which rested on the bayonets of the soldiers and armed workers whom they have deceived'. The only way left was to prise loose the masses from the Bolshevik dictators and their adventure.[5]

Sukhanov's hopes that there might be a way of bridling the Bolshevik dictators began to rise when, in mid-November, the Left SRs began negotiating with them on co-operation in the CEC and eventual Left SR participation in the Council of People's Commissars. Too sanguinely, he welcomed the possible broadening of the government which he greeted in his article 'A New Phase',[6] even urging that those who had walked out of the Congress should drop their 'irresponsible opposition', their 'militant boycott' and instead 'act as true democrats and patriots and engage in organic work'. That, he urged, was not incompatible with their commitment to the Constituent Assembly. But his desperate hopes were shortlived. On 18 November, the day after the article's appearance, the *Novaia zhizn'* editorial already denounced the armed dispersal of the Petrograd Duma 'by the gladiators of rusty Leninism' as a 'new act of civil war'.[7] In the same vein, on 1 December, Sukhanov's signed editorial, 'Civil War',[8] castigated the arrest of leading members of the Kadet party by the 'prosecutors and gendarmes of the Smolny', in flagrant violation of the Kadets' parliamentary immunity as members of the Constituent Assembly. He followed this up in an article, 'Where is the CEC',[9] in which he took the moderate Bolsheviks to task for dismally failing to make common cause with the non-Bolshevik opposition in preventing the CEC from being turned into 'a pathetic parody of a revolutionary parliament' and the soviet regime into 'an evil travesty of the dictatorship of the proletariat'.

When the Left SRs finally joined the *Sovnarkom* (Council of People's Commissars) on 12 December 1917, Sukhanov, reversing his earlier position, sneered at these 'youngsters' who, as Lenin well knew, could easily be wound round his finger and were incapable of any serious opposition. They had, he told them, joined the

Bolshevik government during an 'unheard of outburst of terror' that had witnessed the armed dispersal of the Petersburg Town Duma, the liquidation of the press and the arrest of Kadet members of the Constituent Assembly, and all this while professing to have joined the *Sovnarkom* both 'to strengthen soviet power and to straighten out its policy'. What they had really done, he wrote, was to underwrite Lenin's policy of the 'teeth-smashing fist' and its introduction of preventive censorship and of a 'state of siege' in the capital.[10]

Sukhanov's was a lone oppositional voice in the CEC when on 22 December, Zinoviev, seconded by the extreme Left SR Prosh Proshyan, contrasted the 'revolutionary soviets with the notorious Constituent Assembly' and acclaimed the 'duel between the Constituent Assembly and the soviets' as 'a historical struggle between two revolutions, one bourgeois and the other socialist'. To a constant barrage of Bolshevik jeers, Sukhanov reminded the Bolsheviks and their new Left SR partners of the abrupt change from their support, up to the October revolution, for the 'immediate convocation of the Constituent Assembly' to their post-October slander campaign which proclaimed the Constituent Assembly as 'incompatible with the dictatorship of the proletariat'. What they now had in Russia, Sukhanov insisted, was not the dictatorship of the proletariat but a 'nasty caricature' of one: it had led 'to chaos in every area of the economy, ruined every aspect of social life, paralyzed the schools, hospitals, and theatres, persecuted the press, made arrests, destroyed the banks, law courts and municipal government and unleashed a terror that has reached a point of complete irrationality'.

> We need a government which will unite all the forces of the democracy. [The source] of such a genuine government can only be the Constituent Assembly which must therefore be convened in conditions which will enable it to fulfil its function as a sovereign institution and form a government capable of rescuing the country from the perils it faces.[11]

Having more than an inkling of how the Bolsheviks would deal with a Constituent Assembly in which they would have to confront a hostile majority of SRs and Mensheviks, Sukhanov warned: they who with all their 'millions of bayonets' had proved powerless to cope with even 'the permanent pogroms on the railway stations' and were responsible for a 'policy of general disintegration' should think twice before embarking on 'so risky an experiment and so complicated a surgical operation' as liquidating the Constituent Assembly.[12]

On the eve of the convocation of the Constituent Assembly, Sukhanov and *Novaia zhizn'*, in a spate of editorials and articles, reaffirmed their staunch commitment to All Power to the Constituent Assembly in opposition to the Bolsheviks' All Power to the Soviets As for the soviets, Sukhanov and *Novaia zhizn'* argued, they ought to lend their support to this fortunately radical Constituent Assembly, not as organs of power or administration but rather as the combat organizations of the proletariat and the peasantry against reaction and counter-revolution for which 'anarcho-bolshevism' bore a heavy responsibility. Indeed one of the major tasks of the Constituent Assembly would be to annul all the senseless decrees of the Smolny, trumpeted loudly as 'nationalization' and 'socialization', which had transported Russia back to a 'pre-bourgeois, pre-capitalist and pre-modern situation'.[13]

In a very pessimistic article published on 5 January, the day the Constituent Assembly opened, Sukhanov wondered what function the Bolsheviks had in mind for the Constituent Assembly: was it to serve as 'a consumer co-operative', a 'literary-artistic circle' or as 'an amateur hunting club'. The democracy, he warned, must not play into the hands of the Bolshevik terror by organizing a demonstration in support of the Constituent Assembly: it was unlikely to be impressive or to yield any practical results. The order of the day must be ideological agitation in the mass organizations where disillusionment with the 'disastrous socialism of the Smolny' was beginning to spread.[14]

All he could do on the morrow of the armed dispersal of the Constituent Assembly was to protest both in *Novaia zhizn'* and in the CEC. In his article 'Dispersal',[15] he denounced 'this act of madness' as the 'logical completion' of the October revolution which had begun 'in madness and blindness'. Incapable of running a state administration and a national economy, they had now pinned their hopes 'on the world revolution as the sole rescue belt of the socialist revolution in Russia'. But with that 'experiment on the living body of the Russian people', they had discredited 'our revolution' and done untold harm to the 'international proletarian movement'.

In the CEC, he tried on 6 January to force a debate on a Bolshevik resolution intended to justify and sanction the dissolution of the Constituent Assembly. Sukhanov moved an amendment that the concluding words of the resolution be deleted on the grounds that there was no truth in the resolution's claim that 'the people have no faith in the Constituent Assembly'. Equally untrue was its claim that the Constituent Assembly had refused to recognize Soviet state power 'as that question was never debated'.

When Zinoviev and his Bolsheviks ruled him out of order, he told them 'You cowards are afraid of an honest comment on your despicable resolution.' One soldier, it was reported, raised his gun and pointed it at him. Had it not been for the Bolshevik Moise Volodarsky, who 'jumped over the table' and rescued him, he might well have been lynched by those who had begun to rush forward to manhandle him. Even the writer Zinaida Gippius, no admirer of Sukhanov and his 'wretched *Novaia zhizn''*, was duly impressed and noted in her diary 'one must be fair to Sukhanov: he stood up bravely to the threat of fists and Brownings'.[16]

At the Third Congress of Soviets which opened on 10 January, that is four days after the dispersal of the Constituent Assembly, Sukhanov took issue with Lenin who, in his address to the congress, had hailed the 'revolutionary state power' of the Bolsheviks and proudly acknowledged Bolshevik responsibility for 'terror, dictatorship and civil war'.[17] 'Yes!' he taunted Lenin, 'you have indeed achieved a general breakdown! You have destroyed the entire state mechanism and have replaced it with torrents of unenforceable paper decrees.' Worse still: 'You who in 1917 lauded the democracy are now waging civil war within its very ranks, even against the Internationalists who stood together with you against coalitionism and campaigned for the dictatorship of the democracy.'[18]

The pathetic futility of Sukhanov's lament and of his appeal for socialist solidarity was underscored by shouts from the gallery above: 'We would even have gone against our own fathers and mothers!'[19] Next day Lenin himself answered Sukhanov and his other critics, some of whom had accused him of Anarchism: true, he conceded, in 1917 the Bolsheviks had stood for democracy, but only so long as the revolution was confined to the 'framework of the bourgeois order'. Now, 'when we have seen the first glimmer of socialism, we hold firmly and decisively to the dictatorship of the proletariat'. Dictatorship, he lectured Sukhanov, 'rests always on violence and is savage, harsh and bloody'. What distinguished the Bolsheviks from the Anarchists was precisely the former's commitment to 'the firm revolutionary state power of the toiling masses, the power of a revolutionary state'. As for the complaint that even socialists were being persecuted: 'In the era of parliamentarism these socialists have gone bad, have become antiquated and gone over to the bourgeoisie; they have nothing in common with socialism', Lenin insisted.[20] Indeed, Sukhanov realized, 'It was no more a matter of arguments but of bayonets.'[21] Still, Sukhanov and *Novaia zhizn'* would not let Lenin have the last word. The issue of 21 January carried no less than three articles examining Lenin's Soviet state power and his concept of the dictatorship of the proletariat. In his editorial, Sukhanov indicted Lenin's dictatorship of the proletariat as being nothing but 'a dictatorship of casual gun-brandishing groups and individuals' whose overriding aim was 'the eradication of dissent by way of the strangulation of speech, the liquidation of democratic liberties, arrests, violence and civil war'. Small wonder that the Bolsheviks cavalierly ignored 'their own laws and institutions' notably the CEC, so much so that 'a vicious enemy of Soviet state power could not have contrived a better device to discredit it than this highest legislative organ of the Soviet republic'.[22]

The theoretical arguments against Lenin's dictatorship of the proletariat were marshalled in *Novaia zhizn'* by the historian Nikolai Rozhkov, Sukhanov's colleague on the newspaper, and by the magisterial Karl Kautsky. Both were adamant that the concept was irrelevant and out of place in the democratic revolution taking place in a very backward, largely peasant country such as Russia where conditions for a dictatorship of the majority of the people were still absent. In such a situation, Kautsky insisted, 'the idea of the dictatorship of the proletariat must give way to the idea of democracy'. Admittedly, the urban, industrial proletariat which constituted an intelligent and advanced section of the labouring population could play a leading role in the democratic, republican order established by a democratic revolution, but this social group was a minority in Russia and any attempt to establish a proletarian dictatorship ran completely counter to socialism as the highest form of democracy.[23]

Sukhanov's indictment of the Bolshevik regime, most notably of Lenin's foreign policy, filled the pages of *Novaia zhizn'* throughout

February and March 1918, reaching a climax in two editorials which accused Lenin and his *Sovnarkom* of having 'in a panic and out of fear for their power surrendered in indecent haste to the more than obscene conditions of the German imperialists in the peace negotiations of Brest-Litovsk'. Was 'the hearth of socialism' to be 'rescued for Europe and history upon the snows of Moscow', Sukhanov sneered.

Risking the future of *Novaia zhizn'*, Sukhanov called upon the CEC and its substantial minority of Left Communists and Left SR opponents of the Brest-Litovsk treaty with Germany to 'declare this act immediately null and void'. Worse still, he appealed to what he called the 'conscious democracy' to put the liquidation of 'this government of collapse and shame' on the immediate agenda and then replace it with 'a state power capable of governing and defending the revolution'.[24] The net result of this reckless appeal was the closure of *Novaia zhizn'* for eight days; that it was not closed for longer or altogether was due to a liberal gesture by the Commissariat for Matters of the Press marking the inauguration of Zinoviev's Government of the Petrograd Labour Commune. The condition stipulated for the reappearance of closed-down newspapers was that they 'not spread panic among the population, and not call for the overthrow of the existing state power'.[25] On its reappearance on 2 March, *Novaia zhizn'*'s editorial[26] (unsigned, but written by Sukhanov) proudly recorded the 'unflinching oppositional role' of the paper *vis-à-vis* both the Provisional Government and the Bolshevik regime:

> We have been in opposition to all revolutionary governments and they have taken their revenge to the full. *Novaia zhizn'* was closed down by the democrat Kerensky, in partnership with his erstwhile worthy confidant, the gentleman [Piotr] Palchinsky, at a time when Trotsky sat in the Petropavlovka [the Peter and Paul Fortress] and Lenin was on the run. Subsequently, Lenin, together with his worthy proselyte Trotsky, closed it down while Palchinsky sat in the Petropavlovka and Kerensky was on the run.

Novaia zhizn' would continue to fulfil that 'oppositional role' until such time as Russia had a state power which 'would lead it to socialism and freedom', the editorial continued. 'Punitive measures will neither deter nor change those for whom the pen and the printed word are no pastime or source of worldly goods. They will remain at their posts ... unless they are removed by force.'

One may well wonder why Sukhanov, with his outstanding record of anti-war activity, should with such zeal have rejected the final peace agreement of Brest-Litovsk, a 'noose around Russia's neck', the signing of which, he warned, was tantamount to committing 'suicide'. He had not been in principle against a peace agreement with the 'German imperialists': he had in fact favoured accepting the first joint proposals of 20 December 1917 which sacrificed mainly the Baltic provinces – territory that Sukhanov thought the Russian state could do without. But he found the conditions of the final agreement so unacceptable that he made common cause with the Left Communist and the Left SR advocates of 'revolutionary war' and turned venomously against Lenin's claim that it gave Russia a 'breathing space'. These peace terms, he told Lenin, forced Russia to recognize the independence of the Ukraine and to agree to crippling exports of iron ore and foodstuffs to Germany. In Sukhanov's opinion 'the tearing off from Russia of the rich southern provinces' (as distinct from the Baltic provinces 'inhabited by a non-Russian population') was bound to 'destroy the living organism of the Russian state, depriving it of its essential nourishing juices'. The Bolshevik government should therefore have emulated the example of Belgium and Serbia and even Romania and have refused to submit to Germany's ultimatum especially since Russia was 'in so much better a position to hold out,' he wrote. Further, the democracy of Western Europe on which revolutionary Russia's 'final hopes rested' was now unlikely to rush to the rescue of a Russian democracy that had itself 'trampled on its own principles and its unprecedented achievement and condemned the great revolution to death'.[27] As late as 30 June 1918, Sukhanov continued to denounce the Brest-Litovsk agreement in the pages of *Novaia zhizn'* as a 'crime'. He even upbraided the Menshevik government of Georgia, though it itself had been a 'victim of that crime', for having capitulated to the Germans. It too, like the Bolshevik government, had surrendered to 'the tender mercies of the victors'.[28]

The major themes of Sukhanov's spate of articles and editorials against the peace of Brest-Litovsk were, firstly, his call for a broadening of the government to include other socialist parties and 'democratic groups' which would resist the German onslaught; secondly, his fear that a humiliated and truncated Russia would either be carved up among the imperialist powers or become a colony; and thirdly, his refusal to accept the secession of the Ukraine which he was adamant in regarding as an integral part of Russia. Indeed his total insensitivity to Ukrainian national aspirations is quite remarkable: he sarcastically dismissed their struggle for an 'independent state' as 'fiction,' an 'adventure' embarked upon by 'bourgeois intelligentsia groups' who staked all on the Ukrainian agricultural classes' exhaustion and their craving for peace and a petty-bourgeois order.[29] Indeed, as we saw in Chapter 1, Sukhanov seems to have had very little sympathy for the political independence movements of 'existing and invented nationalities' within the multinational Russian empire.'

With all hope for the broadening and civilizing of the revolution fading and the traumatic humiliation of Brest-Litovsk casting its shadow on the very subdued February revolution anniversary issue of *Novaia zhizn'*, the paper's editorial[30] nevertheless echoed Sukhanov's enduring faith in internationalism:

> We shall arise again! We shall arise for the victory march into the kingdom of freedom hand in hand with our Western brothers whose imminent awakening is ordained by the entire course of history and by the 'insanely' great year of our mighty Russian revolution.

Though often gagged by Yakov Sverdlov, the rock-hard Bolshevik chairman of the CEC, Sukhanov lived up to his gadfly reputation throughout the CEC fourth convocation 20 March–14 June 1918. Thus, as early as 20 March, at the opening session, Sukhanov proposed a debate on 'the situation in the soviet state' as a follow-up to a very gloomy and telling report by Alexander Shliapnikov, People's Commissar for Trade and Industry, his aim, in tune with the editorials and articles of *Novaia zhizn'*, being to expose the Bolshevik regime's disastrous economic performance and put forward an alternative plan of economic reconstruction. That *Novaia zhizn'* plan was predicated on nothing less than the democratization and self-liquidation of the Bolshevik dictatorship.

But Lev Sosnovsky, Menshevik baiter-in-chief, was determined to frustrate Sukhanov and appealed to the assembly to reject his motion for a debate and to refuse him the floor:

Fig. 4.1 Sverdlov

There's only one conclusion to be drawn from comrade [*sic*! I.G.] Sukhanov's remarks: Down with Soviet state power! And we don't need a debate on that in this assembly – this is something [the Sukhanovs] trumpet in the pages of the newspapers and in the streets and they have ample freedom there for that.[31]

As we shall see later, Sukhanov got a better hearing in the CEC in May for his fierce and hard-hitting attacks on the Bolsheviks' agrarian policies. His agrarian blueprint, based on the self-governing activities and economic self-interest of the village commune, was blatantly out of tune with the brutal policies of War Communism, then in its earliest stage. What goaded him beyond endurance was that procession of Bolshevik dignitaries who one by one rose to address the CEC and 'quite openly' turned the procurement crisis simply into a military problem. While Alexander Shlikhter, Extraordinary Food Commissar of Moscow province and certainly no softy, was still speaking the language of 'class struggle', Alexander Tsiurupa, Peoples' Commissar of Food Supplies, laid it down that 'it is only with the gun that we shall procure bread'. And to achieve that, he would rely on the Committees of the Poor in the villages and on the Requisitioning Detachments which 'operate throughout the vast territory of the Russian republic'.[32] His words were echoed by Sverdlov, who put 'the unleashing of civil war in the villages' on the immediate agenda: the village must be split into 'two irreconcilably hostile camps', where 'the poor strata of the population will confront the *kulak* elements'. A climax was reached at the combined session of the Central Executive Comittee, the Moscow Soviet and the trade unions, held in the Bolshoi Theatre on 4 June. Defending the regime's unbending, brutally enforced bread monopoly, Trotsky declared: 'Just as the peasants have been taught to take the land from the land-owners, they will now also be taught that bread is a state possession!' When Sukhanov interjected to question the wisdom of a bread monopoly which prevented bread from reaching the towns, Trotsky dismissed him and the Menshevik critique as 'bourgeois' and proclaimed that 'Soviet state power is organized civil war ... our party stands for civil war and that civil war is now fought over bread!' Turning to Sukhanov, he added: 'There will also be civil war against those who dare to come here and criticize.' When someone ironically interjected: 'Long Live Civil War!', Trotsky answered back in a flash: 'Yes! In the name of bread for the children, the elderly, the workers and the Red Army, in the name of a straight, open and merciless struggle, Long Live Civil War!'[33]

Speaking in the CEC on 29 April and 9 and 14 May 1918, Sukhanov had already told the Bolshevik civil war enthusiasts that the principal cause of the terrible food crisis was precisely the civil war that they had been waging for seven months against the 'democratic organs of self-government'. That civil war, he reminded them, had already begun with the dispersal of the Town Duma of Petrograd in mid-November 1917 and had been followed by the country-wide liquidation of town dumas and rural *zemstva*, all in the name of 'unrealizable goals and principles'. The main and immediate task must therefore be to revive the municipalities, *zemstva* and co-operatives and charge them with recruiting experienced and competent personnel to organize food supply – there could no longer be any room for the 'lickspittles and toadies' of the soviet regime, he urged.

But first of all, he continued, as an emergency measure, the state must relax – if not relinquish – its bread monopoly (which in any case only existed on paper), permit private trade in grain and cease prosecuting the 'bagmen'. Moreover, peasants in the black soil areas should be induced to part with their grain in return for the supply of manufactured goods and of changes in the methods of goods exchange in favour of the peasants. Regardless of the cost, food must be rushed into the non-black-soil areas where people were already dying of starvation. Neither the 'policing forces' in the villages – as Tsiurupa had proposed – nor the soviets, which had become nothing but 'organizations of the dictatorship of armed groups over the village population', were capable of organizing food supplies. These soviets should immediately transfer all their economic and cultural functions to democratic institutions elected on the basis of universal suffrage and then abolish themselves. As for the 'political task' in the village, which was the main item on the agenda of the CEC, he thought it should be summed up as 'Down with the Red Guard Autocracy, and Long Live a Democratic Order!'[34]

Naturally enough, although Sukhanov had for once been heard out in silence, his protests made no impression on the Bolsheviks and he had to watch in impotent despair and anger as they purged the soviets and implemented the brutal requisitioning and coercive sowing policies of War Communism. The profound impact of that experience echoed in his deposition to his chief investigator D.M.

D.M. Dmitriev prior to the Menshevik Trial of March 1931: 'It seemed to me that anything would have been better than the situation then; I was overwhelmed by feelings of the deepest anger and hatred for the Communist authorities ... and when Kronstadt erupted [in March 1921] I was filled with sympathy towards the insurgents and longed with all my heart for their victory.'[35]

On 11 June 1918, three days before he, together with Martov and the few Menshevik and Right SR deputies were expelled from the CEC, Sukhanov squared accounts with the Bolsheviks' much-vaunted 'State Power of the Soviets' both in *Novaia zhizn'* and in the CEC. In his article 'The State Power of the Soviets and the Position of the Working Class', he urged that soviet state power had largely become a fiction. What the Bolsheviks had done to the democratic *zemstva*, to the urban municipalities and to the Constituent Assembly, they were now doing to the soviets and thus 'depriving the working class of its tried and trusted combat organizations'. As a telling example, he cited Fiodor Raskolnikov's own account of the purge of the Soviet of Sormovo where the Mensheviks had won a majority in the elections and the workers had demanded that the defeated, largely Bolshevik executive committee transfer all its affairs to the new Soviet. In reaction, Raskolnikov had assembled the old executive committee and the 'left minority' who together adopted a resolution that 'power must not under any circumstances be handed over' to the Menshevik-SR majority since 'only those organizations committed to the [Bolshevik] soviet platform and ready to carry out those policies in everything may possess power'. Armed with that resolution, the old Bolshevik governing body stayed on in the Soviet 'for purposes of observation and propaganda'.

Where soviets were being emasculated, Sukhanov urged, workers should carry on the struggle for the soviets from within, even though the fight might already be hopeless – and in that situation it was inevitable and rational that there should develop alternative workers' organizations such as Workers Conferences and Assemblies of Factory Representatives: these might become the sole workers' centres defending the revolution against both liquidation by the Bolsheviks and the dangers of bourgeois restoration. Still, they should strive not to be in conflict but rather in contact with the soviets and try to secure proportional representation in the forthcoming Fifth Soviet Congress.[36]

On the same day, when the CEC session opened, Sverdlov accused 'citizen [*sic* I.G.] Sukhanov, a committee member' of having 'distorted the activity of the CEC' when he wrote in that day's *Novaia zhizn'* that the CEC had passed a decree which gave the *Sovnarkom* the right to disband soviets. 'There is not a word of truth in what Sukhanov wrote!', Sverdlov insisted. Before asking for the right to reply to this rebuke by the chairman, Sukhanov commented on the Cassation Decree that had been proposed by Deputy-Prosecutor Nikolai Krylenko and seconded by Sosnovsky. In fact he had already taken issue with the decree on 29 April when he accused Krylenko of misusing it to please Stalin and reverse the inconclusive and embarrassing verdict of the Revolutionary Tribunal in Stalin's imprudent libel action against Martov: 'Your motion,' he told Krylenko, 'has defiled the Soviet republic and disgraced Soviet jurisprudence in the eyes of the whole world, of the International and of history.' Now, he sneered at the elaborate decree as an example of the fictitious character of Soviet justice: 'Our supreme Soviet institutions dealt quite often and at length with the problem of the law courts and of legal rights – to such an extent that one might even be tempted to think that this testifies to a particular respect for law and law courts.' But in fact all basic judicial activity totally ignored the proper legal institutions. 'We have a press tribunal, but it is really the Cheka that deals with these matters and also puts people to death without a trial.' The problem as he saw it was not one of justice and injustice, but of the absence of due process, and the law court that Krylenko's decree would set up was not a legal institution but an organ designed to mete out summary justice to political opponents.[37]

Having first fired that broadside against Soviet justice, Sukhanov next asked for permission to reply to the 'grave accusation' made by Sverdlov. When the assembly refused him that right, he said: 'I very much regret that I will have to take recourse to newspaper polemics rather than explain my point here, which I could do in just three minutes.' After some further debate, the chairman did give him the right to speak and he read from the decree which gave the People's Commissar for Food Supplies 'the right to initiate procedures to disband local soviets'. To underline his point, he added that the government's Left SR partners had voted against the decree 'because it effectively and formally abolishes Soviet state power'. 'It was on that basis,' he said, that 'I included the lines that the *Sovnarkom* really has the right to disband local soviets.' Turning on Sosnovsky, who had argued that the final version of the decree made no mention of the right to disband soviets, Sukhanov declared: 'Citizen Sosnovsky does himself honour when he maintains that Soviet state power still does exist.

But I insist that the opposite is true – what exists here is not Soviet state power which has long been abolished, but rather a police autocracy of the Bolshevik-controlled CEC which is opposed to the majority of workers and peasants and maintains its power with the methods of mediaeval barbarism!'[38]

Three days later, Sosnovsky relished the privilege of delivering a speech in the CEC supporting the motion to expel the Mensheviks, including Sukhanov, and the Right SRs:

These international citizens [*sic!* I.G.] who speak here as representatives of the soviets, this wretched handful of obstructors [uproar from the Right], who organize conferences of representatives and in the name of the proletariat work on public opinion ... Better to have them on the other side of the barricade, with bombs, with rifles, rather than have them here in the Soviet as hypocritical friends of the working class, as so-called revolutionaries, so-called socialists. In the name of that clarity, in the name of that precise delimitation and fencing off of revolutionaries from counter-revolutionaries, I invite the CEC to adopt a decision to show this counter-revolutionary party its place outside the doors of revolutionary organizations, on the other side of the barricade [applause].[39]

In all fairness it should be recorded that the Left SR members of the CEC did not vote for the motion.

A month later, the fate of *Novaia zhizn'* was sealed when, by the 16 July decree of Nikolai Kuzmin, Commissar for Press, Agitation and Propaganda, the newspaper was closed down for good. There was no point in appealing to Kuzmin's boss Zinoviev who had already, in April 1918, castigated the newspaper's 'treasonable editorials' for 'calling for the overthrow of the Soviet order'. Gorky, *Novaia zhizn''s* official owner, appealed to Lenin, but Lenin reportedly justified the closure by saying that with the civil war flaring up 'any intelligentsia pessimism is harmful'. Likewise, when Kamenev, the more liberal chairman of the Moscow Soviet was approached to permit publication of the Moscow edition of the paper, he refused and added, 'It was a rotten newspaper.'[40]

With his expulsion from the CEC on 14 June and the closure of *Novaia zhizn'* on 16 July 'by the will of the Communist authorities', Sukhanov became for a while unemployed and in August began to write what was to be the first volume of his *Zapiski*, completing it in November 1918. It took him another two years and nine months – until August 1921 – to finish writing the other six volumes, having secured a contract for the entire work with the publisher Zinovii Grzhebin early in 1919.

Politically, Sukhanov was – until late in 1920 – more or less identified with Martov's and the Mensheviks' dual semi-loyal, semi-implacable policy *vis à vis* the Bolshevik regime. True, he was active (together with Olga Domanevskaia, N.Iu. Kapelinsky, Mikhail Brounstein, Osip Ermansky, Boris Ber and Andrei Vyshinsky) in a small, short-lived, oppositional, left faction which urged stronger Menshevik support of the Bolshevik side in the civil war.[41] Still, when the White armies of Alexander Denikin and N.N. Yudenich seriously threatened the Soviet state in October 1919, the Menshevik party called on all its members to mobilize in defence of the 'Soviet republic' and thus in April 1920 Sukhanov was sent to the Urals as both a representative of the Commissariat of Agriculture and as member of the Revolutionary Military Council of Trotsky's First (Ural) Revolutionary Army. There he was also active in the local Menshevik party organization and when its entire committee was arrested by the Cheka on the eve of the elections to the soviets, he cabled Lenin, Trotsky and Dzerzhinsky in protest, asking to be relieved of his duties. That request was discussed at the Politburo meeting on 1 June 1920 and he was released from the Revolutionary Military Council but not from the Commissariat of Agriculture.[42] As representative of that body, as he was later to tell the OGPU investigator prior to his trial in March 1931, he organized a conference which adopted his resolution to drop the policy of requisitioning and replace it with free trade in grain. For this, he claimed, he was attacked in the press and his home was searched by the Cheka, and that decided him on an immediate return to Moscow.[43]

Sukhanov's break with the Mensheviks and his resignation from the party on 10 December 1920 came in the wake of Martov's passionate appeal to the Independent Social Democratic Party of

Germany (USPD) in Halle in October of that year that they reject the Comintern's Twenty-One Points and refuse to join it. Martov argued that the 'non-negotiable' points were avowedly designed to extend and perpetuate the hegemony, organizational and doctrinal discipline of the Russian Communist party over the socialist parties of Europe and make them all serve the interests of the dictatorial and terrorist soviet state.[44]

Sukhanov's letter of resignation[45] noted that he had been and continued to be in agreement with the party's internal and economic policies. But he 'strongly disapproved of its *international* platform, of its position within the *international* labour movement, and of its stand on the world socialist revolution'. The Menshevik party's hostile attitude to the Third International was wrong-headed, especially in view of the 'great events that are developing on an international scale'. There could be no excuse for the Menshevik party's 'cutting itself off from the international proletarian army in its assault on capitalism', he insisted. 'Neutrality' or the artificial creation of a 'third force' were intolerable and criminal, he wrote (a reference to Martov's and Rafail Abramovich's part in the creation of the leftist Vienna Union of Socialist Parties – the so-called Two-and-a-Half International). For him, he said, the critical point had been reached in August 1920 when, just after the Comintern's Second Congress had established that body as 'the mightiest factor and the sole centre of revolution', Martov had gone to Halle to 'unsettle the serried ranks of the proletarian army' and the Menshevik party had sanctioned his appearance there.

I am fully conscious of the odium of breaking with my comrades at the very moment when the hounded RSDRP [i.e. the Menshevik party] is once again being subjected to barbarous and senseless repression. But I cannot carry the even greater burden of accepting the slightest responsibility for the party's position on the most important problem of the world revolution. Nevertheless, I hope to prove that doing my duty as a revolutionary and an internationalist in no way implies reconciliation with the regime or solidarity with the policy of Bolshevik state power.

As for Martov and the Mensheviks, they took the resignation seriously, even though – as Martov put it somewhat ironically in a letter to Axelrod – 'Sukhanov has suddenly discovered his sympathy for the tactics of conquering the Third International by joining it.'[46] As we shall see, it took Sukhanov some time to become reconciled to the October revolution and the Soviet system, longer even to accept the dictatorial 'Jacobin' regime, and longest of all to shed some of his social democratic convictions. On 29 April 1921 he reportedly delivered a lecture in the House of the Press to a large and mostly communist audience in which he enlarged on 'the impossibility of socialism in Russia' and the need for 'a dictatorship of the majority' only to be roundly abused for his 'boring social democratic speech'.[47] A few months later, while writing the seventh volume of his *Zapiski*, he recorded Lenin's victory speech in the Petrograd Soviet on 25 October: Lenin had said, 'We have that powerful mass organization which vanquishes all and will take the proletariat to the world revolution; we must now immediately set out to build a proletarian socialist state in Russia. Long Live the Socialist World Revolution!' Discussing Lenin's two central points: 'the smashing of the old state apparatus' and its replacement by 'the creation of a new administrative apparatus of soviet organizations', and the call to 'build a proletarian socialist state', Sukhanov wondered whether this did not mean 'the complete destruction of the productive forces of the country' rather than 'fulfilling the most urgent task of peaceful reconstruction'. Did it not mean taking upon oneself patently unrealizable commitments in the vast, economically fragmented *muzhik* country.[48]

In February 1921, Sukhanov resigned his post in the People's Commissariat of Agriculture and was appointed to a professorship at Moscow University where he lectured on agrarian economics and led seminars on political economy. It seemed as if one of his early ambitions to become an academic had been fulfilled. But finding that he did not really want to be a scholar, and that being a 'pedagogue' was equally not to his taste, he looked for something more interesting. He was glad when, in March 1922, on Trotsky's recommendation, Georgii Chicherin, People's Commissar for External Affairs, asked him to accompany him to the international Genoa Conference as a member of a large delegation of economic experts. He had already started working in his new position when he was suddenly told that his appointment had been cancelled. No reason was given him. Trotsky then explained to him that, as a 'former Menshevik', he was seen as 'worse' and less trustworthy than a bourgeois expert.[49] This was at best, a half-truth, for the real reason –

which Trotsky did not and could not disclose – was that Lenin himself had vetoed the appointment, even though it had already been approved of and passed by the Politburo. In a 'secret' note to Molotov and members of the Politburo, Lenin insisted on 'the *cancellation*' of the decision of the Politburo of 20 January 'to permit Chicherin to enlist *Sukhanov*': 'Chatterbox Sukhanov can only cause trouble.'[50] Unaware of Lenin's role in the humiliating cancellation of his appointment, Sukhanov nevertheless learned the bitter lesson that he had remained a 'social outcast and renegade in that order which I regarded as my own'.[51]

Having resumed his job in the People's Commissariat of Agriculture, he worked for the most part on representing the *Zemplan* section in various institutions and on the preparation of the Soviet–German trade agreement. There he rubbed shoulders with many in high positions whom he thought in many ways inferior to himself so that, by the end of the summer of 1923, he resigned and left for Berlin 'privately and at my own expense'. He worked there for some time in the libraries preparing the manuscripts of his books on the world economy and a never-published introduction to political economy. He also watched events in Germany which looked as if they were heading for a German 'October'. More important still, he sought and made contact with Communist circles with the intention of joining the German Communist party and finding there 'opportunities to use my talents'. But he was soon 'given to understand that, not being a member of the Russian Communist Party', it was 'Moscow' that would have to approve of his working in the German party. This was another painful setback and with his private means running out, Sukhanov returned to Moscow and in January 1924 he applied for membership of the Russian Communist party. His application, dated 8 January 1924, read:

> Feeling at one with the programme of the RKP(b), I wish to be active in a party organization, to submit to its discipline and to pay membership fees, and I request that you accept me as a member (or candidate) of the RKP. Should it be required I can present the necessary guarantees.[52]

Sukhanov's application was considered by the Organization Bureau of the Central Committee on 12 January 1924 when it was decided 'to refuse the application of N. Sukhanov as a member of the RKP'. No explanation was offered and Sukhanov's biographer, Arkadii Kornikov, could find neither protocol nor stenographic note that might have afforded some reason.[53]

Small wonder that when in February 1924, the head of the Soviet Trade Mission in Berlin, Stoleshnikov, offered him the post of head of the mission's information section, which involved editing its two propaganda journals, he was only too glad to accept. He also hoped to combine that post with work in the KPD, since Bukharin had ascertained for him that the Comintern leadership would raise no objection to that – Bukharin even equipped him with a letter of recommendation to August Thalheimer, one of the KPD leaders and ideologists, suggesting that 'I be employed [to work on] party literature, [since] I was a well-informed economist.'[54] His apparent success in his post – especially as editor of its two magazines in German and in French which targeted industrial circles and trumpeted Russia's economic achievements under the NEP – was more than the party cell in the trade mission could take. Fortunately, in January 1925, the newly appointed Soviet Ambassador to France Leonid Krasin invited him to add the information section of the trade mission in Paris to his Berlin responsibilities. Thus, Sukhanov moved to Paris. But there, the large, influential anti-soviet Russian colony soon began an intensive campaign against him in the press and with the police, clamouring for his expulsion. They portrayed him as a long-standing enemy of France and of the *Entente* whose animosity dated back to his anti-war propaganda of 1915–17. Though Krasin did his best to prevent Sukhanov's expulsion, even intervening on his behalf with Aristide Briand, the French foreign minister, all he achieved was a stay of expulsion until the beginning of October 1925 when the French police gave him final notice to leave within three days. To make matters worse, the German Embassy in Paris refused him permission for a short stop-over in Berlin 'for private shopping' en route for Moscow. All this finally put paid to any hopes he may have nursed for a career in the Soviet apparatus in Western Europe.

All that remained of real significance from this frustrating period was a small popular book on the world economy.[55] There he diagnosed the post-war world economy as caught in the throes of that self-same severe crisis that had already caused the World War and might yet cause another such war. That crisis, he believed, had been brought about by the decay and disintegration of capitalism and bourgeois civilization which in turn suffered from such insoluble contradictions as the over-production of commodities facing shrinking markets. He contrasted that gloomy picture with the economic progress of the Soviet Union under the NEP and predicted that Russia with its vast natural resources and its 'economic policy of socialist construction directed towards the development of its industries' would, in a few years, become 'the richest country in Europe' 'even more independent of Europe than the United States', for it would be 'capable of producing on its own all that it needs'.

Regardless of the serious setbacks that revolution had suffered in Germany, Bavaria, Hungary and Austria, Sukhanov continued to believe that the objective conditions for the international socialist revolution were in evidence. What was still missing were the necessary '*subjective* pre-conditions': 'the international proletariat, gravedigger of capitalism and its slave, has not as yet fulfilled its historical mission – to form itself into battle-columns'. He was still confident that it would do that 'under the banner of the Third International' when it faced up to the dilemma of either perishing under the collapse of bourgeois civilization or readying itself 'for the final assault on the tottering fortress of capitalism'.[56]

5
Knight Errant of the *Obshchina*

In October 1925 Sukhanov returned to Moscow and to his comfortable study in the Second House of Soviets which he continued to share with Galina Flakserman even though they had divorced in 1924. It was still a somewhat more relaxed Soviet Union at the height of the NEP in which many economic planning and research institutions such as *Gosplan*, *Narkomzem* and *Narkomfin* were manned by eminent non-party economists such as Nikolai Kondratev, Alexander Chaianov and A.N. Chelintsev and by friends and colleagues of *Novaia zhizn'* days such as Groman and Bazarov. Sukhanov soon got himself a minor post in the information section of the People's Commissariat of External Trade, where there was, however, very little to be done because of a vast reorganization – he was not even given a desk and a chair. But what really depressed him was 'the atmosphere of suspicion, distrust and dirty tricks that surrounded me – not unlike the situation in [the Soviet Trade Mission in] Berlin'. Thus, in the summer of 1926 he resigned, feeling that he was altogether 'unsuitable for work in the existing Soviet apparatus'. When he tried to return to 'pedagogical work, the university quietly declined'. He kept himself busy with part-time freelance work in publishing firms, continuing with his book on political economy, on a new edition of his *Zapiski*, on his play 'The Year 1917, a Dramatic Chronicle in Five Acts' and on some film scripts.

But, more important to him, he became a member of the Communist Academy, active in its Agrarian Section and thus found himself in the very midst of the agrarian debates of the 1920s. On the agenda was the perennial problem of how to modernize and integrate into a socialist Soviet Union 25,000,000 small peasant households, comprising over 85 per cent of the population, the vast majority of which lived in traditional self-contained, self-governing village communes. Sukhanov entered that debate with views that he had restated and sharpened in a second, corrected and enlarged edition of his major work *On the Problem of the Evolution of Agriculture* first published in 1909 and now republished under the auspices of the People's Commissariat of Agriculture.[1] There he had reaffirmed his theory of the decapitalization of the agrarian economy in both pre- and post-revolutionary Russia and argued for a modernization and socialization of the peasant economy based on the *obshchina*.

His pessimistic, startling and provocative conclusion was that Russia's workers' party, now embarking on the building of socialism, would not find in the countryside 'proletarian cadres [that is, agricultural labourers] organized in the process of agricultural production', but would rather be confronted there by 'vast masses of dispersed and reactionary petty [peasant] proprietors who are hostile to socialism'. No 'simplistic clichés and schemes invoked in the name of a falsely understood Marxism must be allowed to deny and conceal that fact, saddening though it is'. It follows 'that the agrarian programme of a workers' party must always be a peasant programme'. And that meant that apart from satisfying the immediate cultural and economic needs of agricultural labourers, a social group which, anyway, could be expected to decline, the Soviet state's agrarian policy must first and foremost be committed to the support of the self-employed peasantry, for instance by providing it with land, but as collective, rather than as private, property. Moreover, technically superior larger forms of social organization should be encouraged. This could be achieved

> by the banding and fusing together of individual small agricultural units ... Here the basic factor, the necessary condition, is that 'revolution in the means of production' which, in the words of Marx, served as the point of departure in the development of industrial capitalism. Without that condition, a socialization of the agrarian economy is impossible. Here, both the extraeconomic compulsion of the state, as well as the moralist-ratio-

nalist propaganda of the fanatics will be of no avail, but will rather produce a ruinous utopia. But given that revolution in the means of production, a reorganization of agricultural production along socialized lines is quite inevitable.

Just how these reforms could be implemented, Sukhanov left open, vaguely invoking producer co-operatives, 'municipalization', or the state, but 'to deal with it here would be out of place'.[2]

Still, he forcefully spelled out his real preference in 1926 in a major and provocative article significantly called 'The *Obshchina* in Agrarian Legislation' written in response to two draft laws under discussion in the Agrarian Section of the Communist Academy.[3] Sukhanov may also have been encouraged by the publication of three drafts of Marx's letter of 1881 to Vera Zasulich which David Ryazanov, director of the Marx-Engels Institute, had recently discovered and published and which Sukhanov believed provided his championship of the *obshchina* with authentic and weighty Marxian credentials, so much so that he appended a lengthy relevant passage to his article. What Marx had said, and in no uncertain terms, was that the *obshchina*, where land was held in common, provided 'a natural basis for collective appropriation'. Moreover the fact that the *obshchina* co-existed with capitalist technology and production would enable it to acquire 'the ready-made material conditions for co-operative labour organized on a large scale. It could thus, gradually, and with the help of modern machinery, replace its parcellated agriculture with a combined and mechanized form of farming.' The *obshchina* could thus become 'a direct point of departure towards that [socialist] economic system to which modern society is moving; the *obshchina* could thus start a new existence without having first committed suicide.' Thus far the Marx of 1881.[4]

As for Sukhanov, his article was nothing less than an advertisement for the *obshchina* à la Marx as the most suitable instrument for socialization and collectivization provided that it was preserved and enhanced as a legal public institution (state or municipal), thus becoming the 'smallest territorial unit of the socialist state'. But to make this possible, it would be absolutely necessary to repeal the Land Code of 1922 which allowed individual peasant householders to opt out of the *obshchina* and take with them their share in the *obshchina*'s land or its equivalent. Such withdrawal with land,

Sukhanov urged, was tantamount to coercing the *obshchina* to commit suicide. Sukhanov also suggested, possibly to counter Bolshevik prejudice against the *obshchina* as a rival of the weak but state-sponsored rural soviet, that the *obshchina* be merged with the local village soviet and that new arrivals and non-*obshchina* residents be given the right to vote in the *skhod* (the *obshchina*'s general assembly). Having merged with the local village soviet the *obshchina* would thus become 'the basic cell of the Soviet state in the countryside'.

Sukhanov may have had a point, and he seems to have had the Marx of 1881 on his side, for, contrary to all predictions and wishful thinking by Russian Marxists such as Plekhanov, Struve and, of course, Lenin and the Leninists, the *obshchina* had survived capitalism, the Stolypin reforms, the World War, the Civil War, the NEP, as well as the *obshchinophobia* of Soviet agrarian policy. By the time of the agrarian debates of the 1920s, no fewer than some 95 per cent of Russia's peasant households lived in 380,000 peasant communes. In the context of Russia's industrial development and of the Soviet revolution, the *obshchina* could have played an important part in modernizing and socializing soviet agriculture had Sukhanov's necessary condition – a vast injection of technology into the *obshchina* – been met. But Sukhanov's reform programme based on the *obshchina* was not taken seriously at all thanks to a vicious campaign of delegitimation waged against him and his deviant views by the so-called school of Agrarian Marxists, led by Leonid Kritsman, director of the Agrarian Section (later Agrarian Institute) of the Communist Academy and editor of its journal *Na agrarnom fronte*.

It is not surprising that Sukhanov, a fierce critic of War Communism, and subsequently an enthusiastic supporter of the NEP, should have fallen foul of Kritsman, an ardent supporter of War Communism[5] in the 1918–20 period, which he celebrated in his 1925 book *The Heroic Period of the Great Russian Revolution*. There, Kritsman extolled the 'so-called War Communism' of 'the epoch of the Great Civil War' as 'the first grand attempt ... the first step towards socialism', marking nothing less than 'a pre-figuring of the future' [sic! IG]. As for its detractors, Kritsman accused them of 'social-democratic thinking' and of 'utter failure to comprehend the *class* meaning of the great Russian revolution'.[6]

Sukhanov had already been taken to task in 1924, though rather mildly, in the anonymous editorial preface to his book *On the*

Problem of the Evolution of Agriculture for attempting to prove that in pre-revolutionary Russia agrarian capitalism had failed to 'destroy' or even to squeeze the peasant economy. Still, the Communist editor commended the book for its rich source materials and scholarship and was confident that 'the reader of today will know how to cope with Sukhanov's errors'. He justified publication of this unorthodox work by invoking the principle that 'the contest of ideas gives birth to the truth'.[7]

The editor's liberality was not to the liking of Sergei Dubrovsky, a leading Communist agrarian economist and historian who felt so strongly about Sukhanov's 'errors' that in 1925 he published a lengthy article which a year later he worked up into a small book against Sukhanov's work denouncing his theory of the 'decapitalization of agriculture' as nothing less than 'a variant of revisionism'.[8] 'Marxists', Dubrovsky lectured Sukhanov, had 'a double interest' in the development of capitalism in agriculture: by sharpening the class struggle in the village, capitalism helped prepare a peasant revolution, linking it with the proletarian revolution; by promoting the concentration and socialization of production, it would create 'a pre-condition for the future socialization of agriculture'.

Yet the first major attack by the school of Agrarian Marxists proper came in a vitriolic response by M. Kubanin in the very same issue of *Na agrarnom fronte* that carried Sukhanov's article. In 'The *Obshchina* under the Dictatorship of the Proletariat: a Reply to N. Sukhanov',[9] Kubanin accused Sukhanov of 'raising anew the antiquated and frayed banner of infatuation with the *obshchina*' and of harbouring 'the illusions of petty-bourgeois socialists' that it was possible 'in a purely democratic way to transform ancient estate organizations into socialist institutions'. Sukhanov, Kubanin argued, had thus ignored 'the dominant role of the *kulak*s in the *obshchina* and its internal class struggle'. Sneering at Sukhanov's claim that he had Marx on his side, but without making any attempt to come to grips with the import of Marx's draft, Kubanin defined '*Sukhanovshchina*' as synonymous with 'theoretical confusion and eclecticism' and all but excommunicated him:

Sukhanov's theory is purely Socialist Revolutionary and not Marxist-Leninist ... it makes a breach in the totality of Leninist theory and diverts the solution of the peasant problem from Leninist to SR lines. It cannot have any place in our ranks.[10]

Overall, Sukhanov's championship of the *obshchina* stirred very little interest: the Agrarian Marxists rejected it out of hand, while their rivals, the neo-populist economists of the Production-Organization School led by Chaianov and entrenched in the Timiriazev Academy, were more interested in the family farm than in the *obshchina*. As so often in his life, Sukhanov was all alone.

Worse still, when the Agrarian Marxists pushed the problem of alleged class differentiation in the Russian village – and with it the '*kulak* danger' – into the centre of the agrarian debate, Sukhanov's theory of the decapitalization of Russian agriculture, which clearly minimized the *kulak* danger, was completely ignored. Undaunted, Sukhanov went into battle in defence of his theory at a conference on problems of social and economic differentiation in the peasant economy, held early in January 1927 at the Timiriazev Academy. There, he argued that economic differentiation in the village diminishes in the course of economic development and industrialization. Likewise, the number of *kulak* households diminishes with the increase in industrialization. It was the middling peasant, and not the *kulak*, who was the central figure in the contemporary village, and he was the 'social type' around which Soviet agrarian policy should be focused. If the Agrarian Marxists were right, and agrarian capitalism were to increase in step with economic development, then to attempt to fight capitalism in the village would be so much tilting at windmills. Were it true that the historical course of events would favour rural capitalism and the *kulak* class, then one should not even attempt to curb the *kulak* 'by means of extra-economic compulsion: history, fortunately, was not on the side of the *kulak*, but against him', Sukhanov urged.[11]

With the atmosphere at the conference still rather civilized and abiding by the rules of academic discourse and debate, criticism of Sukhanov was still quite restrained. True, M. Sulkovsky, soon to become the secretary of the Communist Academy, drew attention to the '*narodnik* smell that emanated from Sukhanov's paper',[12] while A. Gaister, deputy director of its agrarian section, pronounced Sukhanov's methodology 'completely wrong', since it ignored all forms of capitalist exploitation and of 'village capitalism in gestation'.[13]

Far worse followed when Sukhanov launched a direct attack on Kritsman and his school. It took the form of a sarcastic comment on Kritsman's paper 'Class Groupings of Peasant Households' read in the Communist Academy in the same month:[14]

> Many, many years ago, comrade Kritsman (who was not alone in this) was shell-shocked by one sentence in the second chapter of Lenin's *Development of Capitalism in Russia* which read 'The peasantry ceases to exist, it is transformed on the one hand into a proletariat and on the other into a bourgeoisie.' And ever since, Kritsman has been knocking himself out in the search for capitalism in the peasant economy, determined to find it wherever it does and does not exist. It is with regret that I state that this is characteristic not only of Kritsman alone.

Referring to Kritsman and his school's attempt to extend the concept of agrarian capitalism to include also the hiring out of draught animals and agricultural implements, as well as the leasing of land, Sukhanov urged that this form of exploitation was ephemeral and largely the result of the devastation and impoverishment caused by the World War and the Civil War. Economic recovery, linked to well-organized state supplies of implements and livestock was bound to liquidate that form of exploitation. This type of capitalism, he assured Kritsman, was not dangerous and would be overcome, but its existence must not meanwhile be permitted to influence economic policy, nor must it be dealt with by 'special measures'.

Watching the procurement crisis of 1927/28, and horrified by Stalin's use of those 'extreme measures' known as the brutal 'Ural-Siberian method' – 'their hands at your throat and their knees on your chest'– Sukhanov set out his own alternative programme in a paper 'On the Economic Pre-Conditions for the Improvement of Agriculture' which he read in the Communist Academy on 4 December 1928.[15] The paper in the first place offered a specific solution to the crisis, but it was also motivated by Sukhanov's harrowing fears that Stalin's extreme measures, combined with 'the reinforced offensive against the *kulak*' proclaimed by the 15th Communist Party Congress of December 1927,[16] foreshadowed a massive return to the brutalities of War Communism 'when all economic laws were abrogated'. The system of 'equivalent exchanges' which he advocated – whereby the peasant would receive in exchange for some of his grain (30 per cent or so) an agreed quantity of consumer goods imported by the state – was conceived as a rational appeal to the economic interests of the peasant. He had already, so he claimed, presented his scheme to members of the Politbureau and to 'a long line of the most authoritative leaders of our economic policy' who had 'heard him out, but had not listened'.[17] That should not have surprised him, for even 'rightists' such as Aleksei Rykov, Nikolai Bukharin and Mikhail Tomsky would have been wary of being identified in any way whatever with Sukhanov and his non-conformist arguments and schemes. A year earlier already he had known that it was 'sufficient for me to put forward an idea to have it rejected out of hand'.

As was his habit, Sukhanov, before expounding his scheme, brushed aside some official and current explanations of the procurement difficulties such as 'the somnolence of our procurement agencies', 'the break-up of large, modernized landowners' estates', 'the fragmentation of peasant households', 'the general degeneration in peasant farming'. He, for one, was sure that peasant farming had actually improved and become more mechanized. He certainly stuck out his neck when he ridiculed those who attributed the crisis to 'the machinations of the *kulaks*'. 'For the life of me,' he exclaimed, 'I cannot reconcile myself to the idea that some miserable three per cent (*kulak* peasants) are capable of standing up to and frustrating the might of our state apparatus.' That figure, recognized as a given in times of prosperity, was inflated so grossly in times of crisis as to include as *kulaks* all those who 'had made the merest elementary farm improvements' and even those who 'had acquired a radio receiver'. It was from the peasants' loss of all economic incentive to increase the marketable production of grain that the present difficulties sprang. And as long as 'every unit of peasant agricultural produce remains unmatched by a corresponding unit of industrial consumer goods', no measures, including agro-technical improvements, would prove effective: 'without that corresponding equivalent to satisfy peasant demand not one additional *pud* of grain will be produced', he insisted. Since soviet industries were for the moment incapable of and not planned to satisfy the peasants' demand for manufactured consumer goods, those goods would have to be imported by the state. Such imports would have to be financed by agrarian exports. When delivering their grain, peasants would receive part of the payment due them in the form of an entitlement to imported goods that would be channelled to the villages by co-operatives and state agencies. The following objectives, Sukhanov insisted, could thus be achieved: grain, instead of rotting away while being hoarded or being fed 'uneconomically' to livestock or turned into home-brewed vodka, would now be produced in ever-increasing quantities; receipts from export and import duties would grow; the *kulak*, the middleman, would be eliminated by rational economic means since he would be unable to supply goods that the state alone could import by retaining a monopoly in external trade. Further, increasing agricultural surpluses could eventually be used to finance industrialization. And finally, the realization of his scheme, Sukhanov urged, would give the state 'powerful leverage for an agrarian policy to encourage the production of crops it was particularly interested in'. To strengthen his argument, Sukhanov drew attention to the imbalance that existed in the years 1925/26 between the village sector which, while accounting for 80 per cent of Russian exports received a mere 20 per cent of imports. Stressing that many details of his scheme remained to be worked out, Sukhanov suggested that his ideas be tried in some few areas which had substantial grain surpluses.

For once, Sukhanov and his paper were taken seriously. The first discussant, Pogossky, found what Sukhanov had had to say 'interesting in the highest degree'; still, he wondered whether he had not gone too far in brushing aside the view that Russia's peasant agriculture was in the process of degeneration; after all, the significant decline in grain production since 1927 gave some credence to that view. Had not Sukhanov drawn too fantastic a picture of the peasant 'with pencil in hand, calculating whether the quantity of consumer goods corresponded to the quantity of marketable grain'? Would not his scheme of direct exchange or barter have a disastrous effect on an already weakened national currency?[18]

The second discussant, Groman, who in principle approved of Sukhanov's scheme, thought that in the present crisis it was 'unrealistic' to expect it to solve the problem of agrarian underproduction. Sukhanov's plan was predicated on an abundant supply of grain available for export. It should have been tried out and 'could have proved very effective' in a good year such as 1926, but not now when there was a deficit of 200,000,000 *pud*s of grain for internal consumption, nor was that situation likely to change in the coming year. Thus, in the absence of exportable grain, consumer goods would have to be purchased abroad on credit. But he, Groman, knew for sure that no such credit would be forthcoming for the import of consumer goods.[19]

Sukhanov's last active public appearance was at the Conference of Marxist-Leninist Agrarian Research Institutes in April 1929 where he was the first to comment on Kritsman's keynote paper, 'An Analysis of the Peasant Household'. Kritsman, Sukhanov urged, had again overstated the role and extent of agrarian capitalism in the Soviet economy. This time he had gone even further to claim that conflicts within the peasant household were a reflection of class antagonism, pitting heads of households against their sons, the former being cast by Kritsman in the role of the exploitative, capitalist employer, while the sons were the exploited proletarian workers. Such novel and wrong-headed interpretations, Sukhanov warned, would blur the distinction between the middling peasant, now assigned the role of capitalist, and the *kulak*. As for Kritsman's denunciation of the *obshchina*, à la Lenin, as a 'hearth of capitalism', Sukhanov pointed out that Lenin, writing in the 1890s, had referred to a very different situation; since then, the capitalist state had been replaced in Russia by a workers' state, while the *obshchina* constituted an agricultural unit with a public legal standing. By a majority vote of its members, the *obshchina* could introduce any form of socialized economy and thus liquidate and absorb its *kulak* elements. In the hands of the proletarian state, the *obshchina* could serve as a powerful instrument for the collectivization of the economy.[20]

In reply, Kritsman singled Sukhanov out as his 'most consistent opponent', whose arguments though 'exceptionally poor and badly grounded', had been adopted in one form or another by all those comrades-critics who at the same time had gone out of their way to dissociate themselves publicly from Sukhanov. And for good measure, Kritsman pronounced Sukhanov 'a political corpse'.[21] Kritsman's verdict was not far from the truth and it was confirmed by Sukhanov himself at the Menshevik trial of 1931 when he complained: 'I felt I had been expunged from public life and that my very name had become something illegitimate and obscene.'[22] It was Vladimir Miliutin, Vice-President of the Communist Academy and a former People's Commissar of Agriculture, who at the April 1929 conference provided Kritsman's vicious verdict on Sukhanov with the backing of a leading Communist dignitary and thus gave it what was virtually the status of an excommunication.

'Sukhanov,' Miliutin said, and 'the serious rightist danger and petty bourgeois deviation' which he represented, compelled him to speak out. Sukhanov's objections to Kritsman's 'so-called exaggeration of capitalism in the village' must lead to a blurring of class antagonism in the village and to a glossing over of the '*kulak*'s offensive ' (*sic!* I.G.). It was wrong to suggest that it was possible to achieve socialism by evolution and so-called 'peaceful renewal'. Therefore, Miliutin insisted, any analysis that uncovered the rise of capitalist elements in the village was of practical and not just theoretical value. Sukhanov, Miliutin continued, had glossed over the class nature of the *obshchina* where *kulak*s and wealthy elements often played that leading role which they failed to play in the village soviet from which they were debarred. Nor could the *obshchina*, with its equalizing redistribution of land, the three-field system and its internal social differentiation serve as a point of departure for the socialist transformation of agriculture. That could only proceed on the basis of collectivization and not by Sukhanov's refurbished old *Narodnik* utopia. 'May God save us from such friends; we shall know how to deal with our enemies', Miliutin concluded.[23]

That put an end to Sukhanov's public role and eight months later, at the December 1929 First All-Russian Conference of Agrarian Marxists, Sukhanov appears to have been silenced, save for one very unwelcome interjection in support of Dubrovsky, although, in what was by now almost a ritual, he certainly figured there as a major object of vilification.

The first attack came from Alexander Shlikhter, who threw at Sukhanov a quotation from his *Zapiski* which cast serious doubts on the wisdom and Marxist credentials of Lenin's October Revolution and his plan to build 'a proletarian socialist state' in the vast, economically fragmented Russia of the *muzhik*.[24]

Shlikhter was followed by Kubanin, who boasted of his early article against Sukhanov whom he now used as a stick with which to beat Dubrovsky. Sukhanov must have listened with glee when an angry Dubrovsky characterized Kubanin as 'a carnivorous, bloodthirsty representative of the bedbug species'.[25] It was now Dubrovsky's turn to smear his enemy, A. Gaister, whom he accused of 'solidarity' with Sukhanov and with 'his erroneous position on the most important question of the role of technology in the development of collective farms:[26]

> True, we cannot develop collective farms without tractors and other agricultural machinery; but must we wait [à la Sukhanov] with mass collectivization until such time as our stores and garages are bursting at their seams with tractors and their spare parts? No, we must not! Yet the Sukhanovs and the Rightists, too, urge us to wait with mass collectivization until that time. Indeed, Sukhanov thus perceives the link between collectivization and machine technology and you, Gaister, are in solidarity with him. And you have failed to point at Sukhanov's principal mistake in this matter – *that is your political error* ... As for myself, you will not find a single instance when I have been in solidarity with Sukhanov.

Understandably enough, Gaister was determined that the stigma should not stick and he made sure that it would not in a lengthy diatribe against Sukhanov which is the most complete extant Agrarian Marxist catalogue of his agrarian sins:[27]

> There is still in our midst one adversary who even now continues to pose as a knight errant: I speak, of course, about N.N. Sukhanov. Sukhanov as you all know is 'an orthodox Marxist' but this 'orthodox Marxist', of course, always has his own interpretation of Marxism ... But on what does Sukhanov build his conception of the development of cooperation? One should remember that his work *On the Problem of the Evolution of the Agrarian Economy* was published in the old days when Sukhanov was a *Narodnik* and had not yet begun to juggle Marxist phrases. That book has even been republished in our Soviet days, edited and with a special foreword by one of our comrades. This is what Sukhanov wrote there: 'Agrarian capitalism exists and flourishes only in a primitive situation. The growth of productive forces and capitalist progress undermine agrarian capitalism. With the development of bourgeois capitalist relations the toiling peas-

antry seeks to become the only class engaged in agriculture.' If one takes Sukhanov's position, it becomes clear that in our country there is no struggle whatever between capitalism and socialism. No capitalism whatever would grow out of the small peasant household. There would, of course, be no struggle whatever within the *kolkhozy* and around them; no class struggle for a socialist transformation and for the remaking (*sic!* IG) of the petty producer. For, according to Sukhanov, the petty bourgeoisie marches straight into socialism. It was no accident that Sukhanov, commenting on Kritsman's paper, said: 'The *obshchina* is the smallest cell of the socialist state; by a majority vote the *obshchina* can introduce any form of a socialized economy, can liquidate and swallow up the *kulak* household.' When you and I talk of class struggle, we mean that we are now in the village in the midst of the fiercest struggle for a socialist transformation of agriculture. But Sukhanov it appears has a simple prescription: you put the question to a vote in the *obshchina* and by a common decision socialism will be introduced. Needless to add this is a purely social democratic way of introducing socialism: no need for class struggle or for proletarian leadership. From this Sukhanov also concluded, in one of his papers, that last year's procurement difficulties were the result of our inability to organize a correct goods exchange with the village. From this proposition, without the slightest attempt to take notice of the relationship of class forces in the struggle for grain, Sukhanov derives his prescription of mass imports of industrial goods to stimulate grain procurements. Essentially, Bukharin fell for Sukhanov's arguments when he suggested that our grain procurement difficulties resulted from our bad planning organization and not from the backwardness and fragmentation of agricultural production and from the class struggle in the village. Thus Bukharin slid down into Sukhanov's position. What fundamental conclusion must we draw from the fact that our adversaries do not spell things out? *In every such case we must see clearly and sharply through the reactionary essence of these Danaian gifts and fight all the more energetically for the fundamentals of Marxist-Leninist agrarian theory.*

Gaister's indictment of Sukhanov was already outdated by the last day of the conference, 27 December 1929, when Stalin's historical speech, 'On the Problems of Agrarian Policy in the SSSR', brutally putting paid to the entire agrarian debate, burst like a bombshell on the 300 delegates assembled there.[28] Apart from sneering at 'bourgeois' economists and their theories, he castigated 'our agrarian theorists' [of the Kritsman and Gaister variety] for having done nothing to prevent 'the free circulation in the press' of bourgeois, petty-bourgeois and 'rightist-deviationist' agrarian theories: worse, they had not even troubled themselves to issue any 'serious, crushing rebuff'. Stalin enjoined all 'truly Marxist and revolutionary agrarian economists' to extirpate and tear out at the roots such anti-scientific theories that 'befuddle the brains of our practical workers' for only 'in the merciless struggle against such theories will the theoretical thought of agrarian Marxists grow and gain in strength'.[29]

Stalin's speech more than confirmed Sukhanov's worst fears: this was the first time that Stalin had openly and bluntly proclaimed '*the policy of the liquidation of the kulaks as a class'.*[30] Yet Sukhanov had consistently minimized the *kulak* danger and had advertised the *obshchina* as 'the best defence against the *kulak'*. What Stalin urged was the replacement of Russia's allegedly 'backward, fragmented and unproductive' peasant holdings by 'planting in the villages large-scale socialist farms *sovkhozy* and *kolkhozy'.*[31] Sukhanov, for his part, had envisaged the modernization and socialization of peasant holdings resulting from their growing together by way of *voluntary co-operation* that was in turn stimulated by great technological benefits. Stalin, quoting Lenin, damned the peasant village commune as 'daily, hourly, massively and naturally giving birth to capitalism and the bourgeoisie'.[32] But Sukhanov's particular contribution to agrarian economics had been his theory of decapitalization: in agriculture, he had postulated time and again that agrarian capitalism was doomed and on the way out. For good measure, Stalin even went so far as to boast that 'in many areas' mass collectivization had been initiated and realized even 'at the handicraft level', with peasants 'simply pooling their [primitive] implements'.[33] Yet Sukhanov had insistently maintained that an essential precondition for collectivization must be the prior availability of modern machinery which would make large-scale co-operative farming attractive to the peasantry because of its tangible benefits.

Stalin's policy speech sealed the fate of 380,000 communal villages, the home and workplace of the overwhelming majority of the country's peasants, indeed of its population. It also marked the end of Sukhanov, their indefatigable champion, who with singular courage had battled the Agrarian Marxists' enormous research effort to delegitimize the *obshchina* as a hearth of capitalism and had thus prepared the party, ideologically and psychologically, for Stalin's brutal assault on Russia's peasantry. Indeed, Sukhanov's last daring venture before he was arrested on 20 July 1930 was his four-week fact-finding journey in May/June of that year in the agricultural areas along the Volga, the Black Sea and the northern Caucasus to see for himself what collectivization had done to the Russian peasantry. That his detractors, led by Kritsman, who hounded, ridiculed and silenced him and finally expelled him from the Communist Academy, themselves soon fell victim to Stalin's purges does not redeem them.

Sadly enough, Western specialist studies of the agrarian debates of the 1920s,[34] with the notable exceptions of Donald J. Male and Naum Jasny,[35] have largely ignored Sukhanov *the agrarian economist* and his lone role and courageous stand in the debates that preceded collectivization; nor have they come to grips with the 'paradoxical situation' to which Moshe Lewin has drawn attention that the *obshchina* which 'stood for all the collectivist aspects of village life and which had been rooted in the village for centuries was given no part to play in the collectivization of the peasantry'.[36]

6
Sukhanov at the Menshevik Trial of March 1931

By 1928, with the end of the NEP which he had enthusiastically embraced, Sukhanov had certainly fallen foul of the Agrarian Marxist establishment. Headed by Leonid Kritsman, and entrenched in the Agrarian Institute of the Communist Academy, they had brought to their knees the distinguished non-Marxist economists of the Production Organization School, Nikolai Kondratev, Alexander Chayanov and A. Chelintsev[1] and had begun to hound their 'Marxist' and Communist rival Sergei Dubrovsky. While during the relatively relaxed mid-1920s Sukhanov's sharp critique of the Kritsman school had still been grudgingly tolerated as a contribution to the agrarian debate, by the latter part of 1928 his non-conformist views and projects were already attracting attention from the Soviet political authorities. Indeed, Sukhanov is on record on at least three separate occasions as having publicly expressed views diametrically opposed to the policies of the Soviet leadership: in a symposium on 'The Achievements and Difficulties of *Kolkhoz* Construction', chaired and introduced by A. Gaister, he had criticized the early attempts at collectivization as lacking the necessary technological base, the agricultural machinery required to make collective farms attractive to peasants, socially stable and economically viable; moreover, he had urged – as an alternative to the 'extreme measures' of the ruthless procurement campaign – the import of scarce manufactured goods to stimulate peasant production of grain and ensure its delivery to the state procurement agencies; and lastly, as we shall see, he had made, a scathing attack on Professor Vladimir Friche's project of a fierce preventive censorship of literature and publishing.[2]

Sukhanov's rather restrained critique of the early phase of collectivization was singled out for a vitriolic attack in the April 1929 issue of the theoretical Communist party journal *Bol'shevik*, where V.K. Astrov, Senior Scientific Fellow in the Institute of History of the Communist Academy, accused him of three major sins: he had closed his eyes to the growth of capitalism in the agriculture of the Soviet Union and had thus provided 'a theoretical cover-up for the *kulak* and his growing importance in the village'; he had cavalierly ignored 'the leading economic role of the dictatorship of the proletariat in the *kolkhoz* movement'. Moreover, under the cover of 'purely technical aspects', he had slipped in a theory which, with its 'class content, was alien to the proletariat and completely ignored 'the social class point of view'.[3]

Worse still, a copy of Sukhanov's paper on 'The Economic Pre-Conditions for the Improvement of Agriculture', which he had read in the Communist Academy on 4 December 1928, was sent to Viacheslav Molotov, Chairman of the Council of People's Commissars, by a certain N. Vinogradov together with the following summary:

> Comrade Molotov! This material deserves to be looked at. The lecturer is Sukhanov. Firstly, he admits indirectly to a degeneration of agriculture, referring to the 'corresponding' authorities [Vinogradov is perhaps referring to the Rightist Aleksei Rykov whom Sukhanov had quoted in his paper. IG]. Secondly, there is not a word on the social-class structure of the village, on the class struggle. Thirdly, not a word on the socialist sector (*sovkhozy, kolkhozy*). Fourthly without imports of foreign [consumer] goods, there will be no development of agriculture.[4]

Two days later, on 6 December, Sukhanov challenged Professor Vladimir Friche, the formidable chairman of the Section of Literature, the Arts and Linguistics of the Communist Academy, who had called for a vigilant preventive and repressive censorship of literature. This feat may well have been part of Sukhanov's desperate quixotic attempt to warn against that hardening of the Bolshevik 'Jacobin dictatorship' which in his view had been extending since the end of the NEP in 1927 from economics to the 'sciences and the arts, the theatre and daily life'. Friche, as his friend the Communist historian Mikhail Pokrovsky wrote in an obituary following his death in September 1929, had already distinguished himself for 'delicately and tactfully' purging 'bourgeois and philosophical idealists' from the Communist Academy and a number of faculties and journals which he headed or controlled, and replacing them with staunch Marxist-Leninists. Not satisfied with this contribution to Soviet academia, he felt duty bound as a 'publicist and Bolshevik' to harass distinguished non-Communist writers, such as Evgenii Zamyatin, Boris Pilniak, Konstantin Fedin and Ilya Ehrenburg, promoting in their stead 'proletarian writers' such as Alexander Fadeev and Fiodor Gladkov who, imbued with 'proletarian consciousness', had extolled 'proletarian heroes' and could be trusted to 'guide the psyche of the reader towards the building of a socialist society and culture'.[5] In pursuit of 'proletarian hegemony over the literature front', Friche delivered a public lecture in the Communist Academy on 6 December 1928 with the ominous title 'Bourgeois Tendencies in Contemporary Literature and the Role of Critique'.[6] There, he tried to document and denounce an allegedly dangerous proliferation of bourgeois-reactionary and nationalist literature in the Soviet Union. What was needed, he insisted, was an iron-clad Marxist-Leninist control of literature and publishing. Very much in tune with Stalin's pronouncement of 9 July 1928, that 'the class-struggle sharpens in step with the forward march to socialism',[7] Friche laid down his guidelines:

In an epoch like this, when the class struggle sharpens both in literature and in life, our Communist critique must uncover and unmask in works of literature, the clear face of the enemy hidden there. Our editors and publishing organizations must be especially on guard when putting out literary productions. None of the leading lights (*'korovannyie' litsa*) of literature can be exempted from the requirements of the hour (*'tselesoobraznost'*) [italics in the original]. We cannot afford the 'luxury' of printing reactionary material which does not serve the interests of the toiling masses. Each and every small book, before it is put out by our publishing houses, must be weighed rigorously on the scales of the needs of the hour, and, finally, good conditions must be created for those cadres of talented writers who are organically bound to our toiling masses, are imbued with our ideology and will produce works that will inspire the masses with the will to rebuild our life.[8]

Fearful that Friche's lecture may well have been the opening shot in an intensified campaign to intimidate and straitjacket Soviet writing and publishing, Sukhanov, a great believer in the freedom of the press and of publishing – he prided himself on the fact that 'throughout the entire revolution, I spoke out for the complete and unlimited freedom of the press' – rose 'all alone' to subject Friche and his lecture to a searching analysis.[9] In the first place, and granted that there were 'bourgeois tendencies' in Soviet literature, Sukhanov wanted to know what were the precise criteria by which 'bourgeois reaction' could be identified. True, anti-Semitism was 'indisputably' black reaction and 'must not be tolerated', but had not Friche gone too far in accusing Pilniak of anti-Semitism on the basis of some more than questionable indicators. In similar cavalier fashion, Friche had quoted the 'pastoral' poems of a Georgian poet and of the peasant writer Nikolai Kliuev as if 'the very motifs' of pastoralism were 'incriminating'; as if the very concept of the village was now to be rendered illegitimate. While it was true that 'we wage a struggle against the backward features of our peasant households, striving to mechanize and modernize them and to find new [organizational] forms for peasant agriculture', nonetheless the village as such, just as the town, might still, he believed, remain an object of 'poetical perception and creativity'. The same applied to those who branded as 'reactionaries' those writers who turned the spotlight on some of the negative features of Soviet life. Must poets and writers be compelled to write in celebration of the heroes of labour rather than expose those who took bribes, squandered public monies and acted as petty tyrants, he asked. A hundred years ago, he went on, such critical satire had been feted as 'progressive'; should it now be branded as criminal?! All this, Sukhanov urged, was a manifestation of panic which saw dangers 'where they do not exist' and which might lead to the 'baby being thrown out with the bath water'.

As if to counter Friche's argument that 'the outburst' of reactionary literature was the beaten class enemy's protest and consolation, Sukhanov drew attention to the fact that reactionary tendencies had made their appearance only during the past two years, 'when we have been experiencing serious economic difficulties', and not during the years 1924 to 1926, which had been 'a period of rapid economic progress'. It was only natural, he urged, that those who had been lying low during the years of 'the grand forward movement of revolution' should now come out of their holes and raise their heads, so that with the appearance of queues in front of the shops 'reactionary tones were to be heard in the [literary] journals'. Therefore, he argued, once the economic difficulties were overcome and the queues disappeared, 'reactionary literature' would also disappear. But to deal with literature in isolation and 'gag and throttle it' would impoverish and strangle both negative and positive literary creativity, unless, of course, one wanted to follow the prescription of Famusov (in Griboedov's *Woe from Wit*): 'If you want to nip the evil in the bud, collect all the books and burn them'! In conclusion, Sukhanov challenged Friche to offer that Marxist analysis of the intensified growth of reaction in literature that had been missing from his lecture.

With his critical comments grown into a counter-paper, Sukhanov had certainly thrown down the gauntlet not only before Friche but also before the entire literary establishment assembled there to listen to and loyally endorse the policy speech and guidelines of the master, Vladimir Maksimovich. Small wonder that they turned their polemical fire against him, with P.M. Kerzhentsev, deputy chairman of the Communist Academy, who chaired the public meeting, setting the tone. He accused Sukhanov of using Famusov and the censorship of Tsar Nicholas as a stick with which to beat those who want to control literature. 'He's telling us that we are just as bad as the *gendarmes* of Nicholas, every bit as evil as the censors who strangled everything that was new and fresh.' That was Sukhanov's real, though disguised position, 'and how like all those who, in the epoch of the dictatorship of the proletariat, do not speak openly'. 'Yes,' he told Sukhanov, 'we do favour throttling. We make no secret of our intent to strangle hostile literary tendencies, because we know perfectly well that in the ideological struggle under the dictatorship of the proletariat it is necessary to have recourse to strangling. We reject outright all Sukhanov's liberal counsels. In our view, we may order Kliuev and Sergei Klychkov to write in praise of industrialization, in praise of the proletariat and in praise of the town even though their hearts may not be in it ... We and Sukhanov occupy very different positions. He believes that some genuine literature will ultimately emerge from free, spontaneous, intellectual creativity with our role being merely to stand and watch from the side. We, however, see ourselves as combatants in a historical battle, a class struggle, and as such we will conduct as active a policy with regard to *belles-lettres* as we do in all other areas.' [applause!]

Other speakers followed suit in the same vein, though more explicitly and brutally. A.A. Isbakh, denounced Sukhanov's suggestion – that one should wait until the economic difficulties had been overcome – as a 'Menshevik conception of revolution and a philosophy of fatalism and pessimism'. Marxist criticism, he argued, should apply three methods in the ideological struggle to influence the literary process: 'transfer certain writers, terrorize others and cut off (*otsech'*) yet others'.

I.M. Nusinov accused Sukhanov of all but justifying 'the rightwing deviation in literature'. Criticism must have recourse to 'all those weapons which Vladimir Maksimovich has outlined' and must not be satisfied to use only the weapon of persuasion. Moreover speeches such as that of Sukhanov must be 'decisively rebuffed ... such criticism is legitimate when it comes from a friend, from a Communist, but criticism aimed at undermining faith is illegitimate, for it is nothing but a malevolent calumny'. I.M. Bespalov, said that he had not originally intended to speak, but having heard Sukhanov, felt that he must tell him that 'in the sharpening of the class struggle within our economy, the question is simply *kto kogo* – who (devours) whom'.

Winding up the debate, Friche denounced Sukhanov's 'non-Marxist, non-dialectical understanding of the growth of reactionary elements in literature'. He urged him to seek the roots of such growth in 'the reaction of all non-socialist, non-proletarian, *kulak*, petty-bourgeois and intelligentsia elements who are ever more tightly squeezed as the position of the proletariat and the socialist economy advances – the more they are squeezed, the more they express their protest in literature.[10]

Having thus challenged major policies of the Bolshevik regime in the process of Stalinization, Sukhanov went even further and, beginning in October 1928, for the next year and a half he regularly hosted Open Sundays in his study in the Second House of Soviets. To that '*salon*' he invited like-minded economists such as Groman, Nikolai Kondratev and Bazarov and a mixed bag of former Mensheviks and SRs including Fiodor Cherevanin, N. Kapelinsky, Osip Ermansky, Tigran Aniev and Pavel Maliantovich, minister of justice in the last coalition government, as well as some of his wife's artistic and literary friends.[11] At those meetings, the burning issues of the day were discussed. Some of those who visited the *salon*, later found themselves under OGPU investigation or together with

Sukhanov in the dock. Small wonder that an anonymous letter in the Nicolaevsky Collection at the Hoover Institution, Stanford, jocularly described Sukhanov's role in his Open Sundays as that of an 'unwitting *provocateur'*.[12] What is surprising however is that at the very same time that he dared so openly to challenge official policies, he also completed his accommodation with the Soviet regime: in January 1927, in a published autobiographical essay, he renounced as 'mistaken, all that I have written until 1921 in my assessment of the Communist Party and of its role in the revolution'[13] – and that certainly included substantial sections of his *Zapiski o revoliutsii*. He followed that up in a pathetic review of the Russian press of 1917 to the point of blackening his very own *Novaia zhizn'* of 1917–18 in which – and for very good reason – he had taken so much pride.[14] At the same time, and in the same vein, he consented to the publication of a new, abridged, edition of his *Zapiski* which was to be edited and annotated by the historian Pokrovsky.[15] The extent to which this edition, which was never published, would have been brought in line with the official Communist version of the 1917 revolution can only be gauged from the play *The Year 1917 – a dramatic chronicle in five acts*. The original text of that play, written by Sukhanov himself, was subsequently 'reworked by him with the assistance of the Honourable Producer ... of the Malyi Theatre, I.S. Platon'. Moreover, Platon, 'without Sukhanov's participation', himself wrote seven scenes of the first, third and fourth acts.[16]

While the play's motto 'How many ages hence/shall this our lofty scene be acted over/in states unborn and accents yet unknown', taken from Shakespeare's *Julius Caesar* (Act III, Scene 1), reiterates Sukhanov's belief in the greatness and universality of the Russian revolution, the play itself, unlike the original *Zapiski*, is filled with mass scenes and is largely concerned with ridiculing the Bolsheviks' adversaries – from the tsarist ministers, the Octobrists and the Liberals, to the Mensheviks and the Socialist Revolutionaries. Not unexpectedly, some of the major Bolshevik figures of the revolution, such as Trotsky, Kamenev and Zinoviev, are totally absent, so that Trotsky's famous 'rubbish bin of history' speech was delivered 'from behind the scenes by the voice of the [anonymous] first member of the Military Revolutionary Committee' who also made the victory speech.[17]

The play's première took place on the eve of the tenth anniversary of the October revolution, whereafter it had a further 44 performances, remaining in the repertoire of the Malyi Theatre for a further year. A reading of the printed text, published in 1928, confirms the verdict of Mikhail Kalinin, chairman of the Executive Committee of Soviets, that 'the language of the play is poor, it lacks lively dialogue and is didactic rather than revolutionary'.[18] While its talented, non-conformist author apparently paid a heavy price for toeing the line to the point of producing an anaemic and castrated play, that certainly did not prevent his political delegitimation. Indeed, the publication of two of his books was suddenly cancelled though both had already been passed by the censors and had taken all other publishing hurdles.[19] The first was the already-mentioned revised and abridged version of the *Zapiski* which had been commissioned by the publications section of the Central Committee of the Communist Party; the second was 'An Introduction to Political Economy', commissioned by the State Publishing House (*GIZ*), which had already been typeset and printed on its hard-won paper allocation – nevertheless its publication was cancelled and the type and printed pages were destroyed. In neither case were the real reasons for cancellation given, although in both cases Sukhanov received the large payments due to him because of the publisher's breach of contract.[20] For him, the fate of his books was 'a manifestation of the regime of terror which was then developing' and he suspected that the publishers feared that their list of publications would be compromised by his very name. His 'Introduction to Political Economy' may also have fallen victim to the instructions of the head of *Glavlit* P.I. Lebedev-Polyansky of 7 March 1927 which prohibited the publication of 'economic literature of an anti-Marxist content' and permitted the publication of 'non-Marxist economic literature only in small editions provided that it was of scientific interest or of practical significance'.[21]

Events reached a climax at the All-Union Conference of Agrarian Marxists at the end of December 1929 when, after more than a dozen speakers had gone through the ritual of denouncing Sukhanov, M. Kubanin, Kritsman's hatchet man, insisting that this was a matter of a 'non-vegetarian nature', questioned the legitimacy of Sukhanov's membership of the Communist Academy. 'Sukhanov', he said, 'is not a Marxist, but our Communist Academy must be Communist in the full sense of the word.' And he urged the drawing of 'the corresponding organizational conclusions'.[22] Sukhanov's fate as an agrarian economist was finally sealed when

Stalin, on 27 December 1929, instructed delegates to the conference on their duty as 'Communist comrades':[23]

The Marxist elaboration of [theoretical problems] enables us to tear out by the roots all varieties of bourgeois theories which, to our shame, are sometimes spread by our Communist comrades and which muddle the heads of our practical workers. Those theories should have been extirpated and thrown out long ago, for only by merciless struggle against them can the theoretical thought of Marxists grow and gain strength.

It was Kritsman himself who, at last, on 17 June 1930, at the plenum of the Communist Academy, moved 'on behalf of the Communist faction' that Sukhanov be expelled from the Communist Academy. Proposing the motion, he said it was more than strange that Sukhanov had not long since been expelled:[24]

As we know, N.N. Sukhanov never was a Marxist: he was a *Narodnik*; he was and remains a Revisionist and he was always hostile to Marxism. Lenin attacked Sukhanov both before and after the October revolution as a representative of anti-Marxist views. Indeed, he did fight Marxism both before and after the October revolution and even within the portals of the Communist Academy itself. And even now he continues to maintain that he is right in his polemics against Marxism. He has thus remained an ideological adversary of Marxism. Therefore, I repeat, his membership of this Marxist-Leninist Academy that was always strange, is by now completely untenable in a time of sharpening class struggle within the country and at a time when the struggle on the ideological front is also becoming ever more fierce. I thus consider that my proposal to expel N.N. Sukhanov from the Communist Academy is more than well-founded.

The hounding, delegitimation and expulsion of Sukhanov by his Agrarian-Marxist colleagues was followed on 20 July 1930 by his arrest by the OGPU, probably in connection with preparations for the trial of a so-called Labouring Peasant Party allegedly led by Kondratev and Chayanov who had themselves been arrested on 17 June. Following their arrest, Sukhanov's colleague and friend the economist Groman was also arrested on 13 July.

Henceforth, and in the absence of any other reliable source of information such as Sukhanov's personal papers or other writings, one way of understanding his position *vis-à-vis* the tightening of the Bolshevik regime and Stalin's onslaught on the Russian peasantry is via a careful, but always sceptical study of the protocols of the preliminary investigations by the OGPU as well as of some of his statements during the Menshevik trial.

On the very day that Sukhanov was arrested, Groman, who had been arrested a week earlier, was questioned about him by the OGPU investigator Yakov Agranov, the notorious and very able head of the Secret Section of the OGPU. Groman reported to Agranov that Sukhanov had had access to emigré and foreign newspapers as a member of the Communist Academy and had also been kept 'well informed by the Moscow correspondent of the *Koelnische Zeitung*, Arthur Just'. 'Every Sunday', Groman testified, 'meetings had been held in Sukhanov's study in the Second House of Soviets,' and he listed the names of those who were usually present.[25]

Just over three weeks later, on 14 August, if not before, Sukhanov himself was investigated by Agranov, who questioned him on Kondratev and on his own political views. Sukhanov denied all knowledge of any Labouring Peasant Party: no one, he said, had ever in his presence referred to himself as being a member of such a party. Moreover, since he, Sukhanov, was known as a revolutionary Marxist and a supporter of the Third International, no leader of such a party would ever have confided in him. 'Even Kondratev, despite our close personal relationship, assumed [erroneously] that I was a member of the German Communist Party.' Sukhanov himself thought that 'should the area of legality ever widen', then the formation of a peasant party would be 'inevitable and legitimate' because of 'the social structure of our country' and the traditions of 'significant cadres of our intelligentsia who would be leading that party'. But such a party, were it to be formed and headed by a Kondratev and his like, would have nothing new to offer by way of ideology or programme compared with the Socialist Revolutionaries or their offshoots and would therefore have to fuse with them.

As for his own views, he shared with Kondratev a negative attitude to the Soviet government's agrarian policy as it had developed since 1927. But in his case, that did not extend to the party's 'general line on industrialization and the collectivization of agricul-

Fig. 6.1 Kondratev

ture', as could be gauged from his own writings. His real quarrel was with the party's 'break with the NEP and its shift towards War Communism' which he believed was 'detrimental to socialism, a threat to socialist construction', and increased 'the danger of [bourgeois] restoration'. Moreover, the economic difficulties that stemmed from such mistaken policies were, he feared, bound to create political upheaval. As a revolutionary socialist who had accepted the October revolution and the system of proletarian dictatorship as guaranteeing the further development of socialism and the prevention of a 'bourgeois restoration', he had, later in 1928, prepared a paper (which was already in the hands of the OGPU) on a programme of 'inevitable and necessary concessions by the regime'. It included the following points: 1) acceptance of the principles of the NEP as practised between 1923 and 1926, and 2) a widening of the area of Soviet legality with a corresponding democratization of the regime of the proletarian dictatorship to be extended to all who accepted the principles of the October revolution and the further development of socialism. Freedom of speech, of the press, of elections and of assembly would be limited to those 'public elements and political parties who accepted the fundamentals of the October revolution'. That meant acceptance of the Soviet Constitution, of the Basic Law on Land, of the nationalization of industries and of the state monopoly of external trade. These were the principles of his 'clipped constitution', Sukhanov told Agranov and, far from being directed against the Soviet system, they were intended rather to save it from upheaval. Recently, however, since the spring of 1929, when government policy had turned increasingly towards 'War Communism', he had lost faith in any possibility of a return to the NEP so long as the present party leadership continued in control. Should the system collapse as a result of economic disaster or military intervention, then, and only then, would it be possible to forge an alliance with parties of the Second International or with a peasant party.[26]

Three days after this, on 17 August, Groman was again investigated by Agranov who asked him about Sukhanov's political views. Sukhanov, Groman said, was convinced that the government's economic policy was leading to the 'degeneration of agriculture and to a food crisis'. In the autumn of 1929, when it was clear that the party was bent on rooting out every last remnant of capitalism, Sukhanov had worked out a programme to preserve the basic achievements of the October revolution such as the nationalization of the land, railways, heavy industry and the state monopoly of external trade. But at the same time, Sukhanov's programme envisaged complete freedom in the circulation of goods and of crafts, a free press and freedom for the trade unions, free elections and a political amnesty (except for those directly involved in intervention). It was Groman's impression that Sukhanov wanted 'a Soviet state power system, but without its soul: i.e. the dictatorship of the proletariat was to be retained only in appearance, but "democratized" in the sense of moving towards bourgeois democracy'. Sukhanov, who had initially been hostile to the October revolution, had gradually moved closer and closer to Soviet state power, so much so that in the wake of the NEP he had, so he told Groman, disowned as 'erroneous' all that he had written against the Bolsheviks. But after the sharp left-turn taken by the Party in the wake of its Fifteenth Congress of December 1927, Sukhanov had turned to the right, Groman thought, in the direction of the 'right-ist deviation' in the Communist party, but later he envisaged the Bolsheviks' 'overthrow' or 'bankruptcy'. And yet, for all that, he would still fight against bourgeois restoration. In Groman's opinion, Sukhanov's position was at best a 'self-deception', for, like his own, it was in fact 'counter-revolutionary'.[27]

What emerges quite clearly from the August interrogations of both Sukhanov and Groman is that there was not so much as a mention of their 'Menshevism' and certainly not of any so-called Union Bureau of the Central Committee of the RSDRP (Mensheviks) which apparently had not as yet been invented in preparation for the Menshevik trial held in Moscow from 1 to 8 March 1931. Nor is there any mention of Menshevism in Stalin's letter to Molotov from his holiday in Sochi (not earlier than 23 August 1930), although that same letter ordered (a month after the event) the 'obligatory arrest of Sukhanov, Bazarov and [Professor] L.K. Ramzin' as well as 'the roughing up of [Galina Flakserman] Sukhanov's wife (a Communist!) who must have known of the scandalous things being carried on in their home'.[28] While it is difficult to establish the causal chain of events and of arrests, it is most likely that the arrests of Groman and Sukhanov were related to Kondratev's so-called (and fictitious) Labouring Peasant Party case. As Stalin's 6 August 1930 letter to Molotov made clear, he attributed 'very great importance' to the case of Kondratev–Groman–[P.A.] Sadyrin (a director of the Gosbank) and he ordered it to be investigated 'with the utmost thor-oughness (*sic*! I.G.) and without haste': 'I have no doubt' wrote Stalin, that 'it uncovers a *direct* link between these gentlemen (through [Grigorii] Sokolnikov and [I.A.] Teodorovich) and the Rightists (Bukharin, Rykov, [Mikhail] Tomsky). Kondratev, Groman and another couple of scoundrels must certainly be shot'.[29]

Some of Sukhanov's testimonies in preliminary investigations – such as those relating to intervention, collectivization, War Communism and Jacobin dictatorship, as distinct from those relat-ing to his fictitious activities in the so-called Union Bureau of the Central Committee of the RSDRP (Mensheviks) – were unusually frank and appear to reflect his real views. Pride of place goes to his testimony on intervention. On 1 October 1930 the investigator, Yosif Chertok, apparently asked him what his attitude to intervention had been during the Manchurian crisis in the latter part of 1929. Sukhanov gave a clear and emphatic answer:

> I am absolutely sure that none of my acquaintances has ever expressed any sympathy whatsoever in my presence for the interventionist plans of the Western powers ... . As for my personal attitude to intervention – if it is still in need of clarification, I have always seen intervention as a most terrible catastrophe which must at all costs be prevented. This is my view today and such it has always been ... . I declare: whoever says that I at any time and in whatever circumstance whether directly or indirectly have expressed myself otherwise or have let it be understood or have secretly harboured a different attitude to intervention from the one I have just indicated – that person is guilty of the worst sort of lie and the greatest infamy.[30]

That emphatic statement may perhaps have been responsible for Sukhanov not having been assigned any direct personal role on 'intervention' during the Menshevik trial; all he apparently had to do was to confess to a very general and indirect involvement when, at the trial, he declared that 'for me, the acceptance of Menshevism also meant the acceptance of interventionism, for I could not and cannot separate one from the other'.[31]

Sukhanov identified the 'extreme measures' of War Communism (1918 to 1920) as the original sin of Bolshevik economic policy. As he put it during his interrogation and in his autobiographical deposition of 29–30 January 1931, War Communism was

> an elementary economic absurdity: it aimed at forcing the petty producer to produce and exchange his commodity without getting anything in return, something that can only be achieved under conditions of a fully-fledged slave economy.[32]

And he regarded the Communist Party, 'the progenitor of the idea and policy of War Communism', as responsible for 'the greatest calamities and evils that any government can inflict on its country'.

It filled him with particular 'hatred and anger' even though it did not prevent him from being active in 'organic work' in the Soviet apparatus.[33] But, as we shall see, he extended his frequent use of the term War Communism to describe the Bolsheviks' brutal procurement campaigns, the *dekulakization* and forced collectivization of the 1928 to 1930 period.

If War Communism was Sukhanov's shorthand for all Bolshevik economic policies based on 'extra-economic compulsion', he used the term 'Jacobin dictatorship' as a synonym for the Bolshevik dictatorial *regime*, as distinct from the Bolshevik Soviet *system*, for he had accepted the latter and tried to make it his own.

As early as autumn 1917, so Sukhanov claimed during the 29–30 January 1930 interrogation, he had warned that 'the Bolsheviks in power' were bound to form a Jacobin dictatorship.[34] And, as it emerged from his *Zapiski o revoliutsii*, it was the Bolsheviks' 'naked Jacobinism, the tactics of total Jacobinism' – which deterred him from throwing in his lot with them.[35] Even when the NEP was inaugurated in March 1921, he had at first been sceptical, for he had not thought it was compatible with and could survive in a Jacobin dictatorship.[36] He soon realized, however, that he had been wrong and he became an enthusiastic NEP supporter and propagandist. But in 1928–29 when he witnessed the tightening up of the regime and the return to what he thought were the economic policies of War Communism, he came back to his earlier view, because of his realization that analogous with the Jacobin dictatorship of the French Revolution

> inherent in a Jacobin dictatorship is a thoroughly terrorist project [extending] to all spheres of state activity, politics, law, the economy and culture, also inherent in it is – a catastrophic finale.[37]

Armed with his conceptions of War Communism and Jacobin dictatorship, on 22 January 1931, Sukhanov presented his investigator Dmitriev with a detailed and remarkable survey of collectivization, most likely in answer to the question of what his views on the subject were.[38] That survey was based on a month-long fact-finding journey to the Volga area, the Northern Caucasus, the Black Sea region and the Crimea (an area he knew well from high-school vacation trips) undertaken between mid-May and 14 June 1930 'with the aim of seeing everything for himself, to make sure of many things, and to draw conclusions' as he reported to Boris Bogdanov during his visit to Simferopol in June 1930. Sukhanov, painted a vivid picture:[39] there were vast under-sowings, even worse grain collections, approaching famine, and peasants abandoning their homesteads in such numbers as to constitute a mass exodus (he saw 80,000 in Stalingrad), here and there (in the Northern Central Black Soil region) some peasant uprisings, a general increase in discontent ... '. He prefaced his testimony of 22 January 1931[40] with his long-held agrarian credo that 'the socialization and organization of agriculture on collectivist foundations is historically legitimate and inevitable because of the technical-economic superiority of large-scale over small-scale farming'. But, he insisted, 'real collectivization' must be preceded by 'a revolution in the means of production, and based on new technology, on the machine.' Therefore, the Soviet government's attempts 'to plant collective farms relying purely on manual labour but without a prior transformation of the technical base are harmful, reactionary and a revival of old *narodnik* utopias'. Not surprisingly, he did not mention that other condition – that the peasants, attracted by benefits derived from mechanization, would band together and work the land collectively where previously, though they owned it in common, they had worked it individually.

Sukhanov then proceeded to characterize the first phase of collectivization which he considered had lasted until the spring of 1928: it had been 'insignificant and inconsequential economically, politically and ideologically'. These early collective farms were isolated enterprises lavishly supplied by the state for show purposes; they sometimes prospered on state funds but were economically and commercially unprofitable.

The second phase, which he saw as lasting from the beginning of 1928 until the autumn of 1929, was one of mass collectivization. The state had been unable to supply those collective farms with even the most ordinary means of production to say nothing of anything more advanced and they had had a negative effect on the economy as well as proving costly to the state. Indeed, contrary to the conclusions of the Central Statistical Administration, these farms had produced lower yields per acre than had individual holdings in the same areas.

The third phase of the collectivization movement, which had begun in autumn 1929, far exceeded all plans and expectations in terms of the numbers of peasants involved. And this had come about because it had coincided with the procurement campaigns with their intolerable and ruinous requisitioning raids which caused a mass flight of peasants into collective farms. The peasants thought that, as had happened before (during the first and second phases), the state would not only not harm them but might even provide them with assistance in the collective farms. The flight into the *kolkhozy* had gone hand in hand with the degradation of the peasantry, as panic sales of inventory, notably livestock, wiped out an enormous part of the peasants' basic capital. Thus, collectivization had become a major disaster for the village and had dealt a tremendous blow to the country's productive forces. Moreover the collective farms of the third phase were unorganized and unworkable and the state had no means whatever to provide any significant assistance. The slogan 'Liquidation of the *kulaks* as a class' had naturally enough resulted in the so-called *dekulakization* which supplied the tens of thousands of collective farms with implements and whatever other means of production there were. The net result was a redivision of property supported and sanctioned from above, in the course of which the upper and prosperous half of the village was expropriated in favour of the lower and collectivized half. The result of that was likely to produce a catastrophic increase in difficulties and distress.

Sukhanov's incisive and damning analysis of collectivization remained buried in the files of the OGPU's preliminary investigation of 22 January 1931.[41]

Until there is a fully-fledged study of the Menshevik show trial of March 1931, it is only possible to reach some tentative assessment of the motives of its organizers and stage-managers.[42] Indeed, the term 'Menshevik trial' is somewhat of a misnomer. Apart from the indisputable fact that the so-called Union Bureau of the RSDRP (Mensheviks) never existed, of the fourteen defendants only one – Vladimir Ikov, could still have been regarded at the time as a Menshevik; Alexander Finn-Enotaevsky had a Bolshevik past; Aron Sokolovsky had been a member of the United Jewish Socialist Workers party (known as *Varainikte*); Mikhail Yakubovich and Kirill Petunin had been Mensheviks only until the end of 1920, while all the others, including Sukhanov and Groman, had long ago even formally severed their ties with the Menshevik party, and had loyally served the Soviet state in important positions on the State Planning Commission, the Supreme Economic Planning Council, the Commissariat of Trade, the Central Trade Union Council, and as professors in academic institutions. What seems already well-established is that the Menshevik trial formed part of a series of grim show-trials that began with the so-called Shakhty trial of May–July 1928, when a large number of non-Communist and foreign engineers working in the Donets Basin were tried for industrial sabotage and wrecking allegedly on orders from abroad; that was followed by the trial, in 1930, of the so-called Industrial Party allegedly led by Professor L.K. Ramzin, director of the Thermo-Technological Institute, who was accused of interventionist and wrecking activities; and a secret trial in December 1930 of the so-called Labouring Peasant Party, allegedly led by Kondratev and Chayanov.

What all these trials have in common is that responsibility for the procurement crisis, the failure of economic planning, the galloping inflation, the goods famine and the long queues in front of the shops was pinned on the alleged sabotage and wrecking activities of non-Communist specialists (*spetsy*) employed as planners, managers and economists. They were conducted against a backdrop of a vicious and vast press campaign of vilification of the fellow-travelling intelligentsia which reached its climax in a pamphlet *Onward to the Struggle against Wrecking* published in one million copies, printed in bold type and written by none other than the State Prosecutor Krylenko. Here, Krylenko called for 'proletarian vigilance' and appealed to 'every worker and conscious peasant' to take an active part in purging all the enemies of Soviet state power from all Soviet institutions so that their places could be taken by 'our worker-promotees, our Red specialists'.[43]

But what distinguished the Menshevik trial from its predecessors was its political-international dimension which connected it with Stalin's and the Comintern's offensive against the alleged 'social-fascism' of the social democratic parties of the West organized in the Second Socialist International and against the pathetic remnants of Menshevism in Russia and in emigration, cast in the role of the 'All-Russian battalion of international social fascism'.[44] It thus seems to have formed part of Stalin's attempt to use the world economic crisis and the 'revolutionized situation' and 'the hoped-for collapse of the social democratic illusions of the working masses' to turn 'the fraternal Communist parties ... into large mass parties of the working class'. But the world crisis, Stalin urged, had also increased the 'danger of intervention' and the temptation of the capitalist imperialists to solve all problems at 'the expense of the USSR, the citadel of revolution'; they were enlisting 'our experts' to serve as the 'agents of foreign states' and organize wrecking in preparation for military intervention.[45] Stalin's call was, of course, taken up in July 1930 and in April 1931 by the Comintern which diagnosed 'the unbroken process of the evolution of [Social Democracy] towards fascism' which had culminated in efforts to 'prepare a blockade and a war of intervention against the world's first proletarian state'.[46]

At the Menshevik trial, Krylenko adopted Stalin's terminology and style in his summing up speech on 6 March 1931. He sneered at the defendants, some of them outstanding members of the Russian intelligentsia: 'They call themselves socialists, veteran socialists, learned socialists and on top of all that – scholarly specialists, and they turn into wreckers, worse still – interventionists, socialist wreckers, and on top of that – socialist interventionists ... they are "socialist-fascists"'.[47]

Pravda next morning promptly congratulated Krylenko, 'Prosecutor of the Proletarian Revolution' on having exposed 'with facts and documents the treacherous role of the Menshevik-Interventionists, the All-Russian detachment of social fascism' who, with their wrecking work, dare to 'stir up hunger, ruin and discontent in the country'.[48]

What must have been particularly hurtful to Sukhanov was the prominent and treacherous role of Maxim Gorky in the campaign against the non-Bolshevik intelligentsia in general and specifically against Sukhanov himself after his and Bazarov's arrest had been reported in the newspapers. On 2 November 1930, Gorky wrote from Sorrento to his friend the Deputy Chairman of the OGPU Genrikh Yagoda:

I am not surprised that that lad Sukhanov, with his morbid self-love and his adventurer's psychology, finds himself in the dock – though I can't understand how Bazarov's scepticism would land him in the same position ... . I would have loved to travel to the trial just to take a look at the ugly mugs of the has-beens and to listen to their speeches. But I fear that I have neither the strength nor the time, for there is so much work to be done.[49]

On the same day that he wrote to Yagoda, Gorky also wrote to Stalin, telling him how 'deeply shocked' he was by the reports of 'new acts of wrecking' and 'the role of rightist tendencies in them'. He thanked Stalin for his note of 24 October and for his greetings and in particular for 'the new materials on wreckers' that Stalin had collected and was sending him after hearing that he was writing 'a play about wreckers'. He, Gorky, had almost given up on the play: 'It is not working; there is little material.'[50]

Stalin followed up his promise on 10 January 1931 with material on 'Kondratev' [presumably in connection with the latter's so-called Labouring Peasant Party] and on 'the Mensheviks' [presumably in connection with the so-called Union Bureau of Mensheviks]. But, Stalin begged Gorky, 'Don't take the contents of the documents too much to heart as their heroes do not deserve it. After all, there are worse scoundrels around than these tricksters.'[51]

But for whatever reason, Gorky – despite Stalin's prodding – did not write the envisaged play, 'Somov and Others', but instead, on 15 November, he published a ferocious article in *Izvestiia* under the title 'If the Enemy Does Not Surrender – One Exterminates Him'.[52] In that piece, Soviet Russia's foremost writer called for a civil war of extermination against 'the large numbers of traitorous [experts]' who, in the service of 'the scheming bandits of European capitalism' engaged 'in wrecking inside the Soviet Union'. Their places, he noted with relish, were already being taken by 'hundreds of talented promotees – shock workers, worker-correspondents, writers and inventors' who continued to rise from the ranks of the working class and the peasantry to form their 'own new intellectual cadres'. One month later, on the thirteenth anniversary of the Soviet press, he followed this up with an article, 'In Lieu of Greetings',[53] graced by a large photograph of himself. There, as a 'veteran newspaperman', he congratulated fellow Soviet journalists 'on their brilliant role' in the 'energetic and aggressive' battle of exposure, notably of the 'has-beens' … .and of hounding them to despair. For, 'to reduce the enemy to despair is one half of the victory! And for this, comrades, I salute you!' Gorky, it is assumed, was obliquely fingering Sukhanov,

Bazarov and Groman, his former colleagues and friends on the *Sovremennik*, the *Letopis'* and *Novaia zhizn'*.

Judging by Sukhanov's performance at the trial, the special contribution its managers had assigned to him was to highlight and expose the treacherous role played by Western social democracy and Menshevism: their 'specific function' was to neutralize the resistance of the European working class to the preparation for a war of intervention against the Soviet Union, by, for example, brainwashing them with 'the fairy tale of Red imperialism'. One major task of the trial of the 'Menshevik-Interventionists' was, as *Pravda* and *Izvestiia* put it again and again and in banner headlines on their front pages, 'to put into the pillory of history the Dans and Abramoviches, the Gromans and Sukhanovs, the entire social-fascist International who have ruined the national economy of the proletarian state and have prepared intervention and war'.[54]

Sukhanov, with his superb knowledge of Menshevism and European socialism, and with his journalistic talent, produced, in his final speech, a very tendentious potted history of Menshevism, a depressing mixture of half-truths and plain lies which attributed Menshevism's alleged fall from grace and subsequent history of betrayal to its very birth in 1903. He prefaced his indictment with a ritualistic genuflection to Lenin:

Just as [George] Cuvier, the experimental naturalist, could completely reconstruct the evolution of an antediluvian animal by means of one vertebra or tooth, so Lenin, the greatest revolutionary of all times and nations, was already able to discern, as early as the [second] congress [of the RSDRP] in 1903, that barricade which divides revolutionary socialism from the Mensheviks' alliance with the bourgeoisie. For this, Lenin had to have been a prophet, for all he had to go on was [the division between the future Mensheviks and Bolsheviks on] the first point of the party statute [which defined party membership]. I regard this as one of the greatest manifestations of Lenin's genius which enabled him to build his party in a manner all his own and never before seen in history, and then to lead it towards the first, never before heard of, proletarian victory. Lenin's prophecy soon came true. That barricade which he had already discerned in 1903, divided and still divides the Menshevik liquidators [of the underground party], reformists, defensists [during the war], allies of the bourgeoisie [in 1917], [today's] wreckers and interventionists from revolutionary socialism … . Thus, in order to achieve bourgeois restoration, the Mensheviks even now, as earlier, use military intervention and disorganization.[55]

Sukhanov, with his indictment of Menshevism, and of his own alleged role as one of the five leading members of the Union Bureau, certainly lived up to the expectations of the trial's organizers. But, unlike his co-defendants who co-operated meekly with the prosecution, Sukhanov, while accepting general responsibility for the counter-revolutionary activities of the Union Bureau, denied all Krylenko's accusations of involvement – 'on a par with the other defendants' – in 'concrete acts of wrecking'. That cat-and-mouse play between Krylenko and Sukhanov centred on two issues: in the first place, Krylenko sought to implicate Sukhanov in 'concrete organizing and wrecking activities', while Sukhanov insisted on his largely theoretical, ideological and literary role as a member of the 'General Staff' of the Union Bureau, admitting only to some very minor organizational and technical assignments; these Krylenko and the Deputy Prosecutor G.K. Roginsky went to great lengths to inflate. Secondly, Krylenko, making ample use of Sukhanov's confessions during the preliminary investigations from mid-January throughout February, inflated Sukhanov's so-called *salon* or 'Open Sundays' as having served as a recruiting ground for 'knocking together a counter-revolutionary army' and subsequently as a meeting place for the leaders of the Union Bureau, Professor Ramzin's Industrial Party and the Labouring Peasant Party where they allegedly plotted the creation of a counter-revolutionary alliance or *bloc*. Sukhanov, for his part, parried Krylenko's accusations by minimizing and trivializing 'my so-called *salon* with its three chairs and tea [served] without sugar' where the action was limited to discussions of the burning issues of the day.[56]

Only once did Sukhanov appear to get the better of Krylenko. At issue was his alleged major role in the 'negotiations' between the Union Bureau and the Industrial Party on co-operation and co-ordination of their 'counter-revolutionary' activities. In his deposition during the preliminary investigation of 26 January 1931, Sukhanov had confessed to holding a lengthy meeting with Ramzin in the latter's home where they discussed 'tactics for the overthrow of the dictatorship of the proletariat'. He also admitted to having phoned and called on Ramzin on three occasions to collect 'a subsidy for the Union Bureau to be used for wrecking' – the money totalling fifty thousand rubles. Altogether, Sukhanov confessed to

> being grievously guilty of direct contacts with [the Industrial Party], fully aware that it was a capitalist organization and engaged in espionage [against the Soviet Union]; that I personally received monies from it for the purpose of overthrowing the dictatorship of the proletariat and destroying the workers' state in the interests of international capital.[57]

Krylenko, in presenting the indictment – which he signed on 23 February 1931 – paraded Sukhanov's deposition as evidence of relations with and agreements between the Union Bureau and the Industrial Party and as an example of Sukhanov's 'more practical role in wrecking and financing'.[58] But in court, during the evening session of 3 March, Sukhanov insisted under cross-examination that he had 'opposed the very idea of a *bloc* [with the Industrial Party]. My attitude to such a *bloc* was totally negative' even to the extent of trying to sabotage it. But he did admit that he had subsequently 'capitulated', not feeling himself strong enough and 'knowing that in the end my demands would remain unfulfilled'. When asked by Vladimir Antonov-Saratovsky, a member of the court and a veteran Bolshevik, to explain what his reasons had been, Sukhanov replied that for someone with 'my views and my history', there could be no possibility at all of any *bloc* with a party which 'was clearly a party of bourgeois restoration ... of the dictatorship of capital ... and obviously fascist'. When pressed further by Antonov-Saratovsky as to why, then, he had allowed himself to be chosen by the Union Bureau to take part in negotiations with the Industrial Party, Sukhanov replied: 'I must say, I was not really chosen for the negotiations.'[59] It was then Ramzin's turn to take the stand (as a witness for the prosecution) and testify to the co-operation between the Union Bureau and the Industrial Party. Referring to the Menshevik leadership group as of 'great value ... since they occupied some senior posts in the State Planning Commission and the Council of the National Economy', he thought that 'as far as I know, right from the beginning, Sukhanov, too, belonged to that group. Personally, I did not conduct any negotiations with Sukhanov and therefore cannot report in any detail on his part in that matter.'[60] Testifying later on a conference (allegedly held in February 1930) of representatives of the two organizations together with the Labouring Peasant Party, Ramzin, apparently poorly briefed, remembered that the 'Mensheviks present included Groman and, it seems, Sukhanov. I say it seems, because I hardly knew Sukhanov and may therefore be mistaken.'[61] Whereupon, Sukhanov, who may well have seen this as his chance to backtrack on his deposition of 26 January, turned 'from his seat' to the court chairman N.M. Shvernik: 'May I put a question?

Shvernik: Please!

Sukhanov: I would like to ask the witness whether he has ever seen me, and if so, where?

Ramzin: I can presently say 'No!'

Krylenko: Have you met?

Ramzin: I think not, and therefore I say it hesitantly: perhaps I have seen him, and perhaps not. Altogether, I saw Sukhanov only once and I have difficulty in recognizing him. I did not state it categorically earlier and now, too, cannot say that Sukhanov was at that conference.

Sukhanov: I would like to know more precisely whether it still seems to the witness that he saw me at that conference?

Ramzin: I can only say that at that aforementioned February conference, there were more Mensheviks present than I can recall. But again I want to repeat that my recollection of people is not good enough for me to state categorically whether or not Sukhanov was at that conference. Perhaps he was, perhaps he wasn't. (Laughter in the hall).

Groman: Sukhanov was not at that conference.

Krylenko: I have a question for Sukhanov. Have you never met Ramzin?

Sukhanov: It seems to me that we have never met.

Krylenko: What representatives of the Industrial Party did you meet?

Sukhanov: On the matter of business negotiations, I met no one. I have been trying to recollect whom I could ever have met who is known to belong to the Industrial Party. But I can recall no such person.

Krylenko: You cannot?

Sukhanov: Exactly.

Krylenko: For the time being I have no more questions for Sukhanov.

Chairman: Comrade Commandant: take the witness [Ramzin] away.[62]

Krylenko must have smarted under the setback that Sukhanov inflicted on him. The next day, at the end of his cross-examination of Sukhanov, he asked him pointedly: 'I am still interested in one question which concerns you personally: does the testimony which you gave here concur with those depositions you made earlier?' Sukhanov: 'Yes!'[63] Thus far the laconic text of the allegedly *stenographic* report of the trial. *Pravda*'s report of that particular incident is not only fuller but also more revealing:

Krylenko: As a result of your confrontation yesterday with Ramzin, I have the impression that some part of your deposition given during the preliminary investigation does not concur with that given here where you claimed that you have never met Ramzin and have never seen him. Yet in your deposition in the preliminary investigation, you testified that you had a meeting with Ramzin. Is there, am I right in seeing a discrepancy here?

The defendant Sukhanov: Such a discrepancy does indeed exist.

Krylenko: What is the explanation for it?

Sukhanov: The explanation is that my deposition at the preliminary investigation did not correspond with reality.

Krylenko: Did not correspond with reality! Why?

Sukhanov: Yes. I think the reason may be understood by the court. The acceptance of monies from a fascist organization for the purpose of wrecking is something I personally regarded as the filthiest thing ever done by the Union Bureau.[64]

The official defence lawyer, I.D. Braude, thus 'explained' the discrepancy between Sukhanov's grudging and occasionally even provocative performance at the trial and the almost unconditional surrender which marked his testimonies during the preliminary investigations:

> There is no doubt that, even when in deepest crisis, this self-loving and self-assured personage, was virtually incapable of giving utterance to any repentance, to any words that might be understood as expressions of cowardice. But there in prison, seated in front of a sheet of paper, working on his deposition for the investigator, there he underwent a tremendous change. There are things which it is far easier to write than to say. And it was there that Sukhanov wrote: 'As a socialist for nearly thirty years I am happy to confess now that I have sinned against socialism and the revolution. But I am deeply unhappy that I realized my errors rather late.' When Sukhanov, whose distinctive characteristics have been delineated here by the Prosecutor speaks like this, it demonstrates just how deep the change and internal crisis in Sukhanov really is.[65]

If Krylenko, in his summing up, saw in Sukhanov 'a distinctive figure in the history of our political movement and struggle', the State Prosecutor himself stands out as a founder, theorist and stage-manager of Bolshevik Russia's treason and show trials from April 1918 until 1931. Following his triumph at the Menshevik trial in that year, he was promoted to People's Commissar of Justice of the RSFSR and, in 1934, to the even higher pinnacle of People's Commissar of Justice of the USSR. There he remained until February 1938 when, in his turn, he was arrested, accused of 'espionage' and of preparing the assassination of 'Bolshevik leaders', and, in July 1938, shot as a counter-revolutionary.[66] His debut as Deputy Prosecutor in the treason trial of Admiral A.I. Shchastnyi, in June 1918, exemplified that mixture of sneering cynicism and cold brutality that marked the judicial career of one of Lenin's 'most ardent Bolsheviks'.[67] When asked how, in the absence of the death penalty which had been abolished on the morrow of the October revolution, Shchastnyi could be condemned to death, Krylenko shot back: 'He was not condemned to death, but to be shot!'[68]

Krylenko took justifiable pride in being one of the originators of what he himself, in his autobiographical essay of 1927, termed Russia's 'show-trials' (*pokazatel'nyie sudy*).[69] Lenin, too, as early as 1922, urged the 'setting up and holding of noisy, model trials in all

Fig. 6.2   Krylenko

the major towns ... convinced of their enormous educational significance'. The court's function, Lenin postulated, was not to eliminate the 'terror, but to validate and legalize it'.[70] In a similar vein, though more brutally, Krylenko's conception of 'merciless revolutionary justice' was to use the courts as 'a most efficient weapon for the defence of Soviet state power, far superior to the club or the gun'.[71] The thread that runs throughout the three solid volumes of his speeches at treason trials shows a savage hatred for the non-Bolshevik, socialist, or anti-Bolshevik intelligentsia which 'entered the revolution waving aloft the slogan of people's power, but which has put its banners to shame and trampled them in the mud'.[72] Against them all, he was intent on handing down the judgement of history. His attitude is best summed up in the words of his pamphlet against wrecking:

> Let the bourgeoisie of the entire world and all its hangers on, inside and outside of the country, know this: our hands do not tremble when we mercilessly crush the coiling reptile of counter-revolution, when we wipe off the face of the earth anyone who dares to stand in the way of our planned socialist construction.[73]

For Krylenko, even 'mere talk' by '[oppositional intellectuals] over a cup of tea as to which order should replace Soviet state power should it collapse – was a counter-revolutionary act',[74] so that Sukhanov, the independent-minded socialist intellectual *par excellence*, proved his ideal victim. Small wonder that in that part of his summing up in the Menshevik trial which dealt with the personalities of the defendants, Krylenko singled out Sukhanov for 'particular and worthwhile detailed attention (before I will deal with the others)':

> Sukhanov is a 'wild one,' not quite an SR, not quite a Menshevik, not quite a Martovite, not quite a Menshevik of the type that stands now before us, but one who, at the same time, possesses sufficient self-assurance and love of himself as to urge him to seek always to play first fiddle. Having failed to gain recognition as a 'prophet' in the counter-revolutionary fatherland, he organized a special salon of his own Sukhanovite counter-revolutionary organization into which, and under the pretext of singing, music and recitations, he drew Mensheviks, Kondratevites and former SRs. For that, he certainly possessed the right talents: being smart, he certainly knew how to throw sand into people's

eyes … . A lover of clever words, he represents a *Khlestakov* type in politics, an adventurer in practice. At the same time, he tried whenever possible to avoid admitting that he has ever done any concrete practical wrecking work, claiming always that he was only a mere 'ideologist and a *littérateur'*.

And here, Krylenko read out a long list of 'concrete wrecking acts' to which Sukhanov had confessed during the preliminary investigations. Then he continued in true Stalinist style:

As for Sukhanov's implication in activities of an organizational character, what do we find here?! Did he have contact with [the alleged emissary of the Menshevik Central Committee in Berlin] M. Brounshtein? Yes, he did. Did Brounshtein give him organizational assignments?! Yes, he did! Did Sukhanov undertake to carry them out?! Yes, he did! Did he partly implement them?! Yes, he did! Did he engage in organizational work to establish contacts with counter-revolutionary organizations?! Yes, he did! He did not even hesitate to tell a deliberate lie to the court [denying that he ever met Ramzin]. True, that was for 'noble considerations', so he told us. But, citizen Sukhanov, we do not need lies. All we need is the truth! What we have here is not an attachment to principles and nobility, but a total lack of principles. For it is a lack of principles that underlies the zig-zags of Sukhanov's politics. That lack of principles is also to be seen in his counter-revolutionary activity when, in all sorts of ways, he emphasized that his ideological work set him apart from the other defendants, whereas in practice he did the same as all the others. That lack of principles has even shown itself in this court room when, in the face of all the facts, he has continued to present himself as nothing but a *littérateur* with his own independent position. I consider that this political *Khlestakovshchina* together with that lack of principle, that pretentiousness and that desire to play first fiddle made Sukhanov into a person whose evolution towards further counter-revolutionary activity will be unlimited. I can find no social usefulness whatever in citizen Sukhanov, nothing that can be set down to his credit, while his social harmfulness has been sufficiently proven. If we add to all this, his membership of the leading group of five in the Union Bureau, that during its sessions he played the role of lecturer and ideologist and at the same time participated in its most conspiratorial conferences, together with that same Brounshtein, the issue is crystal clear: I have not a minute's doubt in contending that our revolution, the world revolution, and furthermore world history, will lose not the least jot if someone like Sukhanov were to disappear from the face of the earth.[75]

Krylenko demanded the 'highest measure of social defence', that is – the death penalty.

Sukhanov began his final plea by repeating his indictment of Menshevism and of the social democratic parties of the Second International, a performance so nasty and demagogic that it would have done a Zinoviev or Karl Radek proud. He certainly thus even improved on the official line, fleshing it out with illustrations that only a Sukhanov could provide: 'the historical mission' of Menshevism was to 'neutralize the major obstacle to intervention and a future war against the USSR' by discrediting the Soviet Union in the eyes of the international workers movement, and this they did by feeding slanderous literature, information and propaganda into the *Vorwaerts* the party newspaper of German social democracy which he termed 'the central organ of international social democracy' and which he said had now become 'the world's most anti-Soviet newspaper'. Sukhanov then proceeded to explain (not quite convincingly), how he, who had fully identified with the October revolution and the Soviet system ever since the introduction of the NEP, had early in 1929 joined the leadership of the Union Bureau knowing full well of its commitment to wrecking and intervention. It had, he pleaded, been an act of despair in reaction to the return in the post-NEP period of the 'extreme measures' of War Communism and to the 'tightening up ... on all fronts' of the Communist regime which had spread 'naturally and inexorably from economics to science, the arts, the theatre and life in general'.[76]

Having listened to Krylenko singling him out as a particularly odious and revolting member of the leadership of the Menshevik Union Bureau and demanding the death penalty, Sukhanov also heard him – amidst thunderous applause from the entire Hall of Columns – exhorting the court to 'treat the defendants with maximum cruelty'.[77] But this did not deter Sukhanov from prefacing his 'last word of the defendant' with a statement that squarely countered Krylenko's long list of 'concrete wrecking acts' to which Sukhanov had allegedly confessed.

First and foremost, I deem it necessary to attest the following before the court: neither during the preliminary investigations nor court proceedings were any accusations whatsoever made against me of having engaged in wrecking as an official employed in this or that institution or as an organizer of wrecking in Soviet organizations. As a wrecker I worked on the general staff [of the Union Bureau] and I therefore bear responsibility as a member of that organization. True, my statement has no judicial significance, nor has it any practical significance in diminishing my guilt. But it has a certain moral significance for me and without making any further comment, I wish that to be noted.

Sukhanov then explained at length how he had been proved wrong in predicting the collapse of the national economy and expecting a Thermidorian counter-revolutionary finale to the revolution. The collectivization drive had, contrary to his expectations, proved a success, there were no political convulsions and the Soviet system had survived despite his 'learned calculations' and pessimistic forecasts. He certainly had been mistaken about the Bolshevik 'Jacobin dictatorship', for as he now realized, 'it was the only state capable of coping with the vast mass of peasant households and petty proprietors, of forcing them to subsidize the towns and feed them, of organizing the peasants and compelling them to serve the revolution and its proletarian vanguard, for a certain period of time'. From this he concluded that if 'the Jacobin dictatorship does not turn into its opposite' (that is, a Thermidorian counter-revolution: I.G.) then 'there has never been a state like this in history, a Bolshevik proletarian dictatorship, capable of realizing such unprecedented goals'.

I still do not know for certain, but I already believe, that the All-Union Communist Party, with its methods, its organization and its policy, has been victorious, and it has triumphed precisely because of the means it has employed. These methods were very harsh; I have no doubt on that score. Indeed they have been so harsh that in the winter of 1929–30 I could no longer take it and wanted to be arrested. But were they really more severe than the methods generally applied throughout history? Will that [Bolshevik] Jacobin chariot prove more brutal than those which rolled over the feudal and bourgeois world? Not at all! Historically speaking, these [Bolshevik methods] have been by no means more severe, and have, evidently, been historically necessary and justified. That is how things were. I cannot make any further declarations. In view of the position taken by the State Prosecutor, I think it entirely inappropriate for me to speak of there being any possible future for me. I only know full well that to the very end I shall hold in the deepest contempt those crimes for which I have been sentenced, harbouring a sense of burning hatred for the very idea of intervention, wrecking and bourgeois restoration and for all those who attempt to implement such ideas. And to the end I shall remain convinced to the depths of my being that our revolution is invincible.[78]

Sentenced, with four other 'ring-leaders' to ten years' imprisonment, Sukhanov and the rest of the defendants were moved to the Verkhne-Uralsk *Politizolator* (political isolation prison). The regime there resembled more that of 'forced vacation homes rather than prisons', as a resolution of the plenum of the Central Committee dated February–March 1937 complained, with inmates associating with each other and discussing current affairs.[79] But Sukhanov and his co-defendants suffered the deep resentment, bordering on hostility, of the collective of 250–300 political prisoners who, organized in party-political factions, had decided to totally boycott the 'scoundrels' (*svolochentsy*), as they were called, according to the report of the OGPU agents planted among the politicals specifically to inform on mutual relations between the two groups and keep them apart.[80] For some time, the boycott was so strict that when the SR Tigran Aniev was caught passing a letter to Sukhanov, whom he knew well and admired from his frequent visits to the '*salon*', the bureau of the SR faction reprimanded him severely: Aniev's application for membership in the faction was rejected and he was warned that should he repeat the offence he risked expulsion from the entire 'socialist collective' and even eviction from their living quarters. Defending himself, Aniev said that he was very fond of Sukhanov and had written the letter to find out whether the newspaper reports about the trial and about Sukhanov were really true. The cryptic reply he had received was 'Dear Tigran: I assure you that all is as it was before.' The OGPU agent interpreted this as an assurance that their personal relations had not been impaired. But one may also perhaps interpret it as referring to Sukhanov's views with which Aniev was so well acquainted.

As the informers reported to their superiors, the politicals had avidly followed both the preparations for the trial and the newspaper reports of its proceedings, closely annotating every scrap of printed information that they came across: at the suggestion of the agents, they had even kept a complete file of the *Pravda* reports of the trial for the benefit of new arrivals. Many of the comments and some of the discussions on the trial referred specifically to Sukhanov who had generally been regarded as the 'outstanding figure' among the defendants with a great reputation for courage and resourcefulness which had been reinforced by his own insistence that he would 'not give in' and by rumours that 'he had stood up to the onslaught of the investigators'. It had therefore been hoped that Sukhanov would show his 'full stature' in the court room and would, in front of the foreign journalists and the whole world, repudiate his confessions and expose the machinations of the OGPU and the farce of a trial.

When, after some delay, the newspaper reports of the final speeches and verdict had arrived and it became evident that not only had the 14 caved in but that they had also informed on each other and on others, the politicals' terrible disappointment and indignation knew no bounds. Some who were in principle opposed to the death penalty were even heard to say that 'it's a pity they don't shoot such scoundrels', the agents reported to their OGPU masters. Sukhanov was singled out for particularly nasty comments: 'What a scoundrel! And he even had the cheek to ask for moral support and promised that he would give in only under torture!'

The central question that now plagued them and became the subject of wide speculation was exactly what means the OGPU had used to break 'those defendants who had held out so staunchly earlier on (for example, Sukhanov)'. Referring specifically to Sukhanov, the question was asked: 'How could he of all people, who knew his own worth and had so fiercely resisted the onslaught of the investigators, so fear death' that he passed up the opportunity of the court room 'to expose the truth and the machinations of the

Cheka'. Fiodor Cherevanin, the old Menshevik and fellow prisoner, who had known Sukhanov for a long time and had been a frequent visitor to his *salon* was completely at a loss to explain Sukhanov's behaviour in court, although he was convinced that he had not been tortured. 'I would rather have expected him to stand up in court and repudiate his confession in full: there are indeed no hypotheses that fit and help us understand Sukhanov's behaviour. Of the entire group of the 14, he was undoubtedly the outstanding figure and therefore his behaviour was truly vile.'[81]

There can be no doubt that Sukhanov complied with the investigators' demand for 'a full and thorough confession' and that he equally 'fully and thoroughly reported to the investigating authorities all that is known to me of my own [criminal activities] and of those of my accomplices', as he put it in his Petition for Pardon of 9 March 1931 to the Praesidium of the Sixth Congress of Soviets.[82] That petition, together with the petitions of the other defendants, was discussed at the session of the Politburo on 15 March 1931 when it was decided to reject it and uphold the verdict of the High Court.[83]

Yet to this day the complaint made by Cherevanin and his fellow politicals still holds: Sukhanov's behaviour remains inexplicable. It was apparently incomprehensible even to the 'sad heroes of the trial', as Anton Ciliga,[84] a Yugoslav Communist who was at the time a prisoner in the *politizolator* reported: 'One day I asked one of the Menshevik defendants how they had been capable of making those monstrous statements [at the trial]. His answer was eloquent: "We ourselves don't understand. It was all like a horrible nightmare."'

While I have been equally puzzled, I have been even more baffled by Sukhanov's final speech and in particular by his eulogy of the Bolshevik Jacobin dictatorship which, as we have seen, was so much at variance with opinions he had expressed only three months earlier in his testimonies to the OGPU investigators, not to speak of the views he had held on a Bolshevik Jacobin dictatorship ever since the 1917 revolution.

In a search for clues to Sukhanov's compliant behaviour, one has no choice for the most part but to rely on a critical study of two largely unsatisfactory sources: the protocols of the Menshevik trial (of 1–9 March 1931)[85] and the protocols of the preliminary investigations of Sukhanov by the OGPU (14 August 1930–23 February 1931).[86] The protocols of the trial, though allegedly a 'stenographic' account of the proceedings, have occasionally been doctored by the editors as is revealed by a comparison of the published text with the original archival materials.[87] Thus, I myself chanced upon a serious discrepancy between the published and laconic 'stenographic' text of the evening session of 4 March 1931[88] and the far fuller newspaper report of the same session in *Pravda*.[89] As for the protocols of the preliminary investigations, while the autobiographical data supplied by Sukhanov seem remarkably accurate, internal evidence suggests that it is likely that some six early protocols (from 20 July 1930, the day of his arrest, to 14 August) are missing, and certainly missing is the protocol for 25 December. Seriously complicating the matter still further is the fact that all the protocols of preliminary investigations of Sukhanov from 14 August until 3 December 1930 are not at all related to the preparations for the Menshevik trial – rather, they relate to 'the case of the counter-revolutionary Labouring Peasant Party and the Sukhanov–Groman Grouping'.[90]

While Nikolai Kondratev, leader of the fictitious Labouring Peasant Party and some of his alleged associates were secretly tried some time in December 1930, Sukhanov, during his investigation on 3 December, 'confessed' to having entered into a '*bloc* with Kondratev and his Peasant Party with the intention of creating a counter-revolutionary political organization' into which he would draw like-minded friends and associates such as Groman and Bazarov. And, for good measure, he also testified that he had begun to draft a leaflet in the form of a Letter to Workers which urged that the present-day policy of '*dekulakization* and grain-procurement' was 'erroneous' from the point of view of socialism. The guiding principle of the platform of that organization, which Sukhanov confessed to having drafted (and Groman confirmed the existence of the platform in his interrogation of 17 August),[91] was 'the preservation of the system of proletarian dictatorship, further socialist development and a guarantee against bourgeois restoration'. This would have required the following concessions by the Communist Party: a return to the economic principles of the NEP as practised from 1923 to 1926; democratization of the proletarian dictatorship to include freedom of speech, the press and elections [to soviets] for all 'public elements' and political parties which are committed to the principles of the October revolution; and an amnesty for political crimes with the exception of direct implication in 'intervention'.[92]

That platform, if indeed it ever existed, probably did reflect Sukhanov's attitudes at that time. But his 'confession' of 3 December to having negotiated a political *bloc* with Kondratev and his Peasant Party[93] was superimposed on his views by the OGPU investigators in order to establish 'a direct link' with the Rightist opposition to Stalin in the party. Small wonder that the protocols were circulated to the members of the Central Committee at Stalin's behest. Nor was it difficult for the OGPU to browbeat Sukhanov into his confession, for they already had information supplied by Groman and Bazarov that Sukhanov habitually hosted a *salon* in which he, together with Groman and Kondratev, took leading parts and which was also frequented by other non-Communist senior civil servants, economists and other experts who all participated in discussions of the 'burning issues' of the day.[94]

Sukhanov's 3 December detailed confession is of especial interest because of what is missing from it – there is no reference whatever to the Union Bureau of the Central Committee of the RSDRP (Mensheviks) even though the investigations of some defendants accused of membership were already in full swing. There is, equally, no reference to Sukhanov's *salon*. Wrecking, spying and interventionist activities are not even mentioned. On the contrary, there is an emphatic statement – included in the protocol of his interrogation of 1 December – testifying to Sukhanov's and his friends' and associates' uncompromising hostility to 'intervention'.[95]

In short, Sukhanov had been let off rather lightly and had not yet been coerced to 'disarm fully'.

There are no protocols of investigations for the period 3 December 1930 to 13 January 1931. But the protocol for 13 January, which refers to the [missing] protocol of 25 December, reports that it contains the following statement by Sukhanov: 'I realize the necessity to disarm in full measure, ideologically and organizationally, before the proletarian state power and to express my sincerest repentance for the crimes committed against it.'[96] This affirmation was reiterated by Sukhanov during the investigation of 13 January and again, in an embroidered version, in that of 22 January.[97] Petitioning for pardon to the praesidium of the Sixth Congress of Soviets on 9 March 1931, he begs that it 'take into account my most sincere and full repentance and my full and thorough disarming'. He had, he said, 'completely and fully admitted my guilt of crimes against the working-class' and had also 'open-heartedly … .informed the investigating authorities of everything known to me of my own activities and also of those of my accomplices and of the entire organization of which I was a member'.[98] The petitions for pardon by Rubin and Groman also contain references to 'open-hearted repentance' and 'unconditional disarming' (Groman) and 'complete disarming' (Rubin). Variations of confessions containing the term 'disarming' – as signifying total and unconditional compliance – were also made by the co-defendants Rubin and Nikolai Vishnevsky during their interrogations on 24 January 1931 and 26 September 1930[99] respectively, in the final speeches by Ivan Volkov, Sukhanov, Lazar Zalkind, Boris Berlatsky and Moise Teitelbaum,[100] and also during the Communist treason trials of the late 1930s. The classical affirmation – if not definition – of 'disarming' is made by Nikolai Bukharin in his 'very secret and personal' letter to Stalin of 10 December 1937:

> Standing on the edge of a precipice from which there is no return, I tell you on my word of honour that I am innocent of those crimes which I admitted to ['treason to the socialist fatherland, the organization of *kulak* uprisings, the preparation of terrorist attacks, membership in an underground anti-Soviet organization … organizing a conspiracy for a palace revolution']. I had 'no way' out other than that of confirming the accusations and testimonies of others and of elaborating on them *otherwise, it would have turned out that I had not 'disarmed'.*[101] (My italics, I.G.)

Why was it only when Sukhanov was being investigated in connection with the case of the Menshevik Union Bureau that affirmations of 'disarming' were wrested from him at least three times? One possible explanation is that, as distinct from the lesser charges levelled against him in the case of the alleged *bloc* with Kondratev, in the case of the Menshevik Union Bureau and his allegedly major role in it, he was expected to confess to crimes that were a complete fabrication and which might even carry the death sentence. At this he balked a number of times, making it necessary for the OGPU to coerce him into 'disarming'. That initial resistance may also explain the bitter disappointment felt by the convicts in the Ural *politizolator* when they learned that

Sukhanov 'who had stood up to the onslaught of the investigators' had abjectly complied at the trial.[102]

As for the methods used to coerce him – I can only assume that it was the arrest of his common-law wife Natalia Nikolaevna Krym-Shakhmalova (née Kitaeva) that may well have served to bring severe psychological pressure on him. On 6 December she was subjected to a house search (they lived separately but met regularly); the next day she was arrested and on 8 December she was interrogated by investigator A.A. Nasedkin. She insisted that her long-standing relationship with Sukhanov had begun in 1926, that it was of an 'exclusively romantic nature' and that while they met regularly and went to the cinema and the theatre, they never discussed politics. On 27 December (note the date) she was charged by Nasedkin with 'membership in the counter-revolutionary Menshevik party, aiming – with other counter-revolutionary organizations (the Labouring Peasant Party and the Industrial Party) – at the overthrow of Soviet power with the help of intervention'. More specifically, she was charged with typing – on the instructions of the Menshevik Centre – 'a variety of party directives and appeals'. She denied all these charges (no date given), but it was only as late as 29 April – that is long after the Menshevik trial was over – that she was convicted of typing – 'on the instructions of Sukhanov, a member of the Union Bureau' – 'a variety of directives and appeals etc for illegal distribution among members of the counter-revolutionary organization'. On 10 May 1931, she was sentenced to five years' imprisonment.[103]

Sukhanov's study, too, was searched on 6 December. During the investigation of 25 December he 'disarmed in full measure, both ideologically and organizationally'. On 28 December he, too, was charged by Nasedkin with

> membership in the counter-revolutionary Menshevik Party which, together with other counter-revolutionary organizations (Labouring Peasant Party and Industrial Party) and with the assistance and guidance of the Central Committee of the Menshevik Party abroad – sought to overthrow Soviet state power by organizing wrecking activity, in preparation for intervention. Citizen Sukhanov was a member of the leading centre (Union Bureau of the Central Committee of the RSDRP) which directed

and led the entire Menshevik Party and the wrecking activity of the counter-revolutionary organization. The Union Bureau of the CC of the RSDRP, of which Sukhanov was a member, maintained links abroad ... .and received from abroad monies for Menshevik and wrecking activities.[104]

It was perhaps then that he was told that in return for his full compliance and 'disarming', his sentence, and/or that of Natalia Nikolaevna, would not be implemented, which may help explain why he finally co-operated with his investigators and confessed to the charges. This explanation may gain credence from the report of a former fellow-convict – a member of the Zionist workers' party (*Poalei Tsion*) – published in the *Sotsialisticheskii vestnik* in 1936 – that Sukhanov, having been boycotted and repeatedly refused admission to the Communist faction, had fallen into a deep depression and had, in despair, bombarded the Executive Committee of Soviets with letter after letter (some of which he circulated among fellow prisoners) demanding that the NKVD keep its promise and restore his freedom. His letter reminded them of the 'services he had rendered to the regime, to the point of even sacrificing his conscience when he consented to play his despicable part in the comedy of the Menshevik trial. He had been assured that the SSSR demanded that and that the OGPU had promised to take account of that sacrifice and had solemnly guaranteed that the sentence imposed by the tribunal would not be implemented.' Having threatened to go on a hunger strike to the death, he had refused food intermittently over a 50-day period during which time the prison authorities were apparently waiting for instructions from Moscow.[105]

Whether as a result of these actions, or for whatever reason (Rubin's 5-year sentence had similarly been reduced by three years and commuted to exile), on 10 March 1935, the Praesidium of the Central Executive Committee of Soviets decided, with regard to 'the application of Sukhanov, N.N. ... to accept the proposal of the NKVD and release him from the *izolator* for the remaining period of the sentence [more than four years] and to transfer him to [a location to be determined] at the discretion of the NKVD'. That organization sent him into exile in Siberian Tobolsk.[106]

True, the evidence cited here is largely circumstantial and anything but conclusive, but it is perhaps strengthened by the parallel and well-documented case of the young scientist Alexander Grintser.[107] Grintser had been arrested and charged with membership in the Menshevik organization and specifically with copying Menshevik documents. His confession came only after the interrogators threatened to arrest his wife and his sick and aged parents – both his wife and father were in fact arrested. Subsequently he twice withdrew his confessions, and was only brought to confess finally and even to inform on others after he had spent a month in the notorious *politizolator* of Suzdal where he was confronted with the denunciations of some of his colleagues, notably that of Mikhail Jakubovich. In a 'personal' letter to OGPU Deputy Chairman Ivan Akulov of 13 June 1932, Grintser wrote 'As I am by political conviction absolutely loyal to Soviet state power, my conscience weighs heavily on me for having falsely informed on others in my testimony during the preliminary investigation when I also vilified my own political convictions and my Soviet work. Having long pondered my behaviour ... I feel duty-bound to lay the whole truth of my case before you.' This he then proceeded to do in some detail, ending by asking Akulov to 'review the decision of the OGPU'. This indeed happened and on 22 December 1932 his 5-year sentence was reduced by one year.

If thus far I have tried to explain why Sukhanov confessed to crimes which he did not and could not have committed, that explanation still leaves unaddressed the question of his public conversion to 'Stalin's revolution', his public acclaim at the Menshevik trial of the Bolshevik 'Jacobin dictatorship' and of its achievements, as well as a somewhat muted endorsement of its 'methods'. That included, of course, that 'all-out collectivization' drive which he had reported on at length and condemned at the preliminary investigation on 22 January 1931. He may have pondered his conversion for some time, but certainly he gave notice of it at the end of his autobiographical deposition which he wrote down on 29 and 30 January 1931. There, considering the possibility that he might be wrong in his pessimistic predictions of a disastrous failure for Stalin's 'New Course' and its forced grain procurements, its 'crushing offensive against the *kulak*', collectivization and the entire Five Year Plan, he wrote that he would then 'capitulate to the Communist Party and gladly devote myself fully to its service'. He concluded his deposition on a note that foreshadowed the words of his final plea speech:

Today I have indications which allow me to believe that the [Bolshevik] scheme is becoming reality. As a revolutionary socialist of almost three decades standing, I am happy to realize now that I have erred in working against socialism and the revolution. I am deeply unhappy that this realization came so late.[108]

At the trial proper, Sukhanov's declaration of his conversion (on 7 March) was preceded three days earlier by that of Kondratev whose own trial had been held in secret in December 1930. To general surprise Kondratev appeared now as a witness for the prosecution, using the witness box to deliver a ritual speech of recantation. His counter-revolutionary errors, he confessed, had been driven home to him when he realized that contrary to his pessimistic expectations the twin drives of speeded-up industrialization and all-out collectivization had been eminently successful. That had led him to a 're-evaluation of values' and forced him to a 'sincere adoption of the General Line [of the Party] of building socialism in one country, including our own, under the conditions of the dictatorship of the proletariat'. And for good measure, he whose advocacy of agrarian reform based on privately owned peasant farms had been denounced since 1928 as '*Kondratevshchina*' – standing for 'the ideology of the *kulaks*' and 'restoration of capitalism' – now justified the 'liquidation of the *kulak* class and total collectivization as the logical inevitable tasks in a consistent reconstruction of agriculture on collectivist foundations'. Worse still, in a sad act of self-abasement, Kondratev dissociated himself from his own eminent past as a brilliant scholar, economist and public figure and 'amidst laughter' in the vast Hall of Columns both denounced and renounced '*Kondratevshchina*'.[109]

It seems to me that Sukhanov's final plea speech of conversion to the Bolshevik 'Jacobin dictatorship' is of one piece with Kondratev's declaration of faith in the 'General Line': it is similarly constructed, conveys the same messages and may equally have been inspired by the investigating authorities even though the language, the degree of self-abasement and, possibly, of compliance, may differ. Indeed, throughout three separate preliminary investigations – those of 13 and 22 January and 20 February – Sukhanov served notice that he would not confess to charges of involvement 'in concrete wrecking activities'.[110] And that refusal was reiterated in his final plea speech at the trial even after Krylenko – in his vicious indictment – had triumphantly presented the court with 'a concrete list of concrete wrecking activities' in which Sukhanov had allegedly participated. Moreover, as we have seen earlier, Sukhanov – even against the relentless questioning of Krylenko – had publicly repudiated all dealings with Professor Ramzin and his Industrial Party to which he had admitted in the preliminary investigation.[111] In a similar vein, the final plea speeches of a number of co-defendants, though far shorter and of lesser intellectual elaboration, repeat the same words and refer to that 're-evaluation of values' that had compelled them to see the light and thus 'to disarm completely and finally and embark on the correct course of building socialism under the leadership of the Communist Party'.[112]

Both the Menshevik Trial of 1931 and the Communist treason trials of 1936–38 have in common the categorical demand that the defendants 'disarm' completely – including making public confessions of guilt as charged, incriminating themselves and 'unmasking' and 'exposing' all possible and impossible associates and 'enemies'. They also have in common that all the accused who were finally brought to trial (as distinct from those who for one reason or another were not) did as they were told and confessed. The public confessions at show trials seem to have followed some prescribed ritual. At the Menshevik trial, it took the form of conversion to the Stalin revolution. In the case of the Communist trials – that of unconditional loyalty and self-sacrificial service to the Party. What distinguishes the Menshevik trial is, of course, the absence of that 'Party mind' which has often been invoked (in the wake of Arthur Koestler's *Darkness at Noon*) to explain, at least in part, why hardened Old Bolsheviks would confess to crimes that they could not have committed.

To me it seems that it was not so much the questionable 'Party mind' that was in operation here, but, more likely, the organized moral pressure combined with terrorist abuse and threats by the comrades in the Central Committee and/or the Politburo who, like a revolutionary tribunal, sat in judgement on the accused. A good example of this is to be seen from the events at the Plenum of the Central Committee of the Party of February–March 1937 scheduled to deal with the 'Rightists' Bukharin, Rykov and Mikhail Tomsky. Since Tomsky had committed suicide, the fire of the 'investigation' was turned on Bukharin and Rykov by a galaxy of Bolshevik leaders and senior functionaries, including Stalin, Molotov and Kaganovich, all harrying them to do their duty by the Party, 'disarm' unconditionally, incriminate themselves and help unmask all enemies notably Trotskyites and Zinovievites.[113] There is of course a vast difference in the scale and the severity of the outcome of the Menshevik and Communist treason trials. A total of 122 people were arrested in connection with the Menshevik trial, 80 of them received prison sentences of between three and ten years,[114] 40 were either released altogether or debarred from living for the next three to five years in 'regime towns', and two were shot. Those tried in the Communist treason trials were for the most part sentenced to death, and millions more were arrested and suffered in the major purges connected with these trials.[115]

While Sukhanov had the leisure to write his early memoirs, the extent of his misery in the *politizolator* emerges all too clearly in his autobiographical 'Notes of an Old Intellectual' where he asks himself time and again: 'How and why did it happen that I, who have dedicated my whole life to the social struggle, to the cause of socialism and to the revolution, should have found myself crushed by the revolution?' In his answer, he blames the philistinism and the petty-bourgeois environment in which he grew up which 'trampled on my will and destroyed the citizen in me' so that he failed to understand 'the dialectics and the contradictions inherent in the proletarian revolution'. That he then proceeds to an all-out justification of the Civil War, the Red Terror, and Stalin's General Line suggests that this unpublished autobiography was either the final capitulation of a broken man and/or that it was written with the idea that the OGPU authorities would read it.[116] Indeed, Sukhanov wrote on 14 April 1931 to Dmitriev, his principal investigator, asking him to return the manuscript of his 'literary memoirs', and telling him that he had written them in jail with the knowledge and permission of the investigators.

Arriving in Tobolsk in May 1935 together with his wife Natalia Nikolaevna (who worked there as a teacher), Sukhanov was employed for four months as a economist and then, until his arrest on 10 September 1937, as a teacher of Russian and German in a school for Tartar children.[117] The charges then filed against him by the local NKVD[118] were that he had engaged in counter-revolutionary propaganda in co-operation with a group of Trotskyites, and had slandered the Soviet Constitution by allegedly saying that 'it was not very different from the constitutions of Hitler and Mussolini', charges which he denied. After more than a year of incarceration in the Tobolsk prison, he was transferred to the Omsk jail and charged there on 3 December 1938 with spying for Germany in 1924 and 1927 when he allegedly provided information on the policies of the government and of the Communist Party; he was further charged with membership in a counter-revolutionary group and with publishing counter-revolutionary leaflets; and finally, it was alleged that he had slandered the Stalin Constitution and the leaders of the Communist Party and of the government. He pleaded guilty to all these charges and his case was passed for further consideration to the Tribunal of the Siberian Military District.[119]

On 7 August 1939 a high-powered delegation of that body arrived in Omsk and, in closed session, with none of those who had informed on him present, found him guilty of most of the charges and sentenced him to 'the supreme criminal punishment – death by shooting, without confiscation of property, because he has none'.[120] Sukhanov on this occasion had denied his guilt, declaring that 'neither my earlier deposition of 3 December 1938 nor the minutes compiled by the investigator in my absence bears any resemblance to the truth'. Dealing with the charges one by one and reducing them *ad absurdum*, he went on:

> I have told the Tribunal nothing but the truth. The preliminary investigation was conducted in a truly shocking manner and that is why I made false depositions and even they have been distorted both in the protocols and in the indictment. I insist that my thoughts and deeds during the period concerned were beyond reproach.[121]

On 29 June 1940 he was shot.

Fifty-two years later, and only after the advent of *glasnost* and the fall of Communism, and long after the death of his wife (in 1973) and his sons (the youngest and last surviving died in 1987), it was only his grandchildren who were privileged to see his rehabilitation.

The Rehabilitation Commission which met on 19 March 1992 found that the preliminary investigation of Sukhanov in the late

1930s had lasted two years although he himself had only been interrogated twice. At his first interrogation, which took place immediately after his arrest in Tobolsk, he denied all the charges of counter-revolutionary activity. A year later, under interrogation on 19 November 1938, he admitted to having worked for German intelligence, to having contact with Trotskyites and to having engaged in anti-Soviet agitation. Noting that Sukhanov had subsequently repudiated the protocol ostensibly recording his interrogations, insisting that it had been compiled in his absence and was a distortion and that it had been conducted in a 'truly shocking manner', the Commission took note of a deposition by B.W. Nasledyshev, the man who was listed as having questioned him in Tobolsk. Testifying on 26 March 1957, Nasledyshev had denied writing the protocol that purported to be a transcript of his questioning of Sukhanov in 1937 and also denied that the signature it bore was his. Further, the Rehabilitation Commission noted that the 'competent organs' had not produced any evidence to prove charges of espionage against Sukhanov. And finally, the Commission noted that K.A. Rublevskii and B.D. Shmalts, formerly of the NKVD staff in Tobolsk, who had been involved in the arrest and subsequent criminal investigation of Sukhanov, had 'violated socialist legality'. Thus, the Commission wrote, 'it has been established that Sukhanov was sentenced for political reasons and without any evidence, entirely on the basis of fabricated materials. In accordance with the law on the Rehabilitation of the Victims of Political Repression of 18 October 1991, Sukhanov is deemed rehabilitated.'[122]

Appendix I

Address of the Petrograd Soviet to the Peoples of the Whole World, 14 March 1917

Comrades, Proletarians and Toilers of all Countries!

We, Russian workers and soldiers, united in the Petrograd Soviet of Workers and Soldiers Deputies greet you most warmly and send you word of a great event. Russia's democracy has overthrown the age-old despotism of the tsar and now joins your family as an equal member and a mighty force in the struggle for our common liberation. Our victory is a great triumph for universal freedom and democracy. The main bulwark of reaction in the world, the *'Gendarme* of Europe', no longer exists. May the earth weigh as heavy as granite on his grave. Long live freedom! Long live the international solidarity of the proletariat and its struggle for final victory!

But our work is not yet completed: the shadows of the old order have not yet vanished and more than a few of our enemies are even now massing their forces against the Russian revolution. The peoples of Russia will express their will in the Constituent Assembly which will be convened very soon on the basis of a universal, equal, direct and secret vote. One may already predict with confidence that a democratic republic will triumph in Russia. The Russian people now possess full political freedom. They can now make their mighty voice heard both in internal government and in foreign policy. Appealing to all nations who have been slaughtered and devastated in this monstrous war, we declare that the time has come to begin a decisive struggle against the grasping ambitions of the governments of all countries. The time has come for the peoples of the world to take into their own hands the decisions about war and peace.

Conscious of its revolutionary power, the Russian democracy declares that it will use all means to resist the policy of conquest of its own ruling classes and it summons the peoples of Europe to united and resolute action for peace. We appeal to our brothers, the proletarians of the German–Austrian coalition, and above all to the German proletariat: from the very first days of the war, they persuaded you that in taking up arms against autocratic Russia you were defending the culture of Europe against Asiatic despotism. Many of you saw this as the justification for your support of this war. Now even this justification has ceased to exist: democratic Russia can no longer be a threat to freedom and civilization.

We will resolutely defend our own freedom against every reactionary encroachment from both within and without. The Russian revolution will not retreat before the bayonets of conquerors and will not permit itself to be crushed by foreign military force. We appeal to you: throw off the yoke of your own autocratic regime as the people of Russia have cast off the tsarist autocracy; refuse to serve as an instrument of conquest and violence in the hands of kings, landowners and bankers! Together, by our united efforts, we shall stop the terrible slaughter that is such a disgrace to mankind and that so blights the great days of the birth of Russian liberty.

Toilers of all countries! Over the mountains of our brothers' corpses, over rivers of innocent blood and tears, across the smoking ruins of towns and villages, across the devastated treasures of culture, we stretch out to you a brotherly hand and call upon you to restore and strengthen international unity. In this lies the guarantee of future victories for all of us and of the complete liberation of all mankind. Proletarians of all countries, unite! (Translated from the Russian text as it appears in *Zapiski o revoliutsii*, vol. 2, pp. 234–5)

Appendix II

Sukhanov's defence of his version of a Bolshevik
coup d'état in the July Days 1917

Eight months after the momentous events of the July Days, Sukhanov used a session of the Central Executive Committee as his opportunity to set the record straight on what he insisted had been all along a Bolshevik plot to seize power on 3 and 4 July 1917. In so doing, he also sought to 'give a small example' of how the Bolsheviks misrepresented events:

> The third of July is always and categorically presented as a peaceful demonstration... but this was no peaceful demonstration; it was a preparation for that overturn which the Bolshevik party subsequently carried out on 25 October ... On 3 and 4 July, in Bolshevik circles, the portfolios of the Bolshevik ministers were distributed (laughter from the audience). On 4 July there was a definite plan to arrest the first [Menshevik-SR] Central Executive Committee. If it did not succeed, that was due only to a purely technical mishap the causes of which are well-known to me (the chairman rings his bell).

(*Protokoly zasedanii Vserossiikogo Tsentral'nogo Ispolnitel'nogo Komiteta 4–go Sozyva. Stenograficheskii Otchet*, Moscow, 1920, pp. 164–5)
    The source of Sukhanov's inside knowledge of what had gone on in 'Bolshevik circles' was none other than his one-time friend of 1917, Anatolii Lunacharsky who, on the morning of 8 July (that is, less than four days after the events in which he himself had figured as a major participant) told Sukhanov the following story – as reported in the *Zapiski o revoliutsii,* vol. 4, pp. 511–6:

> During the night of 4 July, even as Lenin sent a note to *Pravda* calling for a peaceful demonstration, he simultaneously had a definite plan for a *coup d'état*. The government (which in fact would be in the hands of the Bolshevik Central Committee) was to be vested officially in a 'Soviet' ministry made up of distinguished and popular Bolsheviks. For the present, three ministers had been nominated: Lenin, Trotsky and Lunacharsky. This government would immediately issue decrees on peace and land, thus gaining the sympathy of millions in the capital and in the provinces and consolidating its power. An agreement to this effect was reached between Lenin, Trotsky and Lunacharsky while the Kronstadters were making their way from the Kshesinskaia Mansion to the Tauride Palace ... The overturn was to be carried out in the following manner: the

176th regiment, arriving from Tsarskoe Selo ... was to arrest the members of the Central Executive Committee. At the same time, Lenin was to arrive on the scene and proclaim the new state power. But Lenin arrived too late and the 176th regiment was intercepted and 'dispersed'. The overturn had failed.

App. II Lunacharsky

Early in 1920, when Sukhanov sat down to write the fourth volume of his *Zapiski*, he had already checked Lunacharsky's story with Trotsky who 'protested vehemently' and brushed aside both Lunacharsky's version as well Lunacharsky himself who was dismissed as 'a person completely unsuited to such action and conspiracy'. But Trotsky did not leave it at that. Instead, he 'arranged so to speak a confrontation with Lunacharsky' in the course of which he must have questioned him thoroughly. Lunacharsky assured Trotsky that Sukhanov had 'confused matters' and had 'distorted our conversation'. Trotsky followed up this confrontation with a written note to Lunacharsky:

> N.N. Sukhanov has told me that in the third volume [it was actually the fourth, I.G.] of his book on the revolution there is an account of the July Days in which, quoting you and deferring to you personally, he claims that in July the three of us (Lenin, you and I) wanted to seize power and that we set out to do so!?!?!?

On 30 March 1920, Lunacharsky sent Trotsky's note to Sukhanov together with a lengthy letter the gist of which is contained in the following passage:

> Nikolai Nikolaevich! ... Obviously, Nikolai Nikolaevich, you have fallen into profound error, which, for you as a historian, could have unpleasant consequences. Generally speaking a reference to a private conversation is bad documentation... your error was very likely caused by my telling you that, at the decisive moment of the July events, I told Trotsky that I would deem it a calamity and as courting inevitable defeat, were we to be in power just then. Comrade Trotsky, who was always far more resolute and more sure of victory than I was, replied that in his opinion that would not have been so bad at all and that of course the masses would support us. All this was said by way of weighing the situation in a private conversation at a heated historical moment.
>
> I beg you, when you finally edit your History, to give due consideration to my letter so that you yourself do not fall into error and lead others into error.

As for Sukhanov, he affirmed that he 'clearly remembered the story and in the form that Lunacharsky had told it to him' and it is 'in this form that I pass it on to anyone into whose hands this work may happen to fall'. He conceded that the content of his story was not 'a fully established historical fact: I myself may have forgotten, confused or distorted the story, whilst Lunacharsky may have poeticized, mixed up or distorted the reality'. But 'to establish a historical fact precisely is the job of the historian, while I write my personal memoirs and pass the story on as I recall it ... How things were in reality I do not presume to say. I did not investigate the matter ... Let industrious historians sort it all out.'

Not surprisingly, Sukhanov did not yield to the combined pressure of the two People's Commissars. The only concession he was prepared to make 'in the interests of the truth' was 'to print Lunacharsky's letter to me of 30 March 1920, this I do willingly, word for word and in full'. And he further enunciated 'the principle to which I adhere throughout these *Zapiski* is to write down everything I recall and in the form in which I recall it. This will not at all do for the historian. Lunacharsky is right on this. But it is not history that I write.'

Notes

Introduction

1. *Deiateli SSSR i Oktiabr'skoi Revoliutsii. Entsiklopedicheskii Slovar' Russkogo Bibliograficheskogo Instituta Granat,* 7th edition, vol. 41a, Moscow, 1927–29, cols 129–30.
2. A.A. Kornikov *Sud'ba Rossiiskogo Revoliutsionera: N.N. Sukhanov – Chelovek, Politik, Memuarist,* Ivanovo, 1995, pp. 7–28; also *Deiateli,* cols 129–30.
3. *Deiateli,* cols 129–30. Learning from newspapers that Tolstoy had completed the drama *The Living Corpse,* Sukhanov visited Tolstoy on 26 November 1900 and begged him in his own name and his mother's not to embarrass them by publishing it, a plea to which Tolstoy graciously agreed. But his heirs published and staged the play in September 1911, when Sukhanov was in exile in Archangelsk, *Kornikov,* pp. 11–12.
4. *Deiateli,* cols 129–30.
5. N. Sukhanov, *Zapiski o Revoliutsii* (henceforth cited as *Zapiski*), vol. 4, Berlin–Petersburg–Moscow, 1922, p. 28.
6. *Kornikov,* pp. 33–5; *Deiateli,* cols 130–1.
7. *Deiateli,* col. 131; *Zapiski,* vol. 4, pp. 29–30.

1 Champion of the Russian Village Commune

1. Konstantin Levin [Sukhanov], 'O nashei agrarnoi programmy', *Revoliutsionnaia Rossiia,* no. 75, 15 September 1905, supplement, pp. 1–6.
2. Ibid., p. 4.
3. Ibid., p. 5.
4. Ibid., p. 6.
5. Ibid., p. 6.
6. For the debates and the programme, *see Protokoly pervogo s'ezda Partii Sotsialistov-Revoliutsionerov, 1906.*
7. Ibid., p. 194.
8. Ibid., pp. 204–5, 210–12, 238.
9. Ibid., p. 252.
10. [Peter Struve] 'Die Agrarfrage und die Sozialdemokratie in Russland' [Report of Russian-Social Democracy to the London Congress of the Socialist International of 1895], *Neue Zeit ,* xiv, vol. 2, Stuttgart, 1896, pp. 560–6; Lenin, *Razvitie Kapitalizma v Rossii,* 1899, *PSS,* vol. 3, Moscow, 1958, pp. 165–6, 226, 313–15, 322, 381.
11. N. Sukhanov, *Zemel'naia renta i osnovy zemel'nogo oblozheniia (k voprosu o sotsializatsii zemli). S predisloviem V. Chernova,* Moscow, 1908.

12. N. Sukhanov, *K voprosu ob evoliutsii sel'skogo khoziaistva: sotsial'nye otnosheniia v krest'ianskom khoziaistve Rossii*, Moscow, 1909.
13. Sukhanov, *Zemel'naia renta*, p. 12; not surprisingly, Sukhanov ventured on pp. 31–109 into a lengthy and quite aggressive critique of Marx's theory of absolute ground rent and of its Marxist protagonists such as Kautsky, Peter Maslov, Lenin and Nikolai Rozhkov.
14. Sukhanov, *K voprosu ob evoliutsii sel'skogo khoziaistva*, pp. 6–7, 118–19, 120–4, 126, 128, 132, 142, 153.
15. N. Gimmer [Sukhanov] 'Tekhnika i economika v sel'skom khoziaistve', *Zavety* (1913), no. 11, pp. 1–45; 85n.; also *K voprosu ob evoliutsii sel'skogo khoziaistva*, 2nd edition, Moscow, 1924, p. xi.
16. *A.A. Kornikov*, p. 41.
17. Quoted from the police records in *Kornikov*, p. 42.
18. Ibid., pp. 38, 42.
19. N. Gimmer [Sukhanov], 'K teorii razvitiia agrarnykh otnoshenii', *Russkoe bogatstvo*, vol. 10 (1910), pp. 156–79; vol. 11 (1910), pp. 175–94; vol. 12 (1910), pp. 101–25; N. Gimmer, [Sukhanov] 'Po voprosam nashikh raznoglasii', *Zavety* (1912), no. 6, pp. 1–23; no. 7, pp. 1–75.
20. Gimmer 'Po voprosam nashikh raznoglasii', *Zavety* (1912), no. 7, pp. 35–6.
21. N. Gimmer [Sukhanov], 'K teorii razvitiia agrarnykh otnoshenii', *Russkoe bogatstvo*, vol. 12 (1910), pp. 109, 125.
22. 'Po voprosam nashikh raznoglasii', *Zavety* (1912), no. 7, pp. 42–5.
23. Nik. Sukhanov, 'Na dva fronta', *Zavety*, no. 4, April 1913, p. 128.
24. *Kornikov*, p. 45; V.B. Stankevich, *Vospominaniia 1914–1919g*, Berlin, 1920, p. 9; Stankevich also mentions Vasilii Bogucharsky as co-editor.
25. Stankevich to Lenin, 9 (22) March, 1914, in Lenin, *PSS*, vol. 48, Moscow, 1964, p. 410.
26. Nik Sukhanov, 'O Marksistakh i razrushenii obshchiny', *Zavety*, no. 2 (February 1913), p. 40 (reprinted in *Nashi Napravleniia*, 2nd edition, Petrograd, 1916, p. 86).
27. *Nashi Napravleniia*, pp. 110–12.
28. *Nashi Napravleniia*, pp. 60–1.
29. A select few are listed in *Nashi Napravleniia*, p. 7n.
30. V.B. Stankevich, 'Ob'edinenie ili pogloshenie. K voprosu ob edinoi sotsialisticheskoi partii', *Sovremennik*, January 1913, pp. 329–41.
31. *Nashi Napravleniia*, pp. 6–7.
32. N. Rakitnikov, 'K peresmotru nashikh vzgliadov na krest'ianstvo', *Zavety*, no. 1 (1913), pp. 118–35.
33. Viktor Chernov 'Uprazdnenie narodnichestva', *Zavety*, June 1914, pp. 88–124.
34. Lenin, 'Priemy bor'by burzhuaznoi intelligentsii protiv rabochikh', *Prosveshchenie*, June 1914, reprinted in *PSS*, vol. 25, Moscow, 1961, pp. 321–9.
35. Nik. Sukhanov , 'Edinstvo', *Sovremennik*, no. 12 (1914), pp. 69–81.
36. Aleksei Litvin (ed.), *Men'sheviki v Sovetskoi Rossii. Sbornik dokumentov*, Kazan', 1998, p. 140.

37. Lenin to V.A. Karpinsky, 23 May 1914, *PSS*, vol. 48, p. 292.
38. Their work was published as *Arkhangel'skaia guberniia po statisticheskomu opisaniiu 1785 goda (Itogi podvornoi perepisi)*, Archangelsk, 1916.
39. Stankevich, *Vospominaniia*, p. 22.
40. Sukhanov, *Zapiski o revoliutsii*, vol. 1, p. 16.
41. Sukhanov, *Zapiski*, vol. 4, p. 31.
42. 'Voennaia tsenzura o Letopisi', *Letopis'*, nos. 2–4, February–March–April 1917, pp. 425–7.
43. Sukhanov's *Nashi levye gruppy i voina*, Petrograd, 1915, 1916, together with its follow-up *Pochemu my voiuem?*, Petrograd, 1916, which incorporate a number of his anti-war articles, have been used in the preceding listing of Sukhanov's 'victims and their "crimes"'.
44. *Politicheskie Partii Rossii Konets X1X – Pervaia Tret' XX Veka: Entsiklopedia*, Moscow, 1996, p. 588.
45. *Letopis'*, no. 9, 9 September 1916 apologized to its readers that the following writings were prevented from publication by circumstances beyond the editors' control: V. Mayakovsky, 'War and Peace' (third part), Iv. Bunin, poem, 'Arkhistrateg'; R. Arsky, 'The Workers' Movement during the War', M. Lur'e, 'The Rise of Opposition in Germany', A. Kerensky, a letter to the editor.
46. *Nashi levye gruppy i voina*, pp. 107–8.
47. Quoted in Nik. Sukhanov, *Pochemu my voiuem?*, p. 48; *Zapiski*, vol. 2, p. 364n.
48. Michael Melancon, *The Socialist Revolutionaries and the Russian Anti-War Movement 1914–1917*, Ohio State University Press, Columbus, 1990, pp. 83–4.
49. Stankevich, *Vospominaniia*, p. 23.
50. *Nashi levye gruppy i voina*, pp. 24–5.
51. Lenin, *PSS*, vol. 49, pp. 197, 198, 213, 216, 226.
52. V.P. Antonov-Saratovsky, *Pod stiagom proletarskoi bor'by*, Moscow–Leningrad, 1925, pp. 62–3.
53. Nik. Sukhanov, 'K perspektivam mira', *Novaia zhizn'*, no. 35, 6 March 1918.
54. *Protsess kontrrevoliutsionnoi organizatsii Men'shevikov (1–9 marta 1931g.). Stenograficheskii protokol sudebnogo protsessa*, Moscow, 1931, p. 386.

2 Ideologist of the February Revolution

1. Even in recent works of scholarship such as Tsuyoshi Hasegawa, *The February Revolution: Petrograd 1917*, Seattle and London, 1981, p. 423; Ziva Galili, *The Menshevik Leaders and the Russian Revolution*, Princeton, 1989, pp. 57, 59, not to mention Leon Trotsky, *History of the Russian Revolution*, vol. 1, London, 1934, pp. 184–5 and such Soviet works as *Velikaia oktiabr'skaia sotsialisticheskaia revoliutsiia* (3rd edition), Moscow, 1987, p. 505.

2. Nik. Sukhanov, *Zapiski o revoliutsii* (henceforth *Zapiski*), vol. 1 (4th edition), Berlin–Petersburg–Moscow, 1922, pp. 20–7.
3. Ibid., p. 229.
4. Ibid., p. 229n.; he claims to have written an article to that effect for the February 1917 issue of *Letopis'* which, couched in 'ultra-Aesopian' language to pass the tsarist censor, proved unsuitable for publication in the free atmosphere of the February revolution and survived only in galley proof.
5. Ibid., p. 30.
6. Ibid., pp. 235–8.
7. Ibid., pp. 255–6.
8. Ibid., pp. 330–1
9. Ibid., pp. 277–81.
10. Ibid., pp. 382–3, 344.
11. Ibid., p. 346.
12. V.B. Stankevich, *Vospominaniia*, 1920, pp. 77–8, 97.
13. Trotsky, *History of the Russian Revolution*, vol. 1, pp. 183–4.
14. Ibid., p. 184.
15. *Zapiski*, vol. 2, pp. 77–82.
16. Ibid., pp. 82–6.
17. *Zapiski*, vol. 3, p. 225.
18. *Zapiski*, vol. 1, p. 232.
19. *Zapiski*, vol. 2, p. 78.
20. Iu.S. Tokarev, *Petrogradskii Sovet Rabochikh i Soldatskikh Deputatov v Marte-Aprele 1917g.*, Leningrad, 1976, p. 100; *Petrogradskii Sovet Rabochikhi Soldatskikh Deputatov v 1917 godu. Dokumenty i Materialy*, vol. 1, Leningrad, 1991, pp. 204–5.
21. Ibid., p. 88; *Izvestiia*, no. 7, 6 March 1917, p. 4.
22. *Zapiski*, vol. 2, p. 50.
23. Robert Paul Browder and Alexander Kerensky (eds), *The Russian Provisional Government 1917, Documents*, vol. 2, Stanford, 1961, pp. 1042–3.
24. *Zapiski*, vol. 2, pp. 108–9.
25. Ibid., pp. 143–4.
26. Ibid., p. 199; *Petrogradskii Sovet Rabochikh i Soldatskikh Deputatov v 1917 godu. Dokumenty i Materialy*, vol. 1, pp. 205, 268 and 473n.
27. *Petrogradskii Sovet*, vol. 1, pp. 302–4; *Zapiski*, vol. 2, pp. 228–35.
28. Stankevich, *Vospominaniia*, pp. 102–3.
29. *Zapiski*, vol. 2, pp. 199–203.
30. *Petrogradskii Sovet*, vol. 1, p. 467; *Zapiski*, vol. 2, pp. 269–70; Stankevich, *Vospominaniia*, p. 111.
31. Z. Galili , A. Nenarokov, L. Hyamson (eds), *Men'sheviki v 1917 godu*, vol. 1, Moscow, 1994, p. 78n.
32. Ibid., p. 157.
33. *Izvestiia*, no. 25, 26 March 1917; *Zapiski*, vol. 2, pp. 316–7.
34. *Petrogradskii Sovet*, vol. 1, pp. 439–45.

35. Iraklii Tsereteli, *Vospominaniia o fevral'skoi revoliutsii*, vol. 1 , Paris–The Hague, 1968, pp. 36–7.
36. *Izvestiia*, no. 6, 7 March 1917.
37. Vladimir Voitinsky, 'Gody pobed i porazhenii', *MS*, vol. 3, p. 11, Hoover Institution, Stanford.
38. *Rabochaia gazeta*, no. 1, 7 March 1917, p. 4; also *Izvestiia Petrogradskogo Soveta*, 7 March 1917, quoted in Ziva Galili y Garcia, 'The Origins of Revolutionary Defensism. I.G. Tsereteli and the Siberian Zimmerwaldists', *Slavic Review*, vol. 41, no. 3, Fall 1982, p. 472.
39. *Zapiski*, vol. 2, pp. 336–8; Tsereteli, *Vospominaniia*, vol. 1, pp. 45–6.
40. Tsereteli's speech of 21 March is missing from both the protocols of the *Petrogradskii Sovet*, vol. 1 and from a collection of Tsereteli's 1917 speeches edited by St. Ivanovich, *Rechi Tsereteli proizvedeny v 1917g.*, Petrograd, 1917; a section of that speech was however published as late as 1968 in Tsereteli, *Vospominaniia*, vol. 1, pp. 46–7.
41. *Petrogradskii Sovet*, vol. 1, pp. 471–2.
42. *Zapiski*, vol. 2, pp. 334, 370–1.
43. A.G. Shliapnikov, *Semnadtsatyi god*, vol. 3, Moscow, 1994, pp. 98–100; *Zapiski*, vol. 2., pp. 304–5.
44. Tsereteli, *Vospominaniia*, vol. 1, pp. 69–71.
45. *Zapiski*, vol. 2, pp. 363–5.
46. *Petrogradskii Sovet*, vol. 1, p. 600; *Zapiski*, vol. 2, p. 366.
47. Shliapnikov, *Semnadtsatyi god*, vol. 3, p. 102.
48. *Vserossiiskoe Soveshchanie Sovetov Rabochikh i Soldatskikh Deputatov. Stenograficheskii Otchet*, Moscow, 1927, p. 40.
49. *Petrogradskii Sovet*, vol. 1, pp. 616–17; *Zapiski* , vol. 2, p. 369.
50. *Zapiski*, vol. 2, pp. 377–8; *Petrogradskii Sovet*, vol. 1, p. 491.
51. *Zapiski*, vol. 2, pp. 378–9; the text of the resolution is in *Soveshchanie Sovetov*, pp. 311–12.
52. *Petrogradskii Sovet*, vol. 2, Sankt-Petersburg, 1995, pp. 109–10; *Soveshchanie Sovetov*, p. 311.
53. *Petrogradskii Sovet*, vol. 1, p. 620; *Zapiski*, vol. 2, pp. 381–7.
54. *Petrogradskii Sovet*, vol. 1, pp. 620, 623; *Soveshchanie Sovetov* , p. 292.
55. *Zapiski*, vol. 2, pp. 411–14.
56. *Zapiski*, vol. 3, pp. 84–5.
57. *Ibid.*, pp. 89–90.
58. *Petrogradskii Sovet*, vol. 2, p. 19.
59. Tsereteli, *Vospominaniia*, vol. 1, p. 77.
60. *Petrogradskii Sovet*, vol. 2, p. 36; *Zapiski*, vol. 3, pp. 208–9.
61. *Zapiski*, vol. 3, p. 211.
62. *Petrogradskii Sovet*, vol. 2, p. 48.
63. *Ibid.*, p. 39.
64. *Ibid.*, p. 50.
65. *Zapiski*, vol. 3, pp. 206–7.
66. *Petrogradskii Sovet*, vol. 2, pp. 68–9.
67. *Ibid.*, p. 71.

68. Ibid., p. 77.
69. Ibid., p. 79.
70. *Zapiski*, vol. 3, pp. 203–4; Tsereteli, *Vospominaniia*, vol. 1, pp. 83–4.
71. *Petrogradskii Sovet*, vol. 2, pp. 199–200.
72. Ibid., p. 85.
73. *Novaia zhizn'*, no. 1, April 1917.
74. *Zapiski*, vol. 3, p. 246.
75. Browder and Kerensky, *The Russian Provisional Government 1917*, vol. 2, p. 1098.
76. *Zapiski*, vol. 3, p. 246.
77. *Petrogradskii Sovet*, vol. 2, pp. 276–7; *Zapiski*, vol. 3, pp. 287–8.
78. *Petrogradskii Sovet*, vol. 2, pp. 298–9, 310.
79. 'Demokratiia i Vremennoe Pravitel'stvo', *Novaia zhizn'*, no. 3, 21 April 1917.
80. *Petrogradskii Sovet*, vol. 2, pp. 298–9, 310, 322.
81. Ibid., p. 323.
82. Ibid., pp. 320, 327.
83. Nik. Sukhanov, 'Voennyi zaem v sovete rabochikh i soldatskikh deputatov', *Novaia zhizn'*, no. 5, 23 April 1917; *Zapiski*, vol. 3, p. 315.
84. *Zapiski*, vol. 2, pp. 370–2.
85. Tsereteli, *Vospominaniia*, vol. 1, p. 132.
86. *Men'sheviki v 1917 godu*, vol. 1. pp. 207–9
87. N. Sukhanov, 'Koalitsionnoe ministerstvo', *Novaia zhizn'*, no. 8, 27 April 1917; *Petrogradskii Sovet*, vol. 2, p. 414.
88. 'Peregovory o koalitsionnom ministerstve', *Novaia zhizn'*, no. 13, 3 May 1917; 'Novoe pravitel'stvo i demokratiia', *Novaia zhizn'*, no. 14, 4 May 1917.
89. 'Razreshenie pravitel'stvennogo krizisa', *Novaia zhizn'*, no. 14, 4 May 1917.
90. Browder and Kerensky, *The Russian Provisional Government 1917*, vol. 3, Stanford, 1961, pp. 1277–8.
91. N. Sukhanov, 'O nastupatel'nykh deistviiakh', *Novaia zhizn'*, no. 19, 10 May 1917.
92. 'Programma g. Tereshchenko i Rech' g. Ribo', *Novaia zhizn'*, no. 21, 12 May 1917; 'O vernosti pobede i nastuplenii', *Novaia zhizn'*, no. 22, 13 May 1917; 'Russkie lozungi v soiuznikh stranakh', *Novaia zhizn'*, no. 23, 14 May 1917; 'Pravitel'stvo mira ili pravitel'stvo nastupleniia', *Novaia zhizn'*, no. 25, 17 May 1917; these articles reached a crescendo of bitterness and venom in 'Strategiia ili politika', *Novaia zhizn'*, no. 30, 24 May 1917; 'U razbitogo koryta', *Novaia zhizn'*, no. 32, 26 May 1917; 'Peresmotr dogovorov', *Novaia zhizn'*, no. 41, 6 June 1917; 'O polozhenii v armii', *Novaia zhizn'*, no. 49, 15 June 1917; for Martov's concept of 'separate war', *see* Israel Getzler, *Martov*, Melbourne and Cambridge, 1967, pp. 152–3 and 152n.
93. 'Nastuplenie i soiuzniki', *Novaia zhizn'*, no. 55, 22 June 1917.
94. *Men'sheviki v 1917 godu*, vol. 2, pp. 101–2.
95. 'Pobeda Chernova', *Novaia zhizn'*, no. 74, 14 July 1917.

96. 'Krizis', *Novaia zhizn'*, no. 75, 15 July 1917.
97. 'V poiskakh vlasti', *Novaia zhizn'*, no. 78, 19 July 1917.
98. 'Kogda zhe konets?', *Novaia zhizn'*, no. 82, 23 July 1917, unsigned editorial, but most likely Sukhanov's, *see* 'V poiskakh vlasti' which refers to 'the future historian'.
99. 'Novaia koalitsiia', *Novaia zhizn'*, no. 83, 25 July 1917.
100. *Zapiski*, vol. 5, p. 96.
101. *Men'sheviki v 1917 godu*, vol. 2, pp. 447–8, 457.
102. Nik. Sukhanov, 'Novyie soiuzniki', *Novaia zhizn'*, no. 114, 29 August 1917; 'Na ocheredi', *Novaia zhizn'*, no. 115, 30 August 1917; 'Pered resheniem', *Novaia zhizn'*, no. 116, 31 August 1917; 'Na sud', *Novaia zhizn'*, no. 116, 31 August 1917; *Svobodnaia zhizn'*, no. 3, 5 September 1917; see *Zapiski*, vol. 6, p. 60, for Kerensky's responsibility.
103. 'V tiskakh vlasti', *Novaia zhizn'*, no. 135, 23 September 1917, unsigned editorial, but *see Zapiski*, vol. 7, pp. 58–9 for Sukhanov's authorship.
104. 'Uderzhat li bol'sheviki gosudarstvennuiu vlast', 1 October 1917, Lenin, *PSS*, vol. 34, Moscow, 1962, pp. 289–339 – the specific reference to the editorial of *Novaia zhizn'* is on p. 292.
105. 'Grom snova grianul', *Novaia zhizn'*, no. 142, 1 October 1917; *Zapiski*, vol. 6, p. 166.
106. Lenin, *PSS*, vol. 34, p. 339.
107. Nik. Sukhanov, 'Pobeda Tsereteli', *Novaia zhizn'*, no. 137, 28 September 1917.
108. Nik. Sukhanov, 'Grom snova grianul', *Novaia zhizn'*, no. 142, 1 October 1917.
109. Nik. Sukhanov, 'Novyi vyzov', *Novaia zhizn'*, no. 145, 5 October 1917.
110. Nik. Sukhanov, 'Nachalo krizisa', *Novaia zhizn'*, no. 158, 20 October 1917.

3 Chronicler of Russia's Democratic Revolution

1. 'Perhaps the revolution's most famous memoirist', Orlando Figes, *A People's Tragedy: the Russian Revolution 1891–1924*, London, 1996, p. 311; 'The most penetrating and complete eye-witness account of the revolution of 1917', Marc Ferro, *La révolution de 1917*, Paris, 1967, p. 134.
2. Nik. Sukhanov, *Zapiski o Revoliutsii*, vol. 1, Berlin–Petersburg–Moscow, 1922, p. 7, henceforth *Zapiski*.
3. *Zapiski*, vol. 1, p. 126.
4. *Zapiski*, vol. 4, pp. 511–14; vol. 3, pp. 138,139n.; vol. 7, pp. 160, 157.
5. S.P. Melgunov, *Martovskie dni 1917goda*, Paris, 1961, pp. 9–10.
6. I.G. Tsereteli, *Vospominaniia o fevral'skoi revoliutsii*, vol. 2, Paris, 1968, p. 286.
7. P.N. Miliukov, *Vospominaniia* , vol. 2, New York, 1955, p. 322.
8. I.V. Stalin, *Sobranie Sochinenii*, vol. 6, Moscow, 1954, p. 339.
9. Leon Trotsky, *History of the Russian Revolution*, vol. 3, London, 1934, p. 1156.

10. *Zapiski*, vol. 1, pp. 7, 9, 11; vol. 4, p. 513n.
11. *Zapiski*, vol. 1, p. 10.
12. *Zapiski*, vol. 1, p. 9; vol. 2, p. 8; vol. 3, p. 342.
13. *Zapiski*, vol. 3, p. 372.
14. The drastically abridged English edition of Sukhanov's *Zapiski, The Russian Revolution 1917: a Personal Record by N.N. Sukhanov*, edited, abridged and translated by Joel Carmichael, Oxford University Press, London, 1955, has obscured the *leitmotiv* and thesis of Sukhanov's work, not least by omitting the pen portraits of Iraklii Tsereteli and Fiodor Dan, the two principal characters singled out by Sukhanov as bearing heavy responsibility for the tragic failure of Russia's democratic revolution of 1917.
15. *Zapiski*, vol. 3, pp. 243–6.
16. *Zapiski*, vol. 3, pp. 275–6; Stankevich's speech is also reported in Tsereteli, *vospominaniia* , vol. 1, p. 97.
17. *Zapiski*, vol. 3, pp. 293–6.
18. *Zapiski*, vol. 3, pp. 87–9, 138.
19. *Zapiski*, vol. 3, p. 341.
20. *Zapiski*, vol. 3, pp. 308, 339, 315.
21. *Zapiski*, vol. 3, pp. 100–1, 158.
22. *Zapiski*, vol. 3, p. 49.
23. *Zapiski*, vol. 3, pp. 13–17.
24. *Zapiski*, vol. 3, pp. 16–17.
25. *Zapiski*, vol. 3, pp. 52–61.
26. *Zapiski*, vol. 4, pp. 338–43.
27. *Zapiski*, vol. 4, pp. 423–6.
28. *Zapiski*, vol. 4, pp. 430–1.
29. *Zapiski*, vol. 3, p. 56.
30. *Zapiski*, vol. 3, p. 248.
31. *Zapiski*, vol. 7, pp. 22–3.
32. *Zapiski*, vol. 7, pp. 90–2.
33. Zapiski, vol. 7, pp. 75–82, 89–92, 139.
34. *Zapiski*, vol. 7, pp. 71, 90–2, 143, 224–5.
35. *Zapiski*, vol. 4, pp. 27–35.
36. *Zapiski*, vol. 1, pp. 61–77.
37. It has often and seriously been suggested that Sukhanov's tragic fate was to some extent due to Stalin's vindictive fury at being labelled a 'grey blur'. Trotsky went so far as to assert that 'Sukhanov eventually paid for that with his life' (L. Trotsky, *Stalin*, vol. 1, p. 267) That story has been repeated or hinted at ever since, most recently in the 1991 edition of the *Zapiski*, vol. 1, p. 30. Whatever the likelihood that Stalin was motivated by a personal grudge, he certainly had an earlier and weightier cause for a private vendetta against Sukhanov who, together with Martov, had ridiculed him and put him to shame both in the Central Executive Committee and in *Novaia zhizn'* as early as April 1918 in connection with the so-called 'Martov Affair'.

38. *Zapiski*, vol. 3, pp. 136–8, 138n.
39. *Zapiski*, vol. 6, p. 182.
40. *Zapiski*, vol. 6, pp. 342–3.
41. *Zapiski*, vol. 6, pp. 125–33.
42. *Zapiski*, vol. 3, p. 138.
43. *Zapiski*, vol. 2, p. 395; vol. 3, pp. 135–6, 166, 352.
44. *Zapiski*, vol. 3, pp. 131–8.
45. *Zapiski*, vol. 6, p. 20.
46. *Zapiski*, vol. 6, p. 31.
47. *Zapiski*, vol. 5, pp. 12–13.
48. *Zapiski*, vol. 4, pp. 369–70.
49. *Zapiski*, vol. 6, p. 297.
50. *Zapiski*, vol. 6, pp. 298–301.
51. *Zapiski*, vol. 5, pp. 277, 319.
52. *Zapiski*, vol. 5, pp. 360–1.
53. *Zapiski*, vol. 2, pp. 317–18.
54. *Zapiski*, vol. 1, p. 38.
55. *Zapiski*, vol. 1, pp. 130–1.
56. *Zapiski*, vol. 1, p. 133.
57. *Zapiski*, vol. 2, p. 162.
58. *Zapiski*, vol. 2, pp. 319–20.
59. *Zapiski*, vol. 2, pp. 320–1.
60. *Zapiski*, vol. 1, pp. 265–7.
61. *Zapiski*, vol. 3, pp. 20–1.
62. *Zapiski*, vol. 2, p. 321.
63. *Zapiski*, vol. 3, p. 384.
64. *Zapiski*, vol. 3, pp. 382–3.
65. *Zapiski*, vol. 3, p. 443.
66. *Zapiski*, vol. 7, p. 197.
67. *Zapiski*, vol. 7, p. 203.
68. *Zapiski*, vol. 7, p. 203; also Leon Trotsky, *History of the Russian Revolution*, vol. 3, London, 1934, p. 1156, where Trotsky copies his own speech verbatim from the *Zapiski*.
69. *Zapiski*, vol. 7, pp. 252–3.
70. *Zapiski*, vol. 7, pp. 259–60.
71. *Zapiski*, vol. 1, p. 12.
72. *Zapiski*, vol. 3, pp. 32–6; vol. 4, p. 366.
73. 'Referat N.N. Sukhanova', *Sotsialisticheskii vestnik* , no. 9, 5 June 1921.
74. *Zapiski*, vol. 6, p. 253.
75. *Zapiski*, vol. 7, pp. 57–8.
76. *Zapiski*, vol. 6, pp.126–127, 180; vol. 7, pp. 236, 277–8, 226–7, 276–7, 290.
77. *Zapiski*, vol. 6, pp. 252–3.
78. Israel Getzler 'Lenin's Martov', *Revolutionary Russia*, vol. 5, no. 1 (June 1992), pp. 93–4.
79. *Zapiski*, vol. 3, p. 33.

80. Getzler, *Revolutionary Russia*, vol. 5, no. 1, pp. 93–4.
81. Lenin, 'O nashei revoliutsii', *PSS*, vol. 45, pp. 378–82, also 376–7.
82. M. Kubanin 'Obshchina pri diktature proletariata (Otvet N. Sukhanovu)', *Na agrarnom fronte*, nos. 11–12, 1926, p. 111; *Piat'nadtsatyi s'ezd VKP(b) Dekabr' 1927. Stenograficheskii otchet*, vol. 1, Moscow, 1961, p. 149; *Trudy pervoi Vsesoiuznoi Konferentsii Agrarnikov-Marksistov 20/xii-27/xii, 1929g.*, Moscow, 1930, p. 71.

4 In Opposition to the Bolshevik 'Jacobin' Dictatorship

1. *Zapiski*, vol. 7, p. 220.
2. *Men'sheviki v 1917 godu*, vol. 3, pp. 321–2.
3. 'Bol'sheviki pri vlasti', *Novaia zhizn'*, no. 166, 29 October 1917.
4. 'Doloi oruzhie' *Novaia zhizn'*, no. 167, 30 October; 'Krizis novoi vlasti', *Novaia zhizn'*, no. 173, 5 November 1917.
5. 'Diktatura grazhdanina Lenina', *Novaia zhizn'*, no. 174, 7 November 1917.
6. 'Novaia faza', *Novaia zhizn'*, no. 183, 17 November 1917.
7. 'Razgon dumy', *Novaia zhizn'*, no. 184, 18 November 1917.
8. 'Grazhdanskaia voina', *Novaia zhizn'*, no. 190, 1 December 1917.
9. 'Gde zhe TsIK?', *Novaia zhizn'*, no. 196, 8 December 1917.
10. 'Rasshirenie bazisa', *Novaia zhizn'*, no. 199, 12 December 1917; *Zapiski*, vol. 7, p. 240.
11. John L. Keep (ed.), *The Debate on Soviet Power: Minutes of the All-Russian Central Executive Committee of Soviets Second Convocation, October 1917–January 1918*, Oxford 1979, pp. 248–9, 251.
12. 'Kamen' na doroge', *Novaia zhizn'*, no. 211, 28 December 1917.
13. 'Uchreditelnoe sobranie', *Novaia zhizn'*, no. 2, 4 January 1918 (unsigned editorial).
14. 'Piatoe ianvariia', *Novaia zhizn'*, no. 3, 5 January 1918.
15. 'Razgon', *Novaia zhizn'*, no. 8, 8 January 1918.
16. Keep, *Debate on Soviet Power*, p. 266; Zinaida Gippius, 'Chernyie tetrady', *Zveniia: Istoricheskii Almanakh*, Vypusk 2, Petersburg, 1992, p. 52; James Bunyan and H.H. Fisher (eds), *The Bolshevik Revolution 1917–1918*, Stanford, 1934, p. 384.
17. Lenin, *PSS*, vol. 35, pp. 265–6, 268.
18. *Novaia zhizn'*, no. 10, 14 January 1918, p. 3 (Rech' Nik. Sukhanova).
19. Ibid.
20. Lenin, *PSS*, vol. 35, pp. 280–2.
21. 'Razgon', *Novaia zhizn'*, no. 6, 8 January 1918.
22. 'O vlasti sovetov', *Novaia zhizn'*, no. 15, 21 January 1918.
23. *Novaia zhizn'*, no. 15, 21 January 1918, pp. 4–7, N. Rozhkov, 'Diktatura proletariata'; Karl Kautsky, 'Diktatura i demokratiia' (dated Berlin, 3 January 1918).

24. 'Pokornyi final', *Novaia zhizn'*, no. 29, 20 February 1918; 'Kapitulatsiia', *Novaia zhizn'*, no. 30, 29 February 1918.
25. 'Vykhod gazet', *Novaia zhizn'*, no. 41, 14 March 1918, p. 2.
26. *Novaia zhizn'*, no. 31, 2 March 1918 (reprinted in *Zapiski*, vol. 3, p. 233).
27. 'Peredyshka', *Novaia zhizn'*, no. 35, 6 March 1918; 'Samoubiistvo', Ibid., no. 34, 5 March 1918; 'Pered s'ezdom', Ibid., no. 39, 11 March 1918; 'Klochek bumagi', Ibid., no. 33, 3 March 1918; 'K perspektivam mira', Ibid., no. 35, 6 March 1918; but 'K itogam Bresta', Ibid., no. 126, 30 June 1918.
28. 'Kavkazskii Brest', *Novaia zhizn'*, no. 126, 30 June 1918.
29. 'Brest i Ukraina', *Novaia zhizn'*, no. 23, 31 January (13 February) 1918; 'Gde vykhod', Ibid., no. 43, 16 March 1918; 'K perspektivam mira', Ibid., no. 35, 6 March 1918; *Zapiski*, vol. 4, p. 206.
30. 'Godovshchina revoliutsii', *Novaia zhizn'*, no. 40, 27 February (12 March) 1918.
31. *Chetvertyi vserossiiskii s'ezd sovetov rabochikh, krestian'skikh, soldatskikh i kazachikh deputatov*, Moscow, 1919, pp. 48–9.
32. Ibid.
33. Ibid., pp. 252–4, 299–300.
34. Ibid.
35. The protocols of the preliminary investigations by the OGPU have now been published by Prof. A.L. Litvin, in two volumes: *Men'shevistskii Protsess 1931 goda. Sbornik dokumentov v 2-kh knigakh*, Moscow, 1999, henceforth *Men'shevistskii Protsess* . The reference here is to vol. 2, p. 101.
36. 'Vlast' sovetov o pozitsii rabochago klassa', *Novaia zhizn'*, no. 113, 11 June 1918; *Znamiia truda*, 19 May 1918, quoted in William Henry Chamberlin, *The Russian Revolution 1917–1921*, Vol. 1, New York, 1960, pp. 419, 427.
37. *Protokoly zasedanii Vserossiiskogo Tsentral'nogo Ispolkoma 4-go sozyva. Stenograficheskii otchet*, Moscow, 1920, p. 399.
38. Ibid., p. 205.
39. Ibid., pp. 415, 419.
40. Quoted in *Kornikov* , pp. 95–6; *Zapiski*, vol. 3, p. 247.
41. *Men'shevistskii Protsess*, vol. 2, p. 99; Leopold H. Haimson (ed.), *The Mensheviks*, Chicago and London, 1974, p. 217.
42. *Kornikov*, pp. 95–6,101–2; Martov to Eva Broido, 26 June 1920, Nicolaevsky Collection, Hoover Institution, Stanford.
43. 'Delo Soiuznogo Biuro Men'shevikov', Deposition of 29/30 January 1931, *Men'shevistskii Protsess*, vol. 2, pp. 99–100.
44. Getzler, *Martov*, pp. 208-12.
45. Archive of the Central Committee of the Communist Party in the Russian Centre for the Conservation and Study of Documents of Recent History.
46. Martov to Axelrod, 30 January 1921; Martov to Rafail Abramovich, 10 August 1921; Martov to S.D. Shchupak, 5 February 1921 – all in Nicolaevsky Collection, Hoover Institution, Stanford.

47. 'Referat N.N. Sukhanova', Moscow, 29 April 1921, *Sotsialisticheskii vestnik*, no. 9, 5 June 1921.
48. *Zapiski*, vol. 7, p. 178.
49. *Men'shevistskii Protsess*, vol. 2, pp. 101–2.
50. Lenin to Molotov, 22 January 1922, *PSS*, vol. 54, p. 134.
51. *Men'shevistskii Protsess*, vol. 2, p. 102.
52. Quoted in *Kornikov*, p. 109.
53. Ibid.
54. Ibid.
55. Nik. Sukhanov, *Mirovoe khoziaistvo nakanune i posle voiny, 1913–1923gg. Populiarnyi Ocherk*, Leningrad–Moscow 1924.
56. Ibid., p. 103.

5   Knight Errant of the *Obshchina*

1. Nik. Sukhanov, *K voprosu ob evoliutsii sel'skogo khoziaistva*, second edition, corrected and supplemented, Moscow, 1924.
2. Ibid., pp. 256–8.
3. N. Sukhanov, 'Obshchina v sovetskom agrarnom zakonodatel'stve', *Na agrarnom fronte*, nos 11–12, 1926, pp. 97–110.
4. Ibid., p. 110; the three drafts of Marx's letter were published in the *Marx-Engels Archiv*, vol.1, Moscow, 1926, pp. 316–42, also in Karl Marx and Friedrich Engels, *Werke*, vol. 19, Berlin, 1962, pp. 384–406.
5. E.H. Carr, *The Bolshevik Revolution 1917–1923*, vol. 2, London, 1952, p. 379.
6. L. Kritsman, *Geroicheskii period Velikoi Russkoi Revoliutsiii. (Opyt analiza t. n. voennogo kommunizma)*, Moscow, 1925, pp. 9, 75.
7. *K voprosu ob evoliutsii sel'skogo khoziaistva*, second edition, pp. iv–vi.
8. S. Dubrovsky, *Ob odnoi 'raznovidnosti' revizionizma. O teorii dekapitalizatsii sel'skogo khoziaistva, razvivaemoi N.N. Sukhanovym*, Moscow, 1926; only four years later, one of Dubrovsky's books was denounced in a special session of the Institute of Red Professors as a 'variant of revisionism'.
9. M.L. Kubanin, 'Obshchina pri diktature proletariata (Otvet N. Sukhanovu)', *Na agrarnom fronte*, nos 11–12, 1926, pp. 111–26.
10. Ibid., pp. 111, 125–6.
11. Prof. Sukhanov, 'O differentsiatsii krest'ianskogo khoziaistva', *Na agrarnom fronte*, no. 4, 1927, pp. 145–7.
12. *Na agrarnom fronte*, no. 7, 1927, p. 123.
13. Ibid., pp. 124–5, 133.
14. 'Preniia po dokladu L Kritsmana. Rech' t. Sukhanova', *Na agrarnom fronte*, nos 6–7, 1928, pp. 181, 183.
15. 'Ob ekonomicheskikh predposyl'kakh pod'ema sel'skogo khoziaistva', *Vestnik Akademii Nauk SSSR*, no. 9, 1990, pp. 104–11; arkhiv *AN SSSR* F350, Opis' 2, 349.

16. *Piatnadt'satyi s'ezd VKP (b) Stenograficheskii otchet*, vol. 2, Moscow, 1961–62, p. 1436.
17. *Protsess kontrrevoliutsionnoi organizatsii Men'shevikov*, Moscow, 1931, p. 388; also protocol of preliminary investigation of 17 August 1930, in *Men'shevistskii protsess,* vol. 2, p. 56.
18. Arkhiv *AN SSSR* F350, Opis 2, 349.
19. Ibid.
20. Ibid., no. 7, 1929, pp. 101–2.
21. *Na agrarnom fronte*, no. 8, 1929, p. 101.
22. *Protsess Men'shevikov*, p. 390.
23. *Na agrarnom fronte*, no. 7, 1929, pp. 105–6.
24. *Trudy Vsesoiuznoi Konferentsii Agrarnikov-Marksistov*, Moscow, 1930, p. 71.
25. Ibid., p. 315.
26. Ibid., p. 318
27. Ibid., pp. 246–8, 281.
28. Stalin, 'K voprosam agrarnoi politiki v SSSR', *Sochineniia*, vol. 12, Moscow, 1949, pp. 141–2.
29. Ibid., pp. 142–4, 154, 161, 170–1.
30. Ibid., p. 169.
31. Ibid., p. 149.
32. Ibid., p. 148.
33. Ibid., p. 154.
34. Terry Cox, *Peasants, Class and Capitalism. The Rural Research of L.N. Kritsman and his School*, Oxford, 1986; Susan G. Solomon, *The Soviet Agrarian Debate*, Boulder, CO, 1977.
35. D.J. Male, *Russian Peasant Organisation before Collectivisation: a Study of Commune and Gathering 1925–1930*, Cambridge, 1971, pp. 125, 160, 177; Naum Jasny, *Soviet Economists of the Twenties*, Cambridge, MA, 1972, pp. 53, 179–84.
36. Moshe Lewin, *Russian Peasants and Soviet Power: a Study of Collectivisation*, London, 1968, p. 93.

6 Sukhanov at the Menshevik Trial

1. *Trudy pervoi vsesoiuznoi konferentsii Agrarnikov Marksistov*, vol. I, Moscow, 1930, pp. 38–9
2. *See* references in footnotes 6 and 9.
3. *Bol'shevik*, no. 7, April 1929, p. 97.
4. Quoted from the Central Party Archive in *Kornikov*, p. 121.
5. V.M. Friche, *Zametki o sovremennoi literature*, Moscow–Leningrad, 1928, pp. 5–10, 158-65; M.N. Pokrovsky, 'Pamiati tov. Friche [6.9.1929]' *in Marksistskoe iskusstvoznanie i V.M. Friche, Sbornik statei i bibliografiia*, Kommunisticheskaia Akademiia, sektsiia literatury, iskusstva i iazika, Moscow, 1930.

6. V.M. Friche, 'Burzhuaznyie tendentsii v sovremennoi literature i rol' kritiki', *Doklady v Kommunisticheskoi Akademii*, Moscow, 1930, pp. 5–21; *Vestnik Kommunisticheskoi Akademii*, Kniga 31 (1), 1929, pp. 229–30.
7. I.V. Stalin, *Sochineniia*, vol. 11, Moscow, 1949, pp. 170–2.
8. Friche, 'Burzhuaznyie tendentsii...', pp. 20–1.
9. *Zapiski*, vol. I, p. 147; Sukhanov's critical comments on Friche's lecture, as well as the attacks on Sukhanov made by Kerzhentsev, Isbakh, Nusinov and Bespalov, are in the Archive of the Communist Academy *AN SSSR*, F350, Opis' 2, No. 358.
10. Friche's polemical reply to Sukhanov's critique is in F350, Opis' 2, No. 358.
11. *Men'shevistskii Protsess*, vol. 2, pp. 120–6.
12. Nicolaevsky Collection in the Hoover Institution, Box 690-8, Series 279; I owe this reference to Prof. Aleksei Litvin, of the University of Kazan.
13. *Deiateli SSSR i Oktiabr'skoi Revoliutsii: Entsiklopedicheskii Slovar' Russkogo Bibliograficheskogo Instituta Granat*, 7th edition, vol. 41A, Moscow, 1927–29, p. 133.
14. Nikolai Sukhanov, 'Desiat' let tomu nazad', *Zhurnalist*, no. 3, Moscow, 1927, pp. 18–20.
15. *Men'shevistskii Protsess*, vol. 2, p. 108.
16. *1917 God: Dramaticheskaia Khronika v 5 Deistviiakh*, Moscow–Leningrad, 1928.
17. Ibid., p. 149.
18. *Kornikov*, pp. 112–13.
19. *Men'shevistskii protsess*, vol. 2, p. 108.
20. *Protsess kontrrevoliutsionnoi organizatsii Men'shevikov*, Moscow, 1931, p. 390 (henceforth *Protsess Men'shevikov*).
21. Andrei Artizov and Oleg Naumov, *Vlast' i khudozhestvennaia intelligentsiia: Dokumenty i materialy, 1917–1953*, Moscow, 1999, p. 70
22. *Trudy pervoi vsesoiuznoi konferentsii Agrarnikov-Marksistov*, vol. 1, Moscow, 1930, p. 122.
23. I.V. Stalin, *Sochineniia*, vol. 12, Moscow, 1949, pp. 142–4.
24. *Vestnik Kommunisticheskoi Akademii*, vol. 39, 1930, p. 87.
25. 'Materialy po delu kontrrevoliutsionnoi trudovoi krest'ianskoi partii i gruppirovki Sukhanova–Gromana', in Central Party Archive of the Institute of Marxism-Leninism, pp. 112–13.
26. Ibid., pp. 158–61.
27. Ibid., pp. 116–18.
28. 'Pis'ma Stalina Molotovu', *Kommunist*, 11 July 1990 (no. 1363), p. 103. (Galina Sukhanova-Flakserman was arrested on 16 February 1931 and was released on 13 March 1931).
29. Ibid., pp. 102–3.
30. *Men'shevistskii Protsess*, vol. 2, pp. 62–3.
31. *Protsess Men'shevikov*, p. 233.

32. 'Delo Soiuznogo Buro Men'shevikov', Central Archive of the Federal Security Service of the Russian Federation, vol. 9, pp. 124–5 (this text does not appear in the published volume of the preliminary investigations).
33. Ibid., p. 125.
34. *Men'shevistskii Protsess*, vol. 2, pp. 97–8.
35. *Zapiski*, vol. 6, pp. 43, 45; vol. 2, pp. 33, 244; also unsigned editorial 'V tiskakh vlasti', *Novaia zhizn'*, no. 135, 23 September 1917; (for Sukhanov's authorship of the editorial, *see Zapiski*, vol. 7, pp. 58–9); Nik. Sukhanov, 'Bol'sheviki pri vlasti', *Novaia zhizn'*, no. 166, October 1917.
36. *Men'shevistskii Protsess*, vol. 2, p. 101.
37. Ibid., p. 109.
38. Ibid., pp. 82–3.
39. Deposition of Boris Bogdanov on 4 March 1931 in Arkhiv UFSK, Delo no. 5543, Simferopol, 1961, quoted in N.B. Bogdanov, *Moi otets–Men'shevik*, St. Petersburg, 1994, p. 232.
40. *Men'shevistskii Protsess*, vol. 2, pp. 82–3.
41. Ibid.
42. According to Aleksei Litvin, there are at least 58 volumes related to it in the archives of the Federal Security Service of the Russian Federation, *see* Litvin, *Bez prava na mysl'. Istoriki v epokhu Bol'shogo Terrora*, Kazan, 1994, p. 26.
43. N. Krylenko, *Na bor'bu s vreditel'stvom*, Moscow, 1930, p. 16.
44. *Pravda*, no. 64, 6 March 1931; no. 65, 7 March 1931, front page.
45. Stalin, *Sochineniia*, vol. 12, Moscow, 1949, pp. 252–7.
46. *KPSS v rezoliutsiiakh i resheniiakh*, 7th edition, vol. 3, Moscow, 1954, p. 35; Julius Braunthal, *History of the International 1914–1943*, London, 1967, p. 344n.
47. *Protsess Men'shevikov*, pp. 325–6.
48. *Pravda*, no. 64, 7 March 1931, p. 3; no. 66, 8 March 1931, p. 5, but *see* resolutions of Labour and Socialist International of May 1923 against intervention and for recognition of the Soviet government, resolutions that remained in force until the Nazi–Soviet pact of August 1939, Braunthal, *History of the International 1914–1943*, pp. 269–70.
49. Maxim Gorky to Genrikh Yagoda, 2 November 1930, *Neizvestnyi Gor'kii*, Moscow, 1994, p. 172.
50. Gorky to Stalin, 12 November 1930, *Vlast' i khudozhestvennaia intelligentsiia*, pp. 130–1; also Stalin to Gorky, 24 October 1930, Ibid., p. 130.
51. Stalin to Gorky, 10 January 1931, Ibid., p. 142
52. M. Gor'kii, 'Esli vrag ne sdaetsiia–ego istrebliaiut', *Izvestiia*, no. 314, 15 November 1930.
53. M. Gor'kii, 'Vmesto privetstviia', *Izvestiia*, no. 346, 17 December 1930.
54. *Protsess Men'shevikov*, p. 132; *Pravda*, no. 62, 4 March; no. 64, 6 March; no. 67, 9 March; no. 68, 10 March, 1931; *Izvestiia*, no. 62, 4 March; no. 64, 6 March; no. 65, 7 March; no. 67, 9 March, 1931.

55. *Protsess Men'shevikov*, p. 380.
56. Ibid., pp. 134–9, 457.
57. *Men'shevistskii Protsess*, vol. 2, pp. 86–8.
58. *Protsess Men'shevikov*, p. 23
59. Ibid., pp. 169, 172.
60. Ibid., p. 172.
61. Ibid., p. 176.
62. Ibid., p. 153.
63. Ibid., p. 235.
64. *Pravda*, no. 64, 6 March 1931.
65. *Protsess Men'shevikov* , p. 365; Litvin, *Bez prava na mysl'*, pp. 27–8 concludes on the basis of his study of the archival materials that Sukhanov's testimonies at the Menshevik trial were 'edited and distorted' when published in the so-called stenographic report of the trial.
66. *Men'shevistskii Protsess*, vol. 1, p. 33.
67. Lenin *PSS*, vol. 35, Moscow, 1962, p. 377.
68. *Izvestiia*, no. 128, 23 June 1918.
69. *Deiateli SSSR i Oktiabr'skoi revoliutsii*, p. 245.
70. Lenin *PSS*, vol. 44, Moscow, 1964, pp. 396–7, 399–400; vol. 45, Moscow, 1964, p. 190; vol. 54, Moscow, 1965, p. 160.
71. Quoted in Harold Berman, *Justice in the USSR*, revised edition, Cambridge, MA, 1963, p. 136.
72. N.V. Krylenko, *Sudebnye rechi*, 1922–30, Moscow, 1931, p. 259; N.V. Krylenko, *Za piat' let 1918–1922*, Moscow–Petrograd, 1923, p. 54
73. N. Krylenko, *Na bor'bu s vreditel'stvom*, Moscow, 1930, p. 16.
74. Krylenko, *Za piat let*, p. 39
75. *Protsess Men'shevikov*, pp. 356–7.
76. Ibid., pp. 379–92, in particular pp. 381, 383.
77. Ibid., p. 360
78. Ibid., pp. 456–9.
79. J.A. Getty and O.V. Naumov, *The Road to Terror*, New Haven and London, 1999, p. 423.
80. OGPU report on attitudes of politicals in *Politizolator* to the trial of the so-called Union Bureau of Mensheviks and to the 14 defendants, dated 22 July 1931, TsA FSB d. 1123. T. 3, 1. 1–30 signed Sidorov, published in A.L. Litvin (ed.) *Men'sheviki v Sovetskoi Rossii, Sbornik documentov*, Kazan', 1998, pp. 129–41.
81. Ibid., p. 128.
82. Nik. Sukhanov, Petition to Praesidium of Sixth Congress for Pardon, dated 9 March 1931, made available to me by Professor Litvin.
83. *Kornikov*, pp. 131, 186n.
84. Anton Ciliga, *The Russian Enigma*, London, 1955, pp. 226–7.
85. *Protsess Men'shevikov*.
86. *Men'shevistskii Protsess*.
87. A.L. Litvin, 'Sudebnyi protsess nad nesushchestvuiushchei partiei', *Men'shevistskii Protsess* vol. 1, p. 3.

88. *Protsess Men'shevikov*, pp. 169, 172, 183, 235.
89. *Pravda*, no. 64, 6 March 1931.
90. *Men'shevistskii Protsess*, vol. 2, pp. 52–65.
91. Ibid., pp. 52–60.
92. Preliminary investigations of Vladimir Groman by Yakov Agranov, 20 July 1930 and 17 August 1930, in Russian Centre for the Conservation and Study of Documents of Recent History, Fond 17, Opis' 71, delo 30, pp. 112–18.
93. *Men'sheviskii Protsess*, vol. 2, p. 65.
94. Ibid., vol. 1, pp. 46–7, 50–1.
95. Ibid., vol. 2, pp. 62–3, 65.
96. Ibid., vol. 2, pp. 66–7.
97. Ibid., vol. 2, p. 71.
98. *See* fn. 82.
99. *Men'shevistskii Protsess,*vol. 1, pp. 554, 134.
100. *Protsess Men'shevikov*, pp. 456, 459–62.
101. Getty and Naumov, *The Road to Terror*, p. 557.
102. A.L. Litvin (ed.), *Men'sheviki v Sovetskoi Rossii*, pp. 117, 119.
103. *Men'shevistskii Protsess*, vol. 2, pp. 409–12.
104. Ibid., vol. 2, pp. 65–6.
105. *Sotsialisticheskii vestnik*, no. 9 (365), 10 May 1936, p. 15.
106. *Kornikov*, p. 140.
107. *Men'shevistskii Protsess*, vol. 2, pp. 304–7, 390.
108. Ibid., p. 113.
109. *Protsess Men'shevikov*, pp. 208–9.
110. *Men'shevistskii Protsess*, vol. 2, pp. 68, 81, 142.
111. *Protsess Men'shevikov*; *Pravda*, no. 64, 6 March 1931.
112. *Protsess Men'shevikov*, pp. 456, 459–62.
113. Getty and Naumov, *The Road to Terror*, pp. 364–419.
114. *Men'shevistskii Protsess*, vol. 2, pp. 388–98.
115. Robert Conquest, *The Great Terror*, London, 1969, pp. 587–94.
116. Quoted in *Kornikov*, p. 139; 'Delo Soiuznogo Biuro Menshevikov', vol. 38, p. 366
117. Litvin, *Men'sheviki v Sovetskoi Rossii*, pp. 172–4.
118. Ibid., pp. 174–5.
119. Ibid., pp. 175–9.
120. Ibid., pp. 180–1.
121. Ibid., p. 178.
122. Litvin, *Men'sheviki v Sovetskoi Rossii*, pp. 180–1.

Bibliography

Nikolai Nikolaevich Gimmer, alias Sukhanov (he adopted the pseudonym Sukhanov for the first time in 1907 and thereafter used it most of the time).

A. Books and brochures

Chto daet zemlia gorodskomu rabochemu (Moscow, 1907).

Zemel'naia renta i osnovy zemel'nogo oblozheniia (k voprosu o sotsializatsii zemli), s predisloviem V.Chernova (Moscow, 1908).

K voprosu ob evoliutsii sel'skogo khoziaistva: sotsial'nye otnosheniia v krest'ianskom khoziaistve Rossii (Moscow, 1909; 2nd revised edition, Moscow, 1924).

Krest'ianskii biudzhet na Severe (Archangelsk, 1911).

Nashi levye gruppy i voina (Petrograd, 1915).

Pochemu my voiuem? (Petrograd, 1916).

K krizisu sotsializma (Po povodu voennykh vystuplenii G.V. Plekhanova) (Petrograd, 1916).

Arkhangel'skaia guberniia po statisticheskomu opisaniiu, 1785 goda (Itogi podvornoi perepisi) (Archangelsk, 1916).

Pravo na zemliiu (Petersburg, 1918).

Zapiski o revoliutsii, vol. 1 (Petersburg, 1919).

Zapiski o revoliutsii, 7 vols (Petersburg, 1922–23) .

Zapiski o revoliutsii, 3 vols, with Introduction, Annotations and Index, edited by A.A. Kornikov (Moscow, 1991–92).

The Russian Revolution, 1917: a Personal Record by N.N. Sukhanov, edited, abridged and translated by Joel Carmichael, from *Zapiski o revoliutsii* (Oxford, London, 1955).

Mirovoe khoziaistvo nakanune i posle voiny, 1913–1923. Populiarnyi ocherk (Moscow, 1924).

Ocherki po ekonomike sel'skogo khoziaistva (Moscow, 1924).

1917 god: Dramaticheskaia Khronika v 5 deistviiakh (Moscow–Leningrad, 1928).

B. Selected articles

'O nashei agrarnoi programmy', *Revoliutsionnaia Rossiia*, no. 75, 15 September, 1905, supplement pp. 1–6 (published under the pseudonym of Konstantin Levin).

'K teorii razvitiia agrarnykh otnoshenii', *Russkoe bogatstvo*, no. 10 (1910), pp. 157–79; no. 11 (1910), pp. 175–94; no. 12 (1910), pp. 101–25.

'Neurozhai i ego sputniki', *Sovremennik*, no. 10 (1911), pp. 167–76.
'Krest'ianskaia arenda v Rossii', *Sovremennik*, no. 2 (1912), pp. 223–40; no. 3 (1912), pp. 209–38.
'Po voprosam nashikh raznoglasii', *Zavety*, no. 6 (1912), pp. 1–23; no. 7 (1912), pp. 1–45.
'O marksistakh i razrushenii obshchiny', *Zavety*, no. 2 (1913), pp. 23–40.
'K kharakteristike rossiiskogo proletariata', *Zavety*, no. 4 (1913), pp. 321–30.
'Na dva fronta', *Zavety*, no. 4 (1913), pp. 105–33.
'Iz itogov poslednego tsenza Severo Amerikan'skikh Soedinennykh Shtatov', *Zavety*, no. 6 (1913), pp. 39–62.
'K itogam i perspektivam noveishei agrarnoi politiki', *Sovremennik*, no. 11 (1913), pp. 234–42; no. 12 (1913), pp. 243–52.
'Tekhnika i ekonomika v sel'skom khoziaistve', *Zavety*, no. 11 (1913), pp. 1–45.
'Smotr obshchestvennoi agronomii', *Zavety*, no. 11 (1913), pp. 213–20.
'Kesarevo-Kesariiu', *Zavety*, no. 1 (1914), pp. 151–61.
'Neskol'ko slov o narodnichestve', *Sovremennik*, no. 6 (1914), pp. 59–69.
'Neskol'ko slov o marksizme i revizionisme', *Sovremennik*, no. 7 (1914), pp. 66–78.
'Edinstvo', *Sovremennik*, no. 12 (1914), pp. 69–81.
'Vlast' sobytii', *Sovremennik*, no. 1 (1915) pp. 193–206.
'Obshchina i nashi napravleniia', *Sovremennik*, no. 2 (1915), pp. 181–92; no. 3 (1915), pp. 202–19.
'Nuzhni li ubezhdeniia? (Pis'mo v redaktsiiu), *Letopis'*, no. 1 (1915), pp. 323–8.
'Pereval', *Letopis'*, no. 4 (1915), pp. 198–217.
'Russkaia publitsistika o proiskhozhdenii voiny', *Letopis'*, no. 2 (1916), pp. 184–208.
'Interesy Rossii v mirovoi voine', *Letopis'*, no. 3 (1916), pp., 178–97; no. 4 (1916), pp. 183–203.
'Rossiia i ee soiuzniki', *Letopis'*, no. 5 (1916), pp. 145–61.
'Po povodu mirnykh predlozhenii', *Letopis'*, no. 1 (1917), pp. 188–204.
'Nashi zadachy', *Novaia zhizn'*, no. 1, 1 April 1917 (unsigned editorial).
'Koalitsionnoe ministerstvo', *Novaia zhizn'*, no. 8, 27 April 1917.
'V poiskakh vlasti', *Novaia zhizn'*, no. 78, 19 July 1917.
'V tiskakh vlasti' *Novaia zhizn'*, no. 135, 23 September 1917.
'Bol'sheviki pri vlasti', *Novaia zhizn'*, no. 166, 29 October 1917.
'O vlasti sovetov', *Novaia zhizn'*, no. 15, 21 January 1918.
'Obshchina v sovetskom agrarnom zakonodatel'stve', *Na agrarnom fronte*, nos. 11–12 (1926), pp. 97–111.
'O differentsiatsii krest'ianskogo khoziaistva', *Na agrarnom fronte*, no. 4 (1927), pp. 145–7.
'Ob ekonomicheskikh predposyl'kakh pod'ema sel'skogo khoziaistva', *Vestnik Akademii Nauk SSSR*, no. 9 (1990), pp. 104–11.

C. Select autobiographical and biographical publications

'Avtobiografiia' [signed 20 January, 1927] in *Deiateli SSSR i Oktiabr'skoi revoliutsii*. *Entsiklopedicheskii Slovar' Russkogo Bibliograficheskogo Instituta Granat*, 7th edition, vol. 41A (Moscow, 1927–29), cols 129–33.

Autobiographical Deposition written while under investigation, dated 29–30 January 1931, in Litvin, A. (ed.), *Men'shevistskii Protsess, 1931 goda*, vol. 2 (Moscow, 1999), pp. 93–113.

Kornikov, A.A., *Sud'ba Rossiiskogo Revoliutsionera: N.N. Sukhanov – Chelovek, Politik, Memuarist* (Ivanovo, 1995), a pioneering biography.

'Sukhanov', *Velikaia Oktiabr'skaia Sotsialisticheskaia Revoliutsiia*, 3rd enlarged edition (Moscow, 1987), p. 505.

Kornikov, A.A., 'Sukhanov', *Politicheskie Deiateli Rossii:, 1917. Biograficheskii Slovar'* (Moscow, 1993), pp. 311–12.

Erofeev, N. and A. Kornikov, 'Sukhanov', *Politicheskie partii Rossii: Konets xix – pervaia tret' xx veka. Entsiklopedia* (Moscow, 1996), pp. 599–600.

Miller, V., 'Sovremennye razmyshleniia nad starymi memuarami', *Svobodnaia mysl'*, no. 16 (1992), pp. 111–15.

Litvin, A.L., *Bez prava na mysl'. Istoriki v Epokhu Bol'shogo Terrora. Ocherki sudeb* (Kazan, 1994), pp. 26–8.

D. Select polemical publications against Sukhanov

A.V.P., 'Narodnyi sotsializm ili proletarskii', *Russkoe bogatstvo*, no. 12 (1912), pp. 269–301.

Stankevich, V.B., 'Ob'edinenie ili pogloshenie. K voprosu ob edinoi sotsialisticheskoi partii', *Sovremennik*, no. 1 (1913), pp. 329–341.

Oganovskii, N.S., 'S nebes na zemliu', *Zavety*, no. 12 (1913), pp. 1–29.

Chernov, Viktor, 'Uprazdnenie narodnichestva', *Zavety* (June, 1914), pp. 88–124.

Izgoev, A., 'Na perevale. Letopis'nye skandaly', *Russkaia mysl'*, no. 3 (1916), pp. 114–24.

Lenin, 'Uderzhat li bol'sheviki gosudarstvennuiu vlast'? [1 October, 1917], *PSS*, vol. 34 (Moscow, 1962), pp. 290–339.

Lenin, 'O nashei revoliutsii (Po povodu *Zapiski* N. Sukhanova)' [16–17 January, 1923], *PSS*, vol. 45 (Moscow, 1964), pp. 378–82.

Dubrovskii, S.M., *Ob odnoi raznovidnosti revisionizma: o teorii dekapitalizatsii sel'skogo khoziaistva razvivaemoi N.N. Sukhanovym* (Moscow, 1926).

Shliapnikov, R., 'O knigakh N. Sukhanova', *Pechat' i revoliutsiia*, no. 4 (1923), pp. 46–52.

Kubanin, M.I., 'Obshchina pri diktature proletariata (Otvet N. Sukhanovu)', *Na agrarnom fronte*, nos. 11–12 (1926), pp. 111–26.

Kondrat'evshchina, chaianovshchina i sukhanovshchina: Vreditel'stvo v sel'skom khoziaistve (Moscow, 1930).

Friche, V.M., 'Burzhuaznyie tendentsii v sovremennoi literature i rol' kritiki', *Doklady v Kommunisticheskoi Akademii* (Moscow, 1930), pp. 5–21.

E. Archives, protocols, collections of documents, contemporary journals and other reference works

Boris Nicolaevsky Collection at the Hoover Institution on War, Revolution and Peace, Stanford, California.

Russian Centre for the Preservation and Study of Documents of Recent History (formerly Marx-Engels Institute), Moscow.

Central Archive of the Federal Security Services of the Russian Federation, Moscow.

Archive of the Communist Academy, Moscow.

Protokoly pervogo s'ezda Partii Sotsialistov-Revoliutsionerov (1906).

Protokoly zasedanii Vserossiiskogo Tsentral'nogo Ispolnitel'nogo Komiteta 4-go sozyva [1918] Stenograficheskii otchet (Moscow, 1920).

Nalivaiskii, B.I (ed.) *Petrogradskii Sovet Rabochikh i Soldatskikh Deputatov v, 1917 godu: Protokoly i Zasedanii Ispolnitel'nogo Komiteta i Biuro Ispolnitel'nogo Komiteta* (Moscow-Leningrad, 1925).

Vserossiiskoe Soveshchanie Sovetov Rabochikh i Soldatskikh Deputatov. Stenograficheskii otchet (Moscow–Leningrad, 1927).

Pervyi vserossiiskii s'ezd Sovetov Rabochikh i Soldatskikh Deputatov, 1917. Protokoly, 2 vols (Moscow–Leningrad, 1930–31).

Vtoroi Vserossiiskii S'ezd Sovetov Rabochikh i Soldatskikh Deputatov. Sbornik Dokumentov (Moscow, 1957).

Startsev, V.I., B.D. Gal'perina and Iu.S. Tokarev (eds) *Petrogradskii Sovet Rabochikh i Soldatskikh Deputatov v 1917 godu: Dokumenty i Materialy*, vol. 1 (Leningrad, 1991), vol. 2 (Sankt Peterburg, 1995).

Trudy Pervoi Vsesoiuznoi Konferentsii Agrarnikov-Marksistov 20/xii–27/xii, 1929, vol. 1 (Moscow, 1930).

Protsess kontrrevoliutsionnoi organizatsii men'shevikov (1–9 marta, 1931). Stenogramma sudebnogo protsessa. Obvinitel'noe zakliuchenie i prigovor (Moscow, 1931).

Keep, J.L.H. (ed.), *The Debate on Soviet Power: Minutes of the All-Russian Central Executive Committee of Soviets. Second Convocation, October, 1917 to January, 1918* (Oxford, 1979).

Bunyan, J., and H.H. Fisher (eds), *The Bolshevik Revolution, 1917–1918: Documents and Materials* (Stanford, 1961).

Gankin, O.H., and H.H Fisher (eds), *The Bolsheviks and the World War: the Origins of the Third International* (Stanford, 1960).

Kerensky, A.F. and R.P. Browder (eds), *The Russian Provisional Government, 1917: Documents*, 3 vols (Stanford, 1961).

Rozhkov, N.A. and A.L. Popov (eds), *Oktiabr'skii Perevorot. Fakty i Dokumenty* (Petrograd, 1918).

Vompe, P. (ed.), *Dni oktiabr'skoi revoliutsii i zheleznodorozhniki* (Moscow, 1924).

Avdeev, N. *et al.* (eds), *Revoliutsiia 1917 goda. Khronika sobytii,* 6 vols (Moscow, 1923–30).
Galili, Z., A. Nenarokov and L. Kheimson, (eds), *Men'sheviki v 1917 godu,* 3 vols (Moscow, 1994–97).
Galili Z., A. Nenarokov and D. Pavlov (eds), *Men'sheviki v 1918 godu,* vol. 1 (Moscow, 1989).
Ascher, A. (ed.), *The Mensheviks in the Russian Revolution* (London, 1976).
Litvin, A.L., *Men'shevistskii protsess 1931 goda. Sbornik dokumentov,* 2 vols (Moscow, 1999).
Litvin, A.L., *Men'sheviki v Sovetskoi Rossii. Sbornik dokumentov* (Kazan, 1998).

F. Contemporary memoirs and accounts

Dan, F., *Dva goda skitanii, 1919–1921* (Berlin, 1922).
Ciliga, A., *The Russian Enigma* (London, 1955).
Ivanovich, St. (ed.), *Rechi Tsereteli proizvedeny v 1917g.* (Petrograd, 1917).
Reed, J., *Ten Days that Shook the World* (New York, 1935).
Shliapnikov, A.G., *Semnadtsatyi god,* 4 vols (Petrograd, 1923–31).
Shteinberg, I., *Ot Fevral'ia po Oktiabr' 1917g.* (Berlin–Milan [1920]).
Stankevich, V.B., *Vospominaniia 1914–1919g.* (Berlin, 1920).
Tsereteli, I., *Vospominaniia o fevral'skoi revoliutsii,* 2 vols (Paris–The Hague, 1968).

G. Reference works

Acton, E., V.Iu. Cherniaev and W.G. Rosenberg (eds), *Critical Companion to the Russian Revolution, 1914–1921* (London, 1997).
Frankel, E.R., J. Frankel and B. Knei-Paz (eds), *Revolution in Russia. Reassessments of 1917* (Cambridge, 1992).
Jackson, G. and R. Devlin (eds), *Dictionary of the Russian Revolution* (New York, 1989).
Shelokhaev, V.V. *et al.* (eds), *Politicheskie Partii Rossii Konets XIX–Pervaia Tret' XX Veka: Entsiklopedia* (Moscow, 1996).
Shukman, H. (ed.), *The Blackwell Encyclopedia of the Russian Revolution* (Oxford, 1994).

H. Periodicals

Letopis' (Petrograd).
Novaia zhizn' (Petrograd).
Revolutionary Russia (London).
Russkoe bogatstvo (Petersburg).
Slavonic and East European Review (London).
Sotsialisticheskii vestnik (Berlin–Paris–New York).
Sovremennik (Petersburg).
Zavety (Petersburg).

I. Secondary works

Anweiler, O., *Die Raetebewegung in Russland, 1905–1921* (Leiden, 1958).

Burdzhalov, E.N., *Vtoraia russkaia revoliutsiia: vosstanie v Petrograde* (Moscow, 1967).

Carr, E.H., *The Bolshevik Revolution, 1917–1923*, 3 vols (London, 1950–53).

Chamberlin, W.H., *The Russian Revolution, 1917–1921*, 2 vols (New York, 1965).

Chernov, V., *Rozhdenie Revoliutsionnoi Rossii (Fevral'skaia revoliutsiia)* (Paris–Prague–New York, 1934).

Cox, T., *Peasants, Class and Capitalism: the Rural Research of L.N. Kritsman and his School* (Oxford, 1986).

Fainsod, M., *How Russia is Ruled* (Harvard, 1953).

Ferro, M., *La révolution de 1917* (Paris, 1967).

Figes, O., *Peasant Russia, Civil War: the Volga Countryside in Revolution (1917–1921)* (Oxford, 1988).

Figes, O., *A People's Tragedy: the Russian Revolution, 1891–1924* (London, 1996).

Galili, Z., *The Menshevik Leaders in the Russian Revolution: Social Realities and Political Strategies* (Princeton, 1989).

Getzler, I., *Martov: Political Biography of a Russian Social Democrat* (Melbourne–Cambridge, 1967).

Geyer, D., *Die russische Revolution: historische Probleme und Perspektiven* (Stuttgart, 1968).

Geyer, D., *Lenin in der russischen Sozialdemokratie. Die Arbeiterbewegung im Zarenreich als Organisationsproblem der revolutionaeren Intelligenz, 1890–1903* (Cologne, 1962).

Haimson, L.H. (ed.), *The Mensheviks: from the Revolution of 1917 to the Second World War* (Chicago–London, 1974).

Hasegawa, T., *The February Revolution: Petrograd 1917* (Seattle–London, 1981).

Hildermeier, M., *Die Sozialrevolutionaere Partei Russlands: Agrarsozialismus und Modernisierung im Zarenreich (1900–1914)* (Cologne–Vienna, 1978).

Jasny, N., *Soviet Economists of the Twenties: Names to be Remembered* (Cambridge, MA, 1972).

Keep, J.L.H., *The Russian Revolution: a Study in Mass Mobilization* (London, 1976).

Kritsman, L., *Geroicheskii Period Velikoi Russkoi Revoliutsii (Opyt analiza t.n. Voennogo Kommunizma)* (Moscow, 1925).

Lewin, M., *Russian Peasants and Soviet Power: a Study of Collectivisation* (London, 1968).

Liebich, A., *From the Other Shore: Russian Social Democracy after 1921* (Harvard, 1997).

Male, D.J., *Russian Peasant Organisation before Collectivisation: a Study of Commune and Gathering, 1925–1930* (Cambridge, 1971).

Leggett, G., *The Cheka: Lenin's Political Police* (Oxford, 1981).

Pipes, R., *The Russian Revolution, 1899–1919* (London, 1990).

Pipes, R., *Russia under the Bolshevik Regime* (New York, 1995).

Rabinowitch, A., *Prelude to Revolution: the Petrograd Bolsheviks in the July 1917 Uprising* (Bloomington–London, 1968).

Radkey, O.H., *The Agrarian Foes of Bolshevism. Promise and Default of the Russian Socialist Revolutionaries, February–October 1917* (New York, 1958).

Radkey, O.H., *The Sickle under the Hammer: the Russian Socialist Revolutionaries in the Early Months of Soviet Rule* (New York–London, 1963).

Rosenberg, W.G., *The Liberals in the Russian Revolution: the Constitutional Democratic Party, 1917–1921* (Princeton, 1974).

Schapiro, L., *The Origins of the Communist Autocracy: Political Opposition in the Soviet State. First Phase, 1917–1922* (London–Cambridge, MA, 1955).

Schapiro, L., *1917: the Russian Revolutions and the Origins of Present-Day Communism* (London, 1984).

Service, R., *Lenin: a Political Life*, 3 vols (London, 1985–95).

Service, R., *A History of Twentieth Century Russia* (London, 1997).

Solomon, S.G., *The Soviet Agrarian Debate* (Boulder, CO, 1977).

Trotsky, L., *History of the Russian Revolution*, 3 vols (London, 1934).

Wade, R., *The Russian Search for Peace, February–October 1917* (Stanford, 1969).

Index